"Too often ecclesiastical historians have presented the life of the Church almost as though it existed in a vacuum. Here I have made an effort to exhibit it as part of the epic of America, of an America not to be properly understood without it. The Catholic body acted upon America and was in turn acted upon by America. And that Catholic body, which is part of the Mystical Body of Christ, does not consist solely of churchmen. Therefore my design has been to depict, in each successive period, American Catholic activity as a whole and America as a whole, and their relationship to one another."

Author's Introduction

"Dr. Maynard tells us that he has tried to produce a handy ￼pular history of the Church in the United States and it ￼y be said at once that he has succeeded in doing so. It ￼ould interest every intelligent Catholic.

￼'Although there are many glorious pages in the story of the ￼erican Church, it is by no means one of uninterrupted ￼ccess. Some writers concentrate on what is obviously the ￼ccessful part and others, indulging in excessive mourning ￼￼ lost opportunities, tend to underestimate the difficulties ￼hat had to be overcome and the immense sacrifices the great ￼neasure of success attained has required. Dr. Maynard avoids both extremes and while he is candid about our shortcomings he never fails to give credit for merit."

America

Rev. Louis P. Luljak

Theodore Maynard
THE STORY
OF AMERICAN
CATHOLICISM

VOLUME ONE

IMAGE BOOKS

A DIVISION OF DOUBLEDAY & COMPANY, INC.
GARDEN CITY, NEW YORK

IMAGE BOOKS EDITION 1960
by special arrangement with The Macmillan Company

Printing History
The Macmillan Company edition published 1941
1st printing .... October, 1941
2nd printing .... November, 1941
3rd printing .... February, 1942
4th printing .... July, 1943
5th printing .... March, 1946
6th printing .... March, 1948
7th printing .... October, 1949
8th printing .... December, 1951
9th printing .... January, 1954

Image Books edition published September 1960
1st printing .... August 1960

Nihil obstat: Arthur J. Scanlan, S.T.D.
                Censor Librorum
Imprimatur: ✠ Francis J. Spellman, D.D.
                Archbishop, New York
                August 28, 1941

COVER BY RONALD CLYNE
DESIGNED BY JOSEPH P. ASCHERL

Printed in the United States of America

In the United States our religious system has undergone a revolution, if possible, more extraordinary than our political one.

—JOHN CARROLL

CONTENTS

INTRODUCTION

"The Catholic Church," wrote John Gilmary Shea, "is the oldest organization in the United States and the only one that has retained the same life and polity and forms through each succeeding age." Yet it has received, although by far the largest and most vigorous of religious bodies in America, as a rule perfunctory and even slighting notice in most of the standard general histories. Those who have considered the roots of American civilization worth their attention have almost invariably believed those roots to lie in Puritanism, in spite of the fact that Puritanism had been in decline long before the American Revolution occurred. It is still from time to time fiercely (or else smugly) asserted that Americanism is basically Protestant and that only Protestantism is truly American. The story told in these pages should make such an argument untenable, though of course it would be equally absurd to maintain that all that is good in American life derives from Catholic culture. Many factors have contributed to the building of America: here there will be no more than an attempt to give due weight to the Catholic factor.

I cannot, however, refrain from remarking that it is rather curious that men who admit no dogmatic basis in their own lives or their concept of the universe should so often retain a sentimental attachment to the legend that, because certain dissenting Protestant groups sought, among other things, their own liberty of conscience, they were the architects of American religious liberty. There is no special need to complain that, when in a position to enforce their will, they refused liberty to those with whom they happened to disagree—and particularly to Catholics; for their ideas were inevitably conditioned by their time. Instead it may be gratefully acknowledged that their stern adhesion to their personal convictions contributed in the end greatly to bring about an extension of religious liberty to all. But at least candor demands, from their side, the admission that such Catholic groups as came to the American colonies never thought of religious liberty as something that should be exclusively enjoyed by themselves.

In this respect the Catholic settlers of Maryland were Americans from the beginning, whereas the Puritans became Americans only by slow degrees.

The Catholic Church in truth is the natural upholder of American institutions. Not that it is necessarily committed to the democratic machinery of government—for it will coöperate with any political system with which coöperation is possible; but it has found itself more at ease in the United States than in any other nation of the modern world. Its fundamental doctrine that all men are essentially equal can be the only solid foundation of democracy. The Church powerfully helps to preserve the intellectual atmosphere needed for the continued life of the American idea, just as the organization of the Church has, as one of its functions, the maintenance of order and discipline in society.

The discovery of America was made by Catholics, whether the credit be given to Christopher Columbus or Lcif Ericsson. Despite the disappearance of many of the original place names—an example of this is the Santo Espiritu becoming the Mississippi—hundreds of these Catholic names still exist from St. Augustine in Florida (itself so named because it was first seen on Easter Sunday, *Pascua Florida*) to San Francisco in California, from San Antonio to St. Paul. They are perpetual reminders of the Catholic piety that baptized the land. Mass was said here before the first stockade of the white man was built. As John Gilmary Shea, for once permitting himself an epigram, put it: "The altar was older than the hearth."

So far, then, from the Church being an alien institution in America, it might almost be said that American Catholics are often, from one point of view, rather too American. By which I mean that many among them may be charged with accepting too easily those standards of material success and that indifference to the fate of the rest of the world which are the gravest danger to the spiritual ideal of Americanism; though it should be added that, however many of them make this partial surrender, however many of them try to tuck themselves away in a snug smug isolationism, they cannot—belonging as they do to the Universal Church—be ultimately indifferent to universal good. Not by them will it ever be denied that there are things worth fighting and dying for; not by them will it be believed that man lives by bread alone. They may, as individuals, be insensibly affected by the faults for the moment prevailing in the society in which they find themselves.

But there are, for them, limits to the process. In the last issue they may always be depended upon to affirm that, just as supernatural truth is eternally applicable and necessary to every human soul, so the great natural truths upon which America reposes are necessary to social well-being. Of both categories of truth the Church is the custodian, and therefore is one of the strongest bulwarks of American liberty.

It is these distinctively American characteristics in our Catholic history that I hope to draw out along with the distinctively Catholic characteristics of American history. That is why I shall be obliged to reduce my account of French and Spanish missionary and colonizing effort to a bare minimum, and not because I regard it as unimportant or its results ephemeral. On the contrary, it is because the story is so fascinating and so opulent with detail that it must be drastically abbreviated for the sake of giving sharper clarity to the general pattern.

For the same reason the arrangement of the material under diocesan headings—though it has some obvious advantages—is avoided in this book. I must paint with a broader brush than that used by Shea and O'Gorman and can take only the main movements of American Catholic history. Institutions and religious orders, as such, are not dealt with. And a few typical figures stand here as the representatives of the hundreds of bishops and the thousands of priests and nuns and lay people who have labored in the cause of Christ in America. This would seem to be the only way of making those selected stand out. The alternative would have been, in a work of so small a scope, to have cluttered it up with mere names. Finally, matters of social and political interest have been introduced more freely than is usual in a study of this kind, even if my treatment of them cannot be other than summary. Too often ecclesiastical historians have presented the life of the Church almost as though it existed in a vacuum. Here I have made an effort to exhibit it as part of the epic of America, of an America not to be properly understood without it. The Catholic body acted upon America and was in turn acted upon by America. And that Catholic body, which is part of the Mystical Body of Christ, does not consist solely of churchmen. Therefore my design has been to depict, in each successive period, American Catholic activity as a whole and America as a whole, and their relationship to one another.

The method decided upon has grave drawbacks, of which

I am very conscious. Selection implies rejection. For the sake of the pattern I have been compelled to leave out much that I should have liked to have put in. And at this point my resolution somewhat falters before the question asked by Monsignor Guilday, our leading ecclesiastical historian: "What genius indeed could in a few broad strokes of his brush on the canvas give even the highlights of all that has been accomplished by the Church?" Faced with such a question I—who do not profess either genius or learning—have to look for what little consolation is to be discovered in the decisive word "all." The answer is that nobody could give *all*, even did he write a hundred volumes for my one. Yet I may have given enough to enlighten the general reader—the reader for whom this book is intended.

It goes without saying that I could not so much as dream of writing anything like Dr. Guilday's admirable lives of Carroll and England. It will be at once evident that I have not gone, as he has done, directly to archival sources, but have been content to use to the best of my ability the documents so carefully and accurately printed in many monographs. Even so, I quote from them only a decisive sentence or two now and then. My book has been built with blocks other men have hewn from the quarries. Had it not been for them I should not now be building at all. It is, however, just possible that my little bit of architecture, however much it may fail to approximate achievement to intention, may (perhaps through its flaws, if nothing else) suggest to a keener eye and a more skilful hand a hint of what the grand design ought to be.

There is hardly any need for me to apologize for being merely a "literary" historian or—if even that is too much to claim—a popularizer. The cobbler must stick to his last, and I to mine. Every historian must make up his mind what type of history it is that he means to write. The "scientific" historian is often more to be commended for his patient research and his ample documentation than for his literary gifts or his power to bring his subject into focus. Yet it would be unfair to object, in his case, that literary gifts are not greatly in evidence. But would it be too much to ask for work that is of an entirely different kind a similar condonation from scientific historians? I am not writing a doctoral dissertation. Scholars must therefore pardon me, if they can, for not having employed the apparatus of their craft. Footnote references have been reduced to a minimum, in order to save space, and many of these are explanatory of the text rather than bibliographical. The expert will not need such citations, nor will the general reader desire them. If they tend to increase as the book progresses, this is because in its earlier part I am dealing with matters much more often written about than those towards the end. Precisely because the bibliographical information at present available tends to grow scantier as more modern times are approached I thought it advisable to give it more often then.

My temerity, if not shown in other ways, is all too likely to appear in the fact that a layman is entering a department usually reserved for ecclesiastics. However, it may be that my intrusion will find some justification in my detached point of view and, because of that, an independence of judgment; though as a man incurably given to forthright expressions of opinion, I shall be lucky if I do not bring clouds of hornets around my head. I make no plea for mercy on this account: all risks were accepted at the outset. I hope nevertheless that some allowances will be made. Still more do I hope that, whatever errors and omissions and inadequacies appear in what I have written, the book will be of service. A handy popular history of the Catholic Church in the United States is, after all, something that is badly needed. Which is why I have tried to produce one.

Several laymen who are specialists, a number of priests, and even one bishop, have been kind enough to read sections of this book. I do not mention their names (which will probably be to their relief) for the simple reason that they have not seen the whole. Those who have read the entire manuscript and to whose advice I owe much are Fathers Robert McNamara, Professor of Church History at St. Bernard's Seminary of Rochester, N.Y., Florence D. Cohalan of Staten Island (who are also the compilers of the appendix), Edward A. Ryan, S.J., of Woodstock College, and John F. Fenlon, the Provincial of the Sulpicians. I have usually adopted their suggestions, but as I have not always done so, they must not be held responsible for any of my views. The same thing applies to Mr. Van Wyck Brooks and Mr. William Franklin Sands, who also allowed themselves to be burdened. The Rt. Rev. Dr. Peter Guilday, whose health did not permit him to read what I have written, often discussed the book with me during the years in which it was in progress and allowed me to go over the manuscript with him at the end.

As so often before, the Library of Congress has facilitated my work. And Fathers Philip J. Blanc, S.S., of St. Mary's Seminary, Edwin D. Sanders, S.J., of Woodstock, and Hugh Phillips of Mount St. Mary's College have been very generous in the loan of books.

Two students of the Rochester seminary—The Reverend William J. Schifferli and William H. Shannon—gave valuable help in preparing the bibliography. The index has been compiled by my daughter Rosemary. My wife has done a great deal with regard to the revision of the manuscript and the correction of the proofs.

To all of the above I offer my most grateful thanks. This book could hardly have appeared without their assistance.

THE STORY OF AMERICAN CATHOLICISM

CHAPTER ONE

THE DISCOVERY

"That great antiquity America," wrote Sir Thomas Browne in his *Urn Burial*, "lay buried for thousands of years." Had he been able to wait a couple of centuries longer he would have learned that there are few nations who have not claimed —or had the claim advanced for them—that they outstripped Columbus. Some of the early Portuguese and Spanish explorers of the southern continent imagined they recognized negro features among the aborigines. And Las Casas devised for the first time the theory that the American Indians were the lost ten tribes of Israel. Roger Williams and John Eliot chose to amuse themselves with the same notion, as did Lord Kingsborough with elaborate learning in his sumptuously illustrated *Antiquities of Mexico*. The Mormons found it convenient to incorporate the supposition as a part of divine revelation.

We need not linger upon this, any more than we need accept the Platonic legend of Atlantis. It was natural enough for poets to dream of fortunate isles lying in a heavenly calm beyond the furious waters glimpsed from the Pillars of Hercules. What more natural too than that an Egyptian priest should have been invented to give authentication to so fair a fancy! Only the unimaginative would think of taking such things literally.

It is likely enough that Tyrian and Phoenician mariners should have been driven by storms, while on their trading voyages to the coasts of Cornwall and West Africa, far on to the deep, and have touched at the Canaries and the Azores. If it comes to that, it is not only not impossible but quite likely that more than once their ships should have been cast upon the western world. But because this could have happened, we must not affirm that it did happen. The chances are that such ships never returned. If they ever did, the yarns of their sailors were soon transmuted into myth.

In the same way we must dismiss the tradition that St. Thomas the Apostle went eastwards as far as Peru. If he actually got to India it would have been exploit enough; even from the furthest tip of the Asian archipelago the Pacific stretches twice the distance of the Atlantic. Yet we cannot do other than suppose that man first came to America from Asia, most probably from Siberia, much less probably via Polynesia. It is not difficult, however, to surmise that in later ages Chinese and Japanese junks and Malay proas may, like the galleys of Tyre, have been thrown by the winds on the shores of an unknown continent. If so, they no doubt mingled the strain of their own blood with that of the peoples they encountered. But all this is again guesswork; we know nothing positive.

There is greater substance to the Irish legends. St. Brendan may well have made the voyage with which he is credited to the "Land of Delight" or the "Land of Promise"—and this could have been the Chesapeake Bay region, the locality proposed. The name of Columba has, according to some Gaelic zealots, a claim prior to that of Columbus. But the ancient stories were much more probably nothing but the fabrication of some monastic dreamer who, after poring over manuscripts that told of the Fortunate Isles, retold them with an Irish twist. A romancer, in days when there was hardly any line drawn between sober fact and shining fable, was not necessarily a liar. He did not think of himself as writing history. If, as DeCosta points out, the very word "America" in the *Monastikon Britannicum,* proves the reference fraudulent, we need not charge deliberate fraud. It would merely date the scribe's transcription; he could still have been reworking immemorial traditions. Outright rejection would be as unsafe as unqualified acceptance. There is probably this much basis to the Brendan legend: the Irish Saint did make his famous voyage—but to the Azores.[1]

Hardly less legendary is the account of the hero of Southey's epic, *Madoc,* scornfully alluded to by Byron (who always had scorn for everything connected with Southey) as "Cacique in Mexico, and Prince in Wales." He is supposed to have heard, in the twelfth century, of the Norse explorations and to have sailed westwards, to have made a settlement in America of a hundred and twenty men, and to have returned with a larger number—never to be heard of again. There is a far higher degree of certainty attaching to what is related of John Vas Costa Cortereal, who is said to have come to Newfoundland in 1463. The only trouble with that claim is that it was not

[1] A good partial bibliography is appended to Dunn's article, "The Brendan Problem" in the *Catholic Historical Review,* Vol. VI (1921), pp. 395–470.

heard of until 1818. It is reasonably certain that the Pole, John
Skolnow, who was in the Dutch service, did reach Greenland
and Labrador in 1467, and that the Frenchman, Jean Cousin,
was blown out of his way to Brazil twelve years later. For that
matter there must be some truth in the story that the Italian
Zeno brothers reached Greenland in 1394, and then jour-
neyed still further west. They wrote an account of their voyages and this, together with a map (which was confessedly
touched up by the descendant who edited their manuscript),
was published in 1558. Some—perhaps all—of these men may
have reached points in the western world; and there is little
doubt that Basque, Breton and other fishermen often got as
far as the Banks of Newfoundland. It is therefore rather difficult to believe that Columbus had not heard that land lay
beyond the Atlantic, even if such suggestions are indignantly
rejected by those who would give him all the glory of discovering America. That he owed anything to any Iceland predeces-
sor has been as vehemently denied.

The popular notion is that Columbus produced for the first
time (along with his fabulous egg) the concept of the spheric-
ity of the earth. But Albertus Magnus and Roger Bacon,
among others, had argued that the earth was a globe, and so,
centuries before them, had Aristotle and Parmenides and
Pythagoras. It was not, however, with any of them, a matter
which reposed on pragmatic evidence but of intuition and
logic. As the perfect shape was a sphere, they maintained that
the world must be one: it ought to be, therefore it was. For
once such a mode of reasoning was correct. What Columbus
did was to dare to act upon this concept. Scholars under their
lamps might theorize, and sailors under the stars might venture, with simple courage undisturbed by speculation, across
the vast of waters. But they left no settlements of which definite traces can be found; they built no bridge by which others
could follow. Not even the Norsemen did that, though what
they did was notable enough. If they are unable to take anything away from Columbus, there is no need for us to take
anything away from them.

What we know is this. Late in the tenth century a Norse-
man, Eric Thorwaldsson, or Eric the Red, fled as an outlawed
murderer from his country and came to Iceland. There he
heard of a certain Gunnbjörn who had reached a country still
further westward, and to this land he sailed—for Iceland was
now too hot for him—naming it Greenland, in order that so

good a name might attract others to go there. This was sixteen years before Norway became Christian and therefore about 984. That Iceland itself already contained some Christians we may be sure, for we hear that a third of its population was Irish or Scotch.

Eric's son, Leif, returning to Norway in 999, was commissioned by King Olaf Trygvesson, to undertake the conversion of Greenland, to which country he returned with some priests. He himself did not take kindly to the idea of accepting a new faith, and the manner in which his wife Theodhild did so was little to his taste. Nevertheless, like the majority of the inhabitants, he made a formal profession of Christianity.

About a hundred years later we hear of Greenland having a bishopric at Gardar and, though it was often left vacant, there was a succession of bishops well into the sixteenth century, even if many of these appear to have been merely titular or not to have visited their see. One bishop of Gardar was the English Franciscan, Robert Ringman. All of them—except the first few—were suffragans to the Archbishop of Trondhjem, whose see was established in 1152 by Nicholas Brakespeare (Adrian IV), the only Englishman ever to become Pope. At least one of the Greenland bishops, Eric, went to Vinland— that is to the American continent—but did not return. We have the date of this happening—1121.

So much for the missionary effort in the western hemisphere. The bishopric of Gardar is a matter of established history, however many gaps there may be in the record. The ruins of the cathedral have been found, and we hear of two monastic houses and a convent of Benedictine nuns.

There were in spite of this long periods during which no priests were available for Greenland. Then the dead were buried with a pole resting upon their breasts; it was intended to be pulled up, leaving a funnel for holy water to be poured upon the body, when a clerk arrived. As no wheat could be grown either there or in Iceland we learn of Bishop Nicholas asking the Pope in 1237 whether hosts made from other grain might be consecrated and beer used instead of wine. The answer of course being no, the saying of Mass had to depend upon the arrival of supplies from Norway. The gradual decline that overtook the Christian settlements is indicated by a Bull issued by Alexander VI in which he said that he had heard that "no memory of the Christian religion is found except a corporal, which is shown to the people once a year, and on which, it is said, the last priest who officiated there consecrated the body of Christ a hundred years ago."

To rectify the situation Matthias Knutsson, a Danish Benedictine, was appointed in 1492, but we are without information as to whether he actually went to Gardar. The last bishop consecrated was the Franciscan, Vincent Petersson, and this was in 1519. Not long afterwards the Protestant Reformation swept away a Catholicism too feeble to resist.

It is when we pass from Greenland to Vinland that we reach uncertain ground. That Norsemen did come to America is no longer seriously doubted; what remains open to doubt is where they came. The places mentioned in the sagas are not securely identified, and those suggested range all the way from Labrador to Long Island Sound. As for the authenticity of the Norse relics, this has been challenged.[2] Let us glance at both.

According to the sagas, Eric the Red said, "It is destined that I should never discover more lands than this of Greenland," but that his son, "Leif, with his comrades, in all thirty-five men, rigged out their vessel. . . . They first came to the land which Biarne had last [first] discovered, sailed up to it, cast anchor, put out a boat and went on shore; but there was no grass to be seen. There were large snowy mountains up the country, but all the way from the sea up to these snowy ridges, the land was full of snow, and it appeared to them a country of no advantages. Leif said: 'It shall not be said of us, as it was of Biarne, that we did not come upon the land; for I will give the country a name, and call it Helluland.' Then they went on board again and put to sea, and found another land. . . . The country was flat, and overgrown with wood; and the strand far around consisted of white sand, and was low towards the sea. Then Leif said: 'We shall give this land a name according of its kind, and call it Markland.' Then they hastened on board, and put to the sea again with the wind from the north-east, and were out for two days and made land. . . . There was dew upon the grass; and having accidentally gotten some of the dew upon their hands and put it to their mouths, they thought they had never tasted anything as sweet as it was. Then they went on board and sailed into a sound that was between the island and a ness that went out

---

[2] Mr. Edward F. Gray, who knows both the sagas and the New England coast thoroughly, may be correct in his arguments in favor of the Cape Cod region. But he, like Reeves, attaches less weight to the relics than to the sagas.

northward from the land, and sailed westward past that ness."
There follows a description of that country of good grass in
which "day and night were more equal than in Greenland and
Iceland" and of how an exploring party found wild grapes. It
was for this reason that Leif Ericsson called it Vinland. Everything is as matter-of-fact as a ship's log.

Cape Cod is naturally suggested by the "ness that went far
out northward from the land," and the wild grapes (though
they might have been found in the St. Lawrence valley) also
point to New England. On the other hand, the account given
of encounters with the natives fit the Esquimaux better than
the Indians. To which the answer is that both races might have
been seen by the Norsemen and that subsequent accounts confused the two.

In addition to the difficulties of geographical and ethnologi-
cal identification we have the technical problems of textual
criticism. The historical credibility of the sagas must always remain open to question, especially as they contain obvious dis-
crepancies. Dr. Fridjof Nansen simply dismissed them as the
Norse variants of the classical stories about the Fortunate
Isles, into which were woven incidents taken from the Irish
legend of St. Brendan. But this may be too simple an explanation: the writers of the sagas would not have been the first
people to embroider fact. Even Nansen admits that the
Norsemen may well have come to our shores. A moderate judgment would be that legend and historical truth are woven together.

Some Nordic enthusiasts have attempted to place the whole
matter on a more solid basis by examining what purport to be
relics left by the Norsemen. The carvings on the Dighton rock
at Berkeley, Massachusetts, may, after all, be runic, though it
is often maintained that they were made by the Indians. Similarly it is now virtually certain that the stone tower at Newport, Rhode Island, which Rafn firmly believed built by the
Norsemen, was erected late in the seventeenth century for a
windmill by Governor Arnold.[3]

In his recently published *Westland from Vinland*, Hjalmar

---

[3] Dr. D. J. Gallagher of Philadelphia is, however, confident that
"a later generation will not only come to know the fabric as St.
Brendan's Tower, but will reverently dedicate it as such." (*Catholic
Builders of the Nation*, Vol. I, p. 101.) There's antiquity (and temerity) for you! Or is it a case of the Pickwickian "Bill Stumps his
mark"?

R. Holand, presents again all the evidence in favor of the Norse, some of whom he insists made settlements and penetrated far inland. Verendrye, he points out, found to his surprise in 1732 that the Mandan Indians of Dakota had a tradition that white men had previously come among them, that they made a gesture like the sign of the cross, and even seemed to have a tradition about Noah's Ark and the Immaculate Conception. Unfortunately for Holand's thesis all this is about as intangible and unreliable as Verendrye's fancy that he noticed among the Mandans traces of white blood.

We come to something more definite in the fact that Norse swords and battle axes have been discovered in the North-west. Yet even this really proves little. It would not be altogether satisfactory to account for them as having been carried inland after having been purchased on the Atlantic seaboard, but there is nothing to show that they had not belonged to early Scandinavian settlers instead of to the ancient Norsemen. As for the "Kensington Stone" discovered in Minnesota in 1898, though it has often been rejected as a hoax, it is now admitted that it may, after all, be genuine. If that could be put beyond argument, there would be no difficulty in accepting the other evidence as corroborative. For what it is worth, this is the translation of the runic inscription upon which so much else hinges:

Eight Goths and twenty-two Norwegians on exploration journey from Vinland through the West We had camp by [a lake with?] 2 skerries one day's journey from this stone We were and fished one day After we came home found ten men red with blood and dead. Ave Maria Save from evil have 10 of [our band?] by the sea to look after our ship 14 days' journey from this island 1352.

On the face of it it cannot be regarded as other than extremely unlikely that a Norse band could have got so far into the North American continent. All that can be confidently said is that, if they had done so and had left a memorial, it would presumably have been along these lines. But a feeling that there may have been forgery arises. Although the type of Scandinavian immigrant who settled in the North-west five hundred years later can hardly be conceived as knowing enough about runic characters to have been capable of such an inscription, chance may have brought an impish archaeologist among them. What is in favor of the genuineness of the inscription is the circumstances of the stone's discovery—by a farmer who came across it lodged in the roots of a tree. If, as Justin Winsor said of the sagas, one is left with "the suspicion that the story-telling of the fireside has overlaid the reports of the explorer," an even greater suspicion remains that some Norse enthusiast has "faked" the Kensington Stone. Scholars ought to be full of a passion for truth; but they, no less than the unlearned, are sometimes swayed by party passion. Too complete a proof is apt to raise doubts rather than extinguish them. It would be presumptuous of me to say more concerning a matter on which there is no agreement even among specialists.[4]

One point may nevertheless be safely made: whether Leif Ericsson or Christopher Columbus—or even some explorer between their times—is to be regarded as the discoverer of America, the discovery was effected by a son of the Church. The great seafaring career of the English had not yet begun. The only English ships that came in the fifteenth century to the New World were those under the command of John and Sebastian Cabot who, like Columbus, were Italians and of course Catholics. But the English had during this period so slight an interest in exploration that it was not until another century had passed that they followed up the work of the Cabots, whose almost forgotten voyages then became useful in the way of providing England with a claim to the possession of North America. However shadowy such a claim must be considered, it was advanced because of what Catholic navigators had done while England was still a Catholic country. Five years after the first Cabot voyage of 1497 an English priest came to these shores to say Mass for his fellow countrymen.

But after making full allowance for all possible visits—whether voluntary or not—of those who may have preceded Columbus, it would be ungenerous, not to say unjust, to attempt to detract from the Columbian title. Nothing but an unlucky accident gave the name of the boastful Amerigo Vespucci[5] to the New World instead of that of the man who merited it.

---

[4] The course of this controversy may be traced in a bibliography, whose items are arranged in chronological order, in the *Catholic Historical Review*, Vol. VI (1921), pp. 387–391.

[5] It was Martin Waldseemüller who first used the term America. He later tried to correct it to "Terra Incognita" which was of course out of the question as a name. "America" therefore stuck.

In this no wrong was intended to Columbus, though it would seem that he was never very popular among the Spaniards under his command. He was touchy and full of a sense of his own importance, and his administration was so high-handed that he was eventually sent back to Spain loaded with irons. Yet whatever his faults may have been—and he had many of a private as well as a public sort—what stands out to give him glory are his persistent faith and the will and courage to carry out his great enterprise. Under persecution the Christ-bearer[6] could cry, "Why dost thou falter in thy trust in God? He gave thee the Indies!" In this fond belief he died. He did not know that it had been his destiny to have discovered something even more important than the lands of the Orient which had been his goal. He alone among the early explorers had a clear design and the determination to bring it into being.

There is no need here to retell his familiar story. All that may be remarked is that, except for a mishap, for which he cannot be blamed, the northern continent today would probably be Catholic. It had been his intention to strike a course due west, and this would have brought him to the mainland instead of to the Bahamas, from which he turned south to Cuba and Haiti. Had his crew shared his vision they would have allowed him to continue westward. It was only because their mood was so rebellious—due to their terror—that he consented to yield on what he imagined was an indifferent point. The consequence was that Spanish energies were spent, until too late, upon Central America, Mexico and Peru. By the time the continent to the north came to be explored, English and French settlements were being made, and the stupendous chance of Spain was already lost.

Such a reflection is, however, no more than academic. The providence of God had ordained another destiny for America, one of which we can even now see only the beginning and at whose end we can only dimly guess. What had opened in the New World was an undertaking altogether too staggering for any single nation to carry out alone. It was one to which England and France also had to contribute, and of their best. Columbus therefore does not belong exclusively to the Spain he served, but to the world. Bretons, Basques, Norse and Irish—all may have come before him, as the Norse certainly

[6] His sincere apostolic fervor is incontestable, even if Madariaga is correct in maintaining (*Christopher Columbus*, p. 54) that he was a Spanish Jew in origin.

did—but, in that event, they missed the significance of what they had stumbled upon. They left no permanent mark; they made no settlements. That was the achievement of Columbus. It is for this reason that his fame will never die.

CHAPTER TWO

FIRST EXPLORERS AND SETTLERS

If one could only believe that the famous voyage of St. Brendan was to these shores, one would have the satisfaction of crediting the discovery of America to a saint. Martyrs, however, appeared soon enough among the Spanish and French missionaries, and some of these have been formally canonized. As for the *conquistadores*, though they were not as a rule men of blameless private morals—Columbus, for instance, having his Beatriz Enriquez and Cortés a beautiful and intelligent Indian mistress, Marina—at least they were a great deal more than nominal Catholics. They showed their faith on due occasion with dramatic decision, as did the assassinated Pizarro, who died making the sign of the cross in his own blood. All of them had, unlike their Protestant successors on the North Atlantic seaboard, an interest in the conversion of the heathen that went far beyond perfunctory professions. It was one of the main motives of the Spanish Crown to bring a knowledge of the Gospel to the New World. In confidence that this mission could safely be entrusted to the royal hands, the Pope gave—by the Bull *Universalis Ecclesiae Regimini* of July 28, 1508—such wide powers to the Crown that the kings of Spain could regard themselves, each in his turn, as vicars-general to the Vicar of Christ. Not even the lowest ecclesiastical appointment might be made without their consent.

Spanish officials, operating at a distance, could perhaps have ignored the instructions of the Escorial in this matter, as in others, had they chosen to do so. The fact that they carried them out with enthusiasm proves that their interest in the salvation of souls was not less than that of their King. From the beginning the Spanish enterprise, however much it may have had as its object the extension of the Spanish dominions and the obtaining of private gain, never lost sight of the much grander object of making the New World Catholic. Even exploring expeditions, operating in the most difficult terrain, allowed themselves to be burdened with priests who were to preach to the savages. And when settlements had been established, friars and Jesuits were sent in such numbers that the cost of their maintenance (which was borne by the Crown) became as heavy as that of the army. If the search for gold was often feverish and ruthless, a large part of the proceeds went to the support of the missions. The apostolic obligation was never forgotten. Nor should we forget it or fail to do the common justice to the *conquistadores* of recalling their passionate piety. Their conquests were for the kingdom of Christ.

Only a couple of weeks before John Gilmary Shea died in 1892, when the centenary of the Discovery was being celebrated, he insisted upon the Catholic contribution to America's early history. "Who," he asked, "discovered Greenland and had a cathedral church and convent there? Catholics. If Vinland was really part of this country, who discovered and visited it? Leif Ericsson, a Catholic, with his Catholic Northmen, followed by Catholic bishops and priests. . . . Who explored the Atlantic and Gulf Coast of the United States? Catholic navigators: John and Sebastian Cabot; John Ponce de León; Pineda, first to see the Mississippi and name it the River of the Holy Ghost. . . . Who explored the Mississippi from its northern waters to the Gulf of Mexico? The Catholic Franciscan, Hennepin, and Du Lhut, a Catholic; Joliet, a Catholic; Father Marquette, a Jesuit; La Salle and his Franciscan chaplains, Catholics; De Soto, Tristan de Luna, and other Spanish explorers, all Catholics. Who discovered and named the St. Lawrence? Cartier, a Catholic." Proudly he extends his catalogue, naming Champlain and Jogues and Verendrye (who first reached the Rocky Mountains), Menendez, the founder of St. Augustine, and Oñate, the founder of Santa Fé—these our two oldest cities—and the missionaries in Maine and upper New York and Maryland and Texas and California. The list of Catholic heroes is much too long to quote. Shea might well demand, "In this anniversary year who can wipe these glorious names from the obelisk of fame?"

For the moment I put on one side later missionary activities, and all mention of later Catholic explorers, to consider here only the pioneer efforts. Nearly all of these were made by Spaniards. Indeed, it was not until 1534 that the Frenchman, Cartier, entered the St. Lawrence, so preparing an eventual way for the Jesuits and Recollects and Sulpicians of New France. And Cartier was as fervent a Catholic as the *conquistadores*.

The only Protestant attempt at settlement was that effected for a while under Admiral Coligny's direction on the coast of

Florida. As it was a flagrant piece of poaching on the Spanish preserves, Pedro Menendez, the commander of Philip II's *flota*, wiped it out, hanging the garrison with the notice over their heads, "I do this not as to Frenchmen but as to Lutherans"—an atrocity which permitted De Gourgues to hang the Spaniards a little later with the still wittier explanation, "I do this not as to Spaniards but as to murderers."[1] These occurrences took place in 1565 and 1568. The upshot was that St. Augustine, with the rest of Florida, was held by Spain. Only in the distant north did France maintain her foothold, and there it was the true, the Catholic France. The Huguenots were broken at home by the violent popular action that provoked the massacre of 1572, and twenty years later Henry IV found it advisable to accept the Mass to gain Paris and a secure throne. After that, until the first English settlements were effected, the whole continent, whether the explorers and missionaries were Spaniards or Frenchmen, was a field for the planting of Catholicism. Although the political power of these nations was subsequently destroyed, their culture has left an indelible mark and remains to this day as among the deepest and—for that reason—the generally unnoticed foundations of America.

In 1493, a Spanish bishop of Irish extraction, Bernard Boyl, was sent to Haiti as Vicar-Apostolic. The date on which he consecrated his first church—the Feast of the Epiphany, 1494—may be taken as that of the founding of the Catholic Church in the New World. But of course Mass had been said during the two preceding years.

This, however, was in the Indies. The vast continent—as yet untouched except at the Isthmus—was still thought of as an island. Ponce de León was the first to come to the mainland, and as it was on Easter Sunday—*Pascua Florida*—1513, he named it *Tierra Florida*. Of secondary significance was the fact that the magnolias were in full bloom.

Ponce de León, whose valiant name is unluckily associated with the foolish legend of his supposititious search for the Fountains of Youth, came again in 1521, this time with the title of *Adelantado*, to take possession of the country. But he

---

[1] There is no need to make Menendez out a lover of religious toleration. But his celebrated inscription was not altogether an indication of bigotry, as usually represented. He did not want to create a diplomatic incident. The same allowances must be made for De Gourgues.

was wounded in a fight with the Indians and was carried to Porto Rico to die.

In the interval Alonzo Alvarez de Pineda, searching for the strait which it was believed must lead to the South Sea—which Balboa had discovered from his "peak in Darien" on September 25, 1513—had lighted upon the mouth of the Mississippi, but knew no more than that the great river existed.

Two years later—that is, in 1521, shortly after the conquest of Mexico—Vasquez de Ayllon visited the Cape Fear district and returned seven years later with the royal commission to found a colony. Its terms indicate the intention of the Spanish Crown to claim everything that should be discovered north of the Gulf of Mexico. He was also instructed in his *cedula* from Charles V: "Whereas our principal intent in the discovery of new lands is that the inhabitants and natives thereof who are without the knowledge of faith may be brought to understand the truths of our holy Catholic faith, and that they may come to the knowledge thereof and become Christians and be saved, and this is the chief motive you are to bear and hold in the affair." To point his orders more definitely, the Emperor laid down that Ayllon was to take priests and all that was necessary for the divine worship and that the charges were to be paid "entirely from the rents and profits which in any manner shall belong to us from the said land." No provisions could be more explicit.

We have no record of priests having been with Ponce de León or Pineda—though they may have been with either or both—but it is certain that Ayllon, when he sailed in June, 1526, took with him two Dominican Fathers and a lay-brother. It is interesting to note that one of these friars was that Antonio Montesinos who inspired Las Casas to wage his long battle against the enslavement of the Indians. Catholicism may therefore be said to have been introduced in America by the first of the abolitionists. The first settlement was made on the Chesapeake, close to the very spot where the English later founded Jamestown.

We may take 1526, therefore, as the date of the first Mass in the present territory of the United States. For though priests came with the Northmen, and some may even have reached New England, it is unlikely, in view of the difficulty of obtaining wheaten bread and wine in Greenland, that there were facilities for the offering of the Holy Sacrifice in Vinland.

The Spanish settlement on the Chesapeake did not prosper.

Ayllon died before 1526 was out, and in the spring of the following year the hundred and fifty men, who were all that remained of the original six hundred, departed for Hispaniola. Some of their rosaries were discovered fourteen years later by De Soto.

Panfilo de Narváez was the next, and he tried his luck in 1527, landing at Tampa Bay. He, too, had a large force, and brought with him some secular priests as well as Franciscans, with Juan Xuarez as their superior.[2] Unfortunately Narváez was hardly the right man for a missionary expedition. His idea was to fight first and to preach afterwards, and the Indians (as De Soto was later to discover) fiercely resented any intrusion. After trying to penetrate inland, only to encounter forests and swamps, he retreated to Appalache Bay, where he found that the ships that should have been waiting for him had returned to Cuba.

A desperate attempt was made to build new ships, bellows being fashioned from deerskins and the iron of the horses' harness melted down for nails. The horses themselves were killed for food, and their skins served as water bottles while their tails were twisted into ropes for the rigging. With shirts spread as sails and gunwales hardly a handsbreadth above water, the frail craft set out, hugging the shore of the Gulf in a hopeless effort to reach Mexico. Yet they did succeed in passing the mouth of the Santo Espiritu. Then all were wrecked and perished, with the exception of Cabeza de Vaca and four other men.

These survivors were enslaved by the Indians, but gained their favor because of their skill as medicine men. Cabeza de Vaca, in the *relatio* he was afterwards to write, describes a successful operation he performed with an oyster shell. When charms were demanded, efficacious in the curing of disease, he provided what was wanted—salving his conscience meanwhile by saying the Our Father and the Hail Mary over the sick and by making the sign of the cross. The prayers were heard and the medicine man's prestige rose higher than ever.

After six years Cabeza de Vaca and his companions contrived to escape. Clothed in the pelts of dogs, they traversed the plains of Texas, where they were the first white men to see the buffalo and, having crossed the Rio Grande and the

[2] He was a bishop-elect, though not consecrated. (See Engelhardt, *Missions and Missionaries of California*, 1929, Vol. I, 722 *et seq.*)

Conchos, struck southwards from a point near El Paso. From thence they got to the Gulf of California in 1535 and to Mexico the following year. The sensation caused by Cabeza de Vaca's recital when he returned to Spain served to inspire De Soto, retired rich with the spoils of the Incas, with the design of conquering Florida.

He made his preparations carefully, and his fame as a commander in Peru was such that he was in a position, rare among the *conquistadores*, to reject many who offered their services. At the final muster two hundred and twenty-three mounted *hidalgos* were chosen—among whom was a Portuguese contingent, one of whose members, the "Gentleman of Elvas," has left the best of the accounts of the expedition. Four hundred well armed foot-soldiers were also taken.

There is no need for me to enter here upon the military details of this enterprise except to say that De Soto was, Cortés and Pizarro excepted, the ablest of Spanish colonial adventurers, and in a class by himself as a leader of cavalry. He fought several notable actions, among which must be mentioned that of Mabilla; but these and the constant skirmishing in a difficult country against redoubtable warriors gradually depleted his forces. He pressed through Georgia and into the Carolinas, then returned to the coast, laden with what he supposed were valuable pearls. As he lost these along with all his stores at Mabilla, he kept back the news that the ships were waiting in a harbor close at hand. He was afraid that his dispirited men would insist on leaving for home. It was not in his nature to admit failure. Therefore through Alabama, Mississippi and Tennessee his men had to follow him until, at a spot a few miles below the present Memphis, barges were constructed and the great river was crossed in the face of continuous attacks from the raging tribes.

The once gaily dressed *hidalgos* were now in rags. Since the disastrous victory of Mabilla, when the religious supplies were burnt with the rest of the baggage, the priests had been unable to say Mass, for they had decided that Indian corn could not be used for hosts. The best they could do was to say a "dry Mass," wearing vestments of painted deer skins. Nevertheless whenever they met Indians who were sufficiently tractable, they did what they could to convert them—De Soto himself sometimes expounding the mysteries of the Faith. Here and there a friendly chief was baptized with his people, most of these cases occurring to the west of the Mississippi. But there was no time for thorough instruction, the army continuing its march until it reached Oklahoma and even Kansas. There a sword engraved with the name of Juan de Gallegos, one of De Soto's officers, was found hundreds of years later. It bore the proud admonition: "Do not draw me without right; do not sheath me without honor."

Nor was the Spanish sword sheathed without honor. When exactly a year after the discovery of the Mississippi—that is, on May 21, 1542—De Soto died, just turned forty, his heart at last broken under a long series of disappointments, it was Luis de Moscoso, appointed by the commander on his death-bed to succeed him, who was assigned the almost impossible task of extricating those who were left of the men. His problem was made all the greater by the death, about this time, of Juan Ortiz, a survivor of Narváez's expedition, whom by an astonishing stroke of good luck they had found soon after landing. He had been invaluable as an interpreter and guide. Now somehow Moscoso had to make his way back without him to Mexico.

The little Spanish army first tried, like Cabeza de Vaca, to cross the plains of Texas. There they lost their way. Their food was gone. Such enforced guides as they secured deliberately led them astray. Nothing was left but to retrace their steps to the Santo Espiritu.

But now the loss of De Soto diminished their standing among the Indian tribes. When he had been unable to conciliate the savages, he had fallen back upon the expedient of overawing them by letting it be known that he was the Child of the Sun. After he had been buried, secretly at night, between the gates of the stockade, his men had given out that the Child of the Sun was only away on a visit to his father but would soon return. But the keen eyes of the Indians noticed the earth disturbed over the grave. His body had therefore to be exhumed and—again at night and secretly—lowered in skins weighted with sand into the river he had discovered. Luis de Moscoso was unable to claim a divine origin for himself. All he could do was to escape as soon as possible before he was overwhelmed by the Indians.

Spanish resource and courage did not fail. The river flooded their camp and all but undid their work; malaria sapped their energy; nevertheless they persisted and, taking a leaf out of Narváez's book, built boats to descend the river, as they had previously built boats to cross it. Luckily De Soto had had the foresight to save the nails from those barges. Even so, the nails held the thin planks together precariously. They wondered whether such boats would bear the pressure of the sea. All that they had for calking were Indian blankets unravelled into threads, supplemented with what flax they could find and the bark of mulberry trees. Their ropes were twisted from fibres of the same trees. Their sails were a patchwork of buffalo hides. The stirrups of the horses, now useless to them, were hammered into anchors, and the horses themselves were killed for food, except for a few that were set free to become the ancestors of the mustang. Many months before they had slaughtered the last of the pigs De Soto had brought for an emergency.

During the long march—the longest ever made on the American continent, and another Anabasis—some of the men had deserted, preferring absorption into savagery to what seemed a fruitless struggle which could only end with their butchery. Now those who remained—half of the original six hundred— were obliged, for lack of space in the ships, to leave behind almost double that number of Indian converts. These had become attached to their masters and knew only too well what they might expect from their pagan fellows. The kindhearted Gentleman of Elvas criticized this abandonment as cruel, but it had to be, if any were to be saved. All the same, a few privileged officers took away with them their personal Indian servants—a discrimination that was also criticized.

The overcrowded boats had to fight their way down the Mississippi for seventeen days against constantly attacking savages, and then were nearly wrecked by storms in the Gulf. But at last they reached a Christian settlement in Mexico, where the first act of the survivors was to hasten to church to thank God who had so miraculously delivered them. Not a few of them entered religious orders afterwards, probably in fulfillment of a vow.

De Soto's, like many other Spanish expeditions, was stained by some acts of cruelty. The traditional picture, however, of the *conquistadores* as sadistic monsters, is due to Protestant and political propaganda. What is true enough is that, precisely because the Spaniards had won their liberty from the Moorish yoke only by disdaining death, they were not particularly squeamish when they had to inflict it. But nearly always their severities could be justified—by the code of the time—on the ground of military necessity. In the case of De

Soto, he sometimes had to cow the ferocity of the Indians by reprisals; but apart from one occasion, and at a time when his mind may have been unbalanced by illness, there was no wanton bloodshed. He made friends with the Indians when this was at all possible; nor did he forget his missionary object. But it was not possible, while on the march, to plant the seed of the Faith very deep. Those among his converts who survived the wrath of their fellows, no doubt soon relapsed into the crude paganism from which they had been briefly snatched. If he achieved no conquest, at least he opened the door to the settlement of what was afterwards to be known as Louisiana. His was by all odds the most extensive piece of exploration ever carried out on the American continent.

Almost simultaneously, though unknown to De Soto, Francisco Vasquez de Coronado went out to discover the Seven Cities of Cíbola. He too had been inspired by Cabeza de Vaca's stories, of which corroboration was offered by a Christian Moor named Estevanico who had been sent to the north from Mexico to reconnoitre. He learned of the existence of the pueblos, and this seemed to point to some degree of civilized order and also—it was hoped—of wealth.

The authorities in Mexico thought they now had a heaven-sent opportunity for providing an outlet for the turbulent energies of certain undesirable elements in the colony. Therefore they deliberately fostered the idea that riches comparable to those of Mexico and Peru were only waiting discovery. Whether Coronado was himself hoodwinked, or whether he lent himself to the hoodwinking of others, will probably be forever undetermined. One fact makes it clear that, whatever other incentives were used, the purpose was primarily that of colonization: a large number of sheep and cattle were taken along. The force of three hundred Spaniards and a thousand Indian allies had no less than a thousand horses and were provided with six small pieces of ordnance. A fort and a settlement are indicated.

During the year 1540 practically every one of the pueblos in New Mexico and Arizona, as far as the Colorado river, was visited.[3] Upon the whole Coronado behaved with notable humanity, though when he was resisted, he had no hesitation in crushing opposition. Near the present Santa Fé, the Spaniards

[3] Meanwhile another expedition, which went by sea under Hernando de Alarçon, reached the mouth of the Colorado and marched along its course for over two hundred miles.

were told that in the province of Quivira, which had so far
eluded them, gold existed in abundance. In search of it, some
companies set out at the end of April, 1541, and, crossing
western Arkansas—the eastern part of which had been reached
by De Soto—penetrated to southern Nebraska. The nearest
thing they got to gold was a fragment of copper. Except for
a few Indians in Nebraska who lived in wretched huts, none
but nomadic tribes were encountered in that region. A year
later Coronado decided to throw up his task and return to
Mexico.

There the Viceroy, Mendoza, received him coldly—not so
much because he had failed to produce gold as because he had
disobeyed orders. Mexico had gone to considerable expense in
equipping the expedition and had counted upon the colonization of new territories by disorderly men of whom it would
be well rid. Now they were on Mendoza's hands again, and
they had nothing to show. Coronado was relieved of his command and fell with his wife and eight children into poverty.
In 1553 he died, still in his early fifties. Time in due course
has done justice to his name. Though his exploits were less
brilliant than those of De Soto, and his tragedy remains un-
gilded by romance, his reports concerning the regions he
passed through and of the Indians he encountered gave more
solidly valuable information than was contributed by any explorer of his period.

Something needs to be said about the contributions made
by the priests associated with Coronado. When the Moor
Estevanico had made his preliminary survey of the ground, he
was accompanied by Father Mark of Nice who wrote a *relatio*
of their journey. The exaggerations this contained when published (in translation) have been found to be for the most
part interpolations: what Father Mark actually wrote was
sufficiently accurate. Obviously he cannot be held responsible
for the way the Mexican officials touched up his account for
purposes of their own. Shea says of him that "he stands in
history as the earliest of the priestly explorers who, unarmed
and afoot, penetrated into the heart of the country, in advance
of all Europeans—a barefooted friar effecting more, as Viceroy
Mendoza wrote, than well-armed parties of Spaniards had
been able to accomplish."

Mark of Nice was accompanied by Juan de Padilla and
some other priests and lay-brothers when Coronado's column
set out from Culiacan in April, 1540. But about their work

at this time we hear very little, although we may be sure that Mass was offered whenever possible and may suppose that a makeshift chapel was erected. Even Father Mark disappears from view.

When Coronado's evacuation took place, however, something of great importance happened: several of the friars decided to remain behind. Two of these, Father Juan de la Cruz and the lay-brother Luis, stayed in New Mexico. They must have understood their danger; it was willingly accepted as the price to be paid for preaching the Gospel. It is possible that they felt some relief at the departure of the army, among whom were men whose conduct was hardly conducive to the spread of Christianity. They were never heard of again.

We know what happened to Juan de Padilla, the proto-martyr of America.[4] Like many of the missionaries, he was an ex-soldier. His choice was Quivira as a field of labor. With him remained Andreas del Campo, a layman, two Zapoteca Indians from Mexico, named Sebastian and Luke, and an unnamed mulatto. All of them seem to have been Franciscan tertiaries and are referred to as *donandos*, a term roughly corresponding to the *donnés* of the later French missions—lay-assistants to the Fathers.

So long as this group remained with the Quivira Indians they were unmolested. But Padilla yearned for further conquests; his zeal was of the Xaverian kind. Accordingly the five men pressed on to a point which seems to have been in south-western Kansas. There one day they saw coming towards them a band of hostile braves. Padilla at once understood that it was the end.

The Indians were far enough off to give some hope that, if he went on alone, he might detain them long enough to give his companions an opportunity to escape. He therefore ordered Del Campo, who was on horseback, to ride for safety:

---

[4] We must call him that because his is the first martyrdom of which we have definite record, though Juan de la Cruz and Luis were also probably killed. As for the missionaries who were with Narváez, they were drowned, the boat in which they were travelling being afterwards found by Cabeza de Vaca upside down on the beach. The one priest, Asturiano, who got to land may have met a violent death. Several of the priests who accompanied De Soto died during the expedition, though whether from violence or the rigors of the march we do not know. In the absence of this knowledge it is not safe to presume martyrdom.

he at least could easily outdistance pursuers. Even the two Indians and the negro had a good start, though they were on foot. But if they were to escape they must leave him.

Reluctantly they did as they were told. There was no time to argue, and they knew they could not change Padilla's mind. Andreas del Campo was soon out of sight, but Luke and Sebastian, hiding in the tall grass of the prairie, saw everything that happened. When Padilla had almost reached those running towards him he knelt down to meet death. After the savages had done their bloody work the two Indian converts returned. Padilla's body was riddled with arrows. They buried him with Christian prayers. It is from them that we have the details as to what happened. We might note that this first martyrdom was not on the coast but almost in the very center of the continent. By it the whole of America was consecrated to Christ.

"Had the priests with De Soto," says John Gilmary Shea, "been able to say Mass, the march of the Blessed Sacrament and of the Precious Blood across the continent would have been complete." Even so, the Faith had already been preached on the shores of the Chesapeake and from Carolina to the Mississippi and beyond. Priests had also already gone as far north in the South-west as the Colorado River. But the missionaries, up to the year 1542, had been hampered by being attached to an army or a party of exploration. They had not been able before this time to devote themselves entirely to the evangelizing of the Indians.

Soon there were to be many such efforts in the region of the Great Lakes and in the territory claimed by Spain. These will have to be considered in subsequent chapters, as they constitute a story distinct from that of the first adventurers. As forty years were to elapse before the missions, properly so called, got under way in New Mexico, and thirty more before the French Jesuits began their work, it may be as well to notice briefly two other pioneer attempts, both of which ended in martyrdom.

In 1549 a group of Dominicans, under Luis Cancer, received a commission from the Emperor Charles V to go into Florida independent of military support. The royal instructions were that any Indians that had been taken from the country—and Luis de Moscoso and several of his officers, for instance, had taken some—were to be sent back. The Spanish settlers found a means of ignoring an inconvenient provision, but Father Luis sailed from Vera Cruz accompanied by three other friars. At Havana they came across an Indian woman who had been baptized under the name of Magdalena. By returning her to Florida the Emperor's orders would be—to that extent—fulfilled. And she would be useful as an interpreter. It was hoped that the Indians would prove more friendly towards unarmed missionaries than towards invading soldiers. They came to anchor in Tampa Bay.

Already Cancer had managed to conciliate the natives to whom he had preached in Central America; indeed he had succeeded so well that the scene of his labors is still known as Vera Paz. This was enough to encourage him to believe that he might be able to win Florida where armed force had failed. Despite the warnings of the captain of the ship that nobody should go on shore until there was evidence of a friendly welcome, Father Diego de Tolosa did so, accompanied by a sailor named Fuentes who had offered his services as a lay assistant to the missionaries, and the interpreter Magdalena. They did not return.

Then a Spaniard named Muñoz, apparently one of the deserters from De Soto's expedition, swam out to the ship with the news that Tolosa and Fuentes had been murdered. But Magdalena—who was evidently playing a treacherous game—shouted from the shore that the Christians were alive and well. There still was no sign of them.

Father Luis now persuaded the captain to let him disembark, but the sailors in the row-boat took fright when the Indians threatened them and would not go any nearer. Upon this, the priest threw himself into the water and waded to land. He was not going to desert Father Diego and Fuentes if there was any question of their being alive. His only fear was that the captain would insist on carrying him back to Cuba with his mission unaccomplished.

Those on board could see all that happened—the Dominican climbing up the bank of the river mouth, the Indians surrounding him and pulling off his hat, and then, while Father Luis knelt down, clubs and axes descending on his shaven head. What happened to Tolosa and Fuentes was never learned. But no doubt the story Muñoz brought was correct: they, too, had suffered martyrdom.

The fate of these brave men convinced the Spanish Court that it was unsafe to send out missionaries unless they had armed protection. So Tristan de Luna was given authority in

1559 to go to Florida with fifteen hundred men and establish a colony. With the soldiers and settlers, went Pedro de Feria as Provincial-Vicar, four other priests, and a lay-brother. The policy, however, was to be one of conciliation, not of conquest. As Feria wrote before sailing, it was his hope "by good example, with good works, and with presents, to bring the Indians to a knowledge of our holy faith and Catholic truth."

It was not to be. That fall a Floridian hurricane struck them, wrecking seven of the ships and destroying most of the provisions. Despite reinforcements for both the clergy and the army that arrived from Mexico, and a peaceful contact established with some of the tribes—the price paid by the Spaniards being that of joining them as allies against hostile Indians—dissensions arose and the soldiers threatened mutiny against Luna's harsh rule. Things like these made a successful settlement and steady missionary work virtually impossible.

We hear of one highly dramatic scene. Luna had sentenced Ceron, the leader of the malcontents, to death. But on Palm Sunday, when all the Spaniards were at Mass, Father Dominic, one of the friars, made so powerful a personal appeal to Luna from the altar itself that then and there a public reconciliation was effected. All this, however, happened too late. The settlement was evacuated in 1561, and Philip II decided to abandon all further attempts at colonization in Florida. The situation had been further complicated by the intrusion of the Huguenots under Jean Ribault.

If Florida was saved for Spain and the Church, this was mainly due to the vision and energy of Pedro Menendez. He refused to give up. In 1565 he ejected the French and, because he had arrived on St. Augustine's day, he gave the name of the saint to the new Spanish settlement. Though the French in 1568 took their revenge for what they had suffered at the hands of Menendez, the setback was temporary. Florida remained safely Spanish.

Missionary work was now renewed—this time by the Jesuits, sent by their General, St. Francis Borgia, at the request of Philip II. While some of the band were stationed at St. Augustine, or in South Carolina, the main contingent went as far north as the Chesapeake, the group of two priests, two novices and four lay-brothers being led by John Baptist Segura. For their interpreter they had a captured Indian who had accepted baptism and was now known as Luis de Velasco. If the conduct of the precious Magdalena suggests that she was treacherous, there can be no doubt whatever about the conduct of Luis. The fact is that the Floridian Indians, whatever their professions, were simply not to be trusted.

On September 10, 1570, the Jesuits reached the mouth of the Chesapeake, where the Indians seemed to be friendly enough. But the country had suffered famine for six years and the ship had been so sparsely supplied for her voyage that those on board had been obliged to eat two of the four barrels of biscuits intended as food for the missionaries during the approaching winter. When the ship sailed a couple of days later she carried an urgent request that corn be sent for the spring sowing. Yet by the middle of February there was still no sign of any ship, and the Jesuits and their catechumens were living as best they could on roots.

Meanwhile Velasco, the Indian interpreter, had gone to visit his brother, a chief whose village was on the Rappahannock. When he did not return, Segura sent Quiros, the priest, and Mendez and Solis, lay-brothers, to find out what had become of him. They were at once murdered and, four days later, Velasco reappeared at the Chesapeake settlement, wearing the cassock of Quiros and accompanied by savages whose hostile intentions were only too evident. They surrounded the chapel at Axacan that the Jesuits had dedicated to Our Lady. Segura lost no time in preparing those with him for death.

The Indians of the southern regions were not given to inflicting the hideous tortures destined to be suffered by the Jesuits who afterwards worked among the northern tribes. Simple butchery sufficed: the six missionaries died that day. Only an Indian boy named Alonzo escaped. He saw to it that the martyrs were buried together in a trench, each with a crucifix in his hand.[5]

When word reached Menendez of what had happened he sailed in person to the scene of the atrocity and arrested a number of the Indians with the demand that they give up the treacherous Luis for exemplary punishment. Luis, however, was kept concealed, but on the evidence of Alonzo eight men of those directly implicated in the murder were hanged. Before being executed they were baptized by Father Rogel, the missionary who had come with Menendez from St. Augustine.

The disaster decided Francis Borgia. As even the mission at

[5] As Professor Bolton remarks: "Virginia history thus opened not with the founding of Jamestown but with the giving to the world of eight Jesuit martyrs." (*Rim of Christendom*, p. 5.)

St. Augustine was making no headway among the intractable savages, he withdrew his subjects and sent them to Mexico. Menendez, who, whatever his private failings, had been so zealous for the conversion of the heathen, died in September, 1574. Nobody else had the heart for what seemed to be an impossible task. Florida had to wait until 1577 for the arrival of the Franciscans.

The failure was made glorious by martyrdom. It was therefore not a failure under its religious aspect. The abandonment of the Chesapeake region, however, was politically disastrous for Spain. Could it have been held, an effectual barrier would have been erected against the encroachments of the English in Virginia. But not even Spanish energy was quite sufficient to keep its grip on such far-flung territories. It was already becoming as much as the authorities could do to protect the settlements already made in the Indies and Central America from the depredations of Drake. That celebrated pirate sacked even St. Augustine in 1586.

The Spanish ambition was not merely, or even primarily, political. Menendez had written shortly before his death: "After the salvation of my own soul, there is nothing I desire more than to be in Florida and there end my days saving souls." The noble sentiment bares the very heart of the great Spanish dream. Only too often the *conquistadores* are remembered mainly for their severities. It is no more than elementary justice that their spiritual aims should also be borne in mind. Where they succeeded in establishing their power, the Indians were absorbed into Christian civilization, at least according to the extent of their capacity. The policy of extermination had to wait for the coming of English Protestants.

CHAPTER THREE

THE SPANISH MISSIONS

A serious problem confronts any historian who writes of the Church in America. It is that of telling his story according to chronological plan. If he does so in the case of the Spanish missions, he ought to carry his account almost into the middle of the nineteenth century, when Texas and New Mexico and Arizona and Utah (together with parts of Colorado and Wyoming) became part of the United States. If that were done, however, the story of the English colonies of the seventeenth century and of the American Revolution, and also of the reorganization of the Church that was made possible by the Revolution, would have to wait. But as that story cannot wait, I must defer all reference to those great men, Eusebius Kino of Lower California and Junipero Serra of Upper California, until later. The compromise is far from satisfactory, for Spanish missionary effort forms, after all, a continuous whole, continuing even after the independence of Mexico in 1821, though in a feeble and attenuated way. In the high noon of the seventeenth century no less than three thousand missionaries were maintained in its dominions by the Spanish Crown. It is because what was being done in the West and the Southwest did not make any impression upon the American consciousness until after the war with Mexico, that I must accept an interruption as unavoidable. The tyranny of pattern is grievous to be borne, especially when the most drastic chronological limitations will not fully serve. Perhaps 1763, when Florida was ceded to England and Louisiana to Spain, would be a suitable date at which to draw a line. Yet if I took it, I should have to go too far afield. I shall therefore not go beyond the end of the seventeenth century in this chapter, or in the next, the one which will deal with the French missions from Canada.

Though the Dominicans and Jesuits had in turn been obliged to withdraw from Florida—using that term in the wide sense in which it was used then—they had done much that was to be of service to their successors. Sedeño had performed spade work in Georgia; Rogel, in South Carolina. And a Jesuit lay-brother named Baez had already written an Indian grammar and catechism. When the Franciscans arrived in 1577 there was some foundation upon which they could build. Fifteen years later we find eight priests and three lay-brothers at work, though still against almost insurmountable difficulties.

Drake sacked St. Augustine in 1586 and in 1597 there was an Indian massacre in which six of the missionaries perished. Nevertheless when Juan Cabezas de Altamirano visited Florida in 1607 to administer Confirmation—for the first time in this country—the native Christians were already numerous. By 1634 we hear of forty-four missions served by thirty-five Franciscans and of twenty-five thousand native converts. The work continued to flourish so well that in 1655 a bishop was asked for, but was not supplied.

As so often happens, success brought enervation. The absence of a bishop, who would have exercised effective control, resulted in some slackening of effort among the missionaries who, no longer steeled by martyrdom, or even with serious obstacles to overcome, had begun to perform their duties in perfunctory fashion. Calderon, the Bishop of Santiago, who came in 1674 on a canonical visitation, found such ignorance among the Indian converts that it was necessary to issue strict orders—to be obeyed under pain of excommunication—about preaching and the teaching of catechism. He gave, it is true, Confirmation to over thirteen thousand souls and conferred minor orders on seven native clerics. All the same he was clearly not the kind of man to be impressed with mere statistics. He could not fail to notice that the friars had declined from heroism and were all for an easy life free of episcopal regulation.

There were of course other factors operating. The climate was one. Another was that the secular officials did not always give, as in the past, a hearty coöperation. And the relaxation of effort on the part of the missionaries was not unconnected with the decay of Spain. In both cases a magnificent façade remained, while the foundations were being sapped. Probably, too, Florida already divined that it could not maintain itself much longer against the English encirclement. Certainly in California, at an even later period, we find apostolic zeal undimmed. There Spain had not yet been challenged. But after all other explanations have been allowed for, we have to come back to the mysteriously bad effects of success. Catholicism needs a sharp and bracing atmosphere. Where this was provided, as in the new mission fields, a spontaneous heroism was called forth. It always is.

Yet it would be unjust to represent the story of Florida merely in these terms. O'Gorman has described the period, 1625–1700, as the palmy days of the Church in that province. Even before that time—in 1612—Francisco Pareja had written two books in the Timuquan language, to be followed by others, all of which were printed in Mexico. And these, like the letters written by the Florida Indians (which still exist), demonstrate that good work was being done, even if in an increasingly sleepy style. Though the story trails away to a dreary end, it had, at all events, opened in a burst of splendor. Between these two poles what was accomplished was by no means negligible.

But let us turn from this to what happened in the Southwest.

After the retreat of Coronado there was no further attempt, until 1581, to settle New Mexico. Then the Franciscan lay-brother, Augustino Rodriguez, was inspired to go as a missionary and, in his turn, inspired two young Fathers, Francisco Lopez and Juan de Santa Maria, to go with him. It was by them that the name New Mexico was first used. They worked in the vicinity of the present Albuquerque until the two priests were killed. Rodriguez buried them and was himself killed soon afterwards. Again a resplendent failure.

But in 1588 Juan de Oñate, a rich Mexican, married to a lady in whose veins flowed the mingled blood of Cortés and Montezuma, believed he could succeed where Coronado had failed. He therefore asked Philip II to appoint him viceroy of the new province, with a jurisdiction independent of Mexico proper. This was considered a rather tall order, but he did receive the dignity of governorship with the right of transmitting it to his descendants. Although his motive was largely one of personal profit and prestige, he did not neglect spiritual objects, for he recruited ten Franciscans for the missions. When at last he entered his territories—not until 1598 because of various delaying causes—it was with four hundred Spaniards, some of whom were women and children, seven thousand head of cattle, and over eighty carts for the baggage. By 1605 Santa Fé had become the center of administration, the two earlier settlements of San Juan Bautista and San Gabriel remaining subsidiary. Ten years after he had taken possession of his province eight thousand Indian converts had been made and additional priests were working among them.

Ten years later again we hear of Jerome de Zarete Salmeron having composed a catechism in the Jeme language and of having baptized 6,566 of the people. Clearly the progress was rapid; as events were to prove it was more rapid than thorough.

What is rather curious is that Oñate, who had derived most of his wealth from mines in Mexico, neglected to prospect for silver in New Mexico. Instead he and his settlers became ranchers, no doubt fortunately for the country. In a society left relatively free from the contamination of greed a special kind of civilization was able to develop, one in which both Spanish and Indian elements fused. The churches still standing, or their ruins, attest in their architecture and paintings to the character of the resultant culture. Politically New Mexico developed into a province almost as completely isolated from Mexico, under whose nominal jurisdiction it had been placed, as from the English of the Atlantic seaboard.

All this was not accomplished at once or without many setbacks. In 1668 there occurred an explosion of such ferocity as to make it clear that the fusion of cultures was still largely on the surface, that under the facile Catholicism of the Indians, who appeared almost without exception to have accepted the Christian faith, there existed a sullen and sinister paganism.

It has often been charged—usually by the narrower sort of Protestant controversialist—that Catholicism is overlaid with many pagan incrustations. Catholicism, it must be added, is ready to accept the accusation—and even to make it her boast. Only it would change the terms to some extent; it regards the process as a willingness to absorb the true, the good and the beautiful, wherever they may be found, and to indulge all harmless human propensities. The great god Pan is not really dead; he is baptized.

The process of accommodation, however, can easily be carried too far. Catholicism is, in truth, elastic in some of its aspects; but it can be drawn out only so far and no further without snapping. By tolerating too much, and by failing to understand the Indian psychology, the missionaries had, in effect, allowed their neophytes to remain largely pagan at heart. The somewhat careless good humor of the Franciscan friars ought to have been aware that the Catholicism of the Indians did not go very deep; yet they did not unduly trouble themselves, because they hoped that grace, operating among a whole people over a long period, would amply suffice to bring about what their own declining zeal should have made it its business to effect. It is always easier to baptize a man than to instruct him thoroughly.

Moreover, the absence of a bishop, as in the case of the missions in Florida, resulted in clerical laxity. Both provinces of course were nominally under a bishop, but in each case he was so far off as not to know what was going on and unable to exercise the necessary control. The fact is that the missionaries did not want a bishop resident among them. When one had been proposed in 1630 the Franciscans were against his being appointed. And in this they were supported by the civil and military authorities, who were jealous of any jurisdiction save their own. Why interfere when things were going so well! What could be a better sign than that the Tlascaltecos Indians who came to Santa Fé should build their own church and dedicate it to San Miguel de los Tlascaltecos! In this complacency the friars and the secular officers were at one. In particular the Franciscans positively resented all attempts to reform discipline—weak and infrequent as these attempts were—made by their nominal bishop. Their order had established the missions unaided. They had come to regard them as their own preserve. They did not want to be disturbed in their comfortable sloth.

There is of course nothing to be wondered at in this state of affairs. Long afterwards, when the first bishops in the United States were appointed, their authority was often openly flouted by many of the priests and people. During colonial days they had managed to get along without any bishop at all, except for the Vicar-Apostolic in distant London, under whom they had enjoyed a virtual autonomy. And though the parallel between the Church in the young American Republic and the Church in New Mexico must not be carried too far, there are at least points of similarity between the two cases.

Another factor was that the Spaniards were, by now, resting much too heavily upon their heroic past. What nation was more Catholic than themselves? What nation had made more brilliant and extensive conquests in the New World? What nation had done more to propagate the Faith? They were so very orthodox that they were only too often indifferent to personal morals. God would be sure to be indulgent towards those who had rendered Him such signal services.

There were still, they admitted, some dangers to the province from wandering bands of Apaches and Comanches and Navajos, who came down from time to time from their mountain fastnesses to pillage the pueblos. But these were only external annoyances. The authorities shut their eyes to what was going on among the Christian Indians. They failed to remember that these Indians, seemingly so docile, might also have a secret hankering for independence, especially when the Spanish hand was iron upon them. For however tolerant their masters could be in some matters, they were very severe in others. The inconsistency itself was productive of resentment.

It was not that no warnings were received. The authorities received many, and chose to ignore them. Stories were brought of how the same people who had attended Mass on Sunday met secretly at night in their *estufas*, the underground sweathouses, for the practice of pagan rites. The reports were dismissed as exaggerated or distorted. Never is it easy for the white man to enter into the mentality of the Indians—a mentality which appears to have been able to encompass two religions simultaneously. Their Christian piety was fervent. The poor savages loved an ornate ritual. Nothing could exceed their devotion to their favorite saints—especially when they were able to express it, in their own fashion, by means of fantastic ancestral dances. The same dances, however, were performed with an even greater gusto in the *estufas*. The medicine-men were acquiring a deeper influence than the priests.

It is not to be denied that, when a flagrant case of sorcery or devil worship was brought to their attention, the Governor and the friars sternly reproved it, and on occasion used the lash to correct the evil. More often they were content to wink at evils they could not cure, or to deny that the secret paganism could be anything but rare.

The punishments did no good. The Indians perhaps could not comprehend why they should be punished for their obscene heathen dances or for their invocation of devils whose existence was affirmed by the Christians themselves. What was needed was a resolute and systematic effort to destroy paganism at the roots by patient instruction. But that was too much trouble. Punishment that descended only now and then on a few heads, when all were known to be guilty, was merely irritating. The anger of the Indians mounted. Through their secret societies they organized themselves. And knowing, as they did, how great was the prowess of the Spaniards, they allied themselves with the Apaches.

In one of their medicine-men, Popé by name, the Indians

found an able leader. His motive was probably political rather than religious, but he understood that, in order to shake off the Spanish yoke, he must direct his rising against Christianity as well. Church and State were inextricably bound together in the Spanish dominions. It was therefore only by a revival of paganism that Popé could free the people and further his own ambitions.

Suddenly the storm broke. The Indians sought to wash away their baptism with water and the weed they used for soap. The churches were burnt; the Blessed Sacrament was profaned; the name of Christ and His Mother was forbidden. But that the rebellion was not merely (or even mainly) religious in motive is indicated by the fact that the use of the Spanish language was also proscribed and that it was ordered that none of the vegetables and fruits the white man had introduced into the country should be touched. Popé was a clever psychologist.

In the first fury of the rising half the clergy and four hundred white settlers were instantly massacred. Those who escaped crowded into Santa Fé, where they were encircled by almost the entire Indian population. To hold the city was impossible. After a siege of five days the Governor, Otermin, decided that there was nothing for it but to cut his way out and retreat to Mexico.

He had about a thousand souls with him, many of them women and children. No more than a hundred and fifty armed men could be mustered. Only because the Indian memory knew how a force as small had sufficed to rout thousands before, were the Spaniards allowed to pass. El Paso was safely reached. North of that settlement the whole province had been cleared of the whites within a few weeks. The work of nearly a century had been destroyed at a single blow.

Or so Popé and his followers imagined. It might have been so had the Indians been capable of maintaining an organization. But now with the removal of the Spanish order, the tribes reverted to their ancient quarrels. Popé, drunk with power, was ferocious in his tyranny. The Apaches, whom they had accepted as allies, harried them again. And the wrath of heaven manifested itself in a drought. The Indians began to sigh for a return of the prosperity they had enjoyed under the ejected Spaniards. They were at least to be preferred to Popé.

Moreover, not all the Indians, by any means, had really abandoned the Faith. In terror they professed to conform to the triumphant paganism, but secretly they took a leaf out of the book of the medicine-men and gathered in what we might almost call Christian *estufas*. In hidden caverns they preserved the vessels that had been used for Mass and before them they kept candles burning night and day. It was all they could do.

Not until 1692 was a reconquest attempted. Then the new Governor marched in August from El Paso against Santa Fé with a force of sixty Spaniards and a hundred faithful Indians. There was no battle. The fury of the rebellion had long spent itself. The Indians were glad to accept their pardon on condition that they return to the Church.

So drastic had Popé been in his determination to extirpate the last vestiges of Christianity that he had demanded that men give up the wives they had married in church and take other women. The general shuffling, however agreeable it may have been for the moment to the licentious, proved to have drawbacks. Therefore former partners in the majority of instances were very willing to rejoin one another. The children born since the rebellion were baptized. The apostates were absolved. Popé had recently died.

Nevertheless the embers were not quite quenched. The adhesion of many of the Indians was made only under duress. These continued the practice of secret paganism. Again there were warnings about the meetings in the *estufas*. And again the Spanish authorities laughed at those whom they thought too timid. The Indians, having been taught their lesson, would not dare to rise a second time.

But they did, even though the new rebellion of 1696 was that of only a few tribes. These murdered such priests and settlers as fell into their hands, until decisive action drove the rebels into the mountains. The Moqui tribe in Arizona refused submission, as did a part of the Zuñi, and were never brought back into the Christian fold. But by the end of 1700 it may be said that New Mexico had been pacified, except for the recalcitrants holding out in their fastnesses. After that the Spaniards were alert to detect and suppress the slightest sign of crypto-paganism. They, too, had been taught a lesson.

This is not to suggest that no distinctively Indian complexion was forbidden to Indian devotion. On the contrary, they might dance as much as they wished—if that was their way of expressing their piety. They might fill their churches with pictures painted in primary colors, since no other pictures appealed to them. For that matter, many of the forms of Spanish piety appear somewhat startling to the more somber-minded

"Anglo-Saxon." The Catholic religion, being universal, can readily admit full rein to racial temperament. But the Indians were to remember that they were Christians, not pagans. There was to be no creeping off to *estufas*. God, not the devil, was to be worshipped.

It is likely enough that the Indian mind was not capable of forming any very definite notion of the exalted mysteries of the Faith—though, if it comes to that, the knowledge of even the profoundest theologian is imperfect. Benignant heaven demands from no man more than he is capable of giving. The Shepherds were as welcome at Bethlehem as the Wise Men —and got there sooner. The tribes henceforward remained Catholic—to the extent of their capacity.

Rather abruptly I close this chapter with the date 1700; for I must hurry on to my central theme—a distinctively American Catholicism. Within these limitations—chronological and geographical—the best achievements of the Spanish missions cannot receive anything like adequate treatment. But perhaps in this connection I may quote a sentence or two from Herbert Bolton's life of Kino. "The Black Robes of New France counted their conversions by hundreds, or at best by thousands; those of New Spain, working in a more propitious vineyard, numbered their baptisms by hundreds of thousands, or even by millions. . . . The imposing stature of the Jesuits of New France is widely known because they had Parkman as their historian. The Spanish Jesuits in North America await their Parkman."[1] This story—perhaps fortunately for the preservation of my pattern—falls outside it. But I should at least indicate it, since there was some impinging. As it is, I have not had space to do more than sketch in a few of the aspects of Spanish missionary work within the present territory of the United States.

[1] *Rim of Christendom*, p. 4.

CHAPTER FOUR

THE FRENCH MISSIONS

Although the beginning of any attempt at French settlements in America should perhaps be dated from 1534, when Cartier sailed up the St. Lawrence (which he named) as far as Quebec and Montreal, French exploration may, if one chooses, be pushed back to a much earlier point. Apart from Cousin, about whose Brazilian discovery of 1488 there must remain some doubt, there is reason to believe that Breton fishermen—like Basques—knew about Newfoundland before Columbus ever came to the New World. Certainly Denis of Honfleur came to the Gulf of St. Lawrence in 1506, as did Aubert and De Lery during the twelve years that followed. And Giovanni da Verrazano, an Italian employed by France, had reached Cape Fear and had then gone as far as the Hudson ten years before Cartier's first voyage.

Nevertheless Cartier opened the door to Canada, just as Columbus had opened the door to the Western World. And this despite the fact that it was not until 1604 that any permanent French settlement was made. Then Du Guast received from Henry IV a monopoly for colonizing Acadia—which at that time was understood as comprising everything from the Bay of Fundy to a point as far south as Philadelphia—and Champlain made his accurate geographical surveys, mapping, by the way, Plymouth Harbor and naming it for St. Louis, while Pourtrincourt planted a colony at Quebec in 1608 and another in Nova Scotia two years later.

It was, however, not until 1614 that the first priests came out to Quebec—four Recollect friars, and in 1625 the first Jesuits. If all priests had to leave after the capture of Quebec by the English in 1628, the conquest proved only temporary. In 1632 the Jesuits—now without the Recollects—returned. And in 1644, when Montreal was founded by Maisonneuve, a group of Sulpicians were brought over.

A word might be said about this Society. Jean-Jacques Olier had established his seminary at Paris in October, 1642, the foundation being intended to confine itself to conducting seminaries, the work Olier saw to be of paramount importance for his time. In Montreal, however, conditions necessitated the Sulpicians' undertaking parish work as well, which in that city is still in their hands. Moreover, we shall see before long how when, after the outbreak of the French Revolution, Emery, the Superior-General of the Sulpicians, sent a group of his men to set up a seminary in Baltimore, they too were obliged, because of the needs of a new country in which there were so few priests, to go beyond the limitations that had been assigned them. Three of the first four American colleges were theirs, and several of the first American bishops—especially those working on the frontier—were (or had been) Sulpicians. All of them were Frenchmen. The Church in the United States owes a heavy debt to them.

If the Recollects were the first priests to go to Quebec, they were not the first French missionaries in America. These were the Jesuits, whom the Marquise de Guercheville, one of those wealthy and pious women who are accustomed to having their own way, managed to establish in a colony of her own in Maine, since she found that she was unable to induce Pourtrincourt to take them. It is with them that I would begin, were it not that I should have to carry their story to a date later than I have set myself. As the story of the Jesuits in Maine ends tragically in a clash with the New England colonists, it will have to be deferred to a later chapter.

But before we come to French missionary activity it is necessary to glance at the exploration that made this activity possible. It is also necessary to recall the accident that was to prove an almost insuperable obstacle to French expansion and eventually an important contributing factor to the French loss of Canada. This was when on July 29, 1609, Champlain, backing the wrong horse among the Indian tribes, shot dead an Iroquois chief. That he wounded two others at the same time was something on which he may have plumed himself. By doing so he made implacable enemies of the Five Nations. It was they who set themselves to wipe out the Indian allies of the French and subsequently fought beside the English in the war that began in 1755. Had it not been for that shot, the shot of the "embattled farmers" might never have rung around the world. So do historical events hinge on one another.

Despite Iroquois hostility, the French proved to be, even more than the Spaniards, the explorers of America. Where the *conquistadores*, being horsemen, got themselves bogged down in the swamps and forests of Florida, and did not make any real progress until they reached the more open country of the South-west, the French, from the outset, accommodated themselves to the means of transportation provided by northern lakes and rivers. From the St. Lawrence they utilized the water-way that goes, broken only by short portages, by Lake Champlain and Lake George, to the Hudson and so to the Atlantic. They discovered and exploited the system of the Great Lakes that comes—again with only short portages—to the network of rivers flowing into the Mississippi. Their frail birch-bark canoes might almost be called eggshells that cleft a continent. The Spaniards have indeed the credit of discovering the Father of Waters, but they never realized its importance as the key to America, nor would they have been able to use it as the key.

This was what the French did. After Nicollet in 1634 had nearly reached the Mississippi, and the rather shady Des Groseillers and Radisson twenty-five years later had gone still nearer, Joliet and Père Marquette at last got to the river, paddled down it in their canoe, and learned beyond all question that it flowed into the Gulf of Mexico. Du Luth and La Salle completed the process, the one by getting as far as the western shore of Lake Superior, the other—while asserting France's claim to everything on the continent up to the Rockies—by planning means for holding the Great Lakes and the Mississippi against all comers. Soon an unbroken line of forts and trading stations was drawn from Quebec to New Orleans, at once hemming in the English colonies on the Atlantic seaboard and estopping Spain from thrusting eastwards. One would think, looking at the map, that America's destiny was now safely of French determining. Though, in the event it proved otherwise, America remains permanently enriched from France's once having been the chief American power.

Of all elements in the French-American epic beyond all comparison the most romantic is that of the missionary effort. As Thwaites says in his *France in America*, our history "would lose much of its welcome color were there blotted from its pages the picturesque and often thrilling story of the curés and friars of Canada in the French régime." Or to quote Bancroft, "Not a cape was turned, or a river entered, but a Jesuit led the way." Though the sons of Ignatius were not primarily explorers but missionaries, it was from their pens—writing in canoes or the depths of the forests or in smoky wigwams—that we get our greatest wealth of geographical and ethnographical knowledge. It is to the seventy-three published volumes of the *Jesuit Relations* that every historian of the period must go.

Parkman is of course the author who has left us the most vivid account of the Jesuit labors. He does, it is true, now and then indulge in a gratuitous sneer—for he could not quite shake off his Puritan prepossessions—but we must gratefully acknowledge that, except for this, he does ample justice to the men he writes about. He did his work almost too well. Not without justice does Bolton complain that the very title of his book, *The Jesuits in North America,* has obscured from the general reader that there were a still greater number of Jesuits in the Spanish dominions. It is with Parkman's Jesuits—or rather with those of them who worked in what is now the United States—that I am now concerned.

They designed nothing less than the conversion of a continent of the most intractable savages in the whole world. Had France not fallen, the Jesuit ambition might well have been fulfilled. For even after their order was suppressed, when Clement XIV yielded to political pressure in 1773, other Catholic missionaries could have been counted upon to have continued their work. But with French rule ceasing in Canada, soon afterwards to be followed by the American Revolution, the French missionary effort was broken. If again we are obliged to record a failure, it is again a glorious one. The sadness that touches it is due to the fact that the French, more than men of any other nation, understood how to win the Indians. Where the Spaniards forcibly (and therefore imperfectly) converted them, and the English, after having completely ignored their spiritual interests, set about their extermination, the French charmed them and treated them as brothers.

Yet the French were under no illusions with regard to the red man. They knew perfectly well that he was crafty and dirty and cruel and fantastically obscene and a devil-worshipper and (at least ritually) sometimes a cannibal. What they recognized, however, were the fine qualities indicated by the noble bearing of the savage, by his powerful oratory, and by his indomitable courage. The tragedy is that the Indians could not have been Christianized and civilized by the one people capable of that task. As a consequence America has simply thrown away one of the best of its elements.

Apart from the ever-present dangers so cheerfully accepted

by the Black Robes, it was they who had to contend with the ravages wrought by the white man's fire-water, and Indian polygamy and sexual promiscuousness, and the dream super-stition which impelled the Indians to do whatever it was, how-ever violent or wicked or absurd, that their manitou had in-stilled into their minds in sleep. But the Fathers met these difficulties, never baptizing their neophytes (unless at the point of death) until a long probation had proved their faith and their virtue. In page after page of the *Jesuit Relations*, along with much that was a heartbreaking disappointment, they were able to record most touching incidents showing of what devotion and purity the savage breast was capable. One would think, they sometimes exclaim, that these poor people at Mass were members of a religious order! Among others who developed not merely a reasonable decency of behavior but positive sanctity, is one, Catherine Tekakwitha, the Lily of the Mohawks, who may eventually be raised to the altars of the Church.[1]

At first the Jesuits were received, if at all, as medicine-men whose magic had a greater potency than that of the native wiz-ards. This meant, however, that if anything went wrong—espe-cially if a pestilence broke out—the Jesuits were regarded as the authors of the calamity. The Indians did not fail to notice that many of the children—still more, the adults—who were baptized by the Black Robes (who were always very anxious to baptize anyone in danger of death) actually did die. From this they drew their own sinister inference. And the Dutch traders at Fort Orange (the present Albany), to whom they went for a boot-leg trade in strong waters and firearms, inflamed their minds with an active prejudice, which became deep dread, against the sign of the cross. The Dutch, it is true, rescued St. Isaac Jogues and others from their Indian torturers; at the same time they did much to increase the dangers of the Catho-lic missionaries.

Even apart from those created by Dutch Protestants, the Fathers had difficulties enough. Often the Indians would obstinately refuse to listen at all; at other times they would,

[1] Her bones are preserved near Montreal. In the church of the Indian village where they lie, the people sing the responses to the Mass in Iroquois, and the inscriptions on the Stations of the Cross are in the same language. The Fathers there still exhibit ancient plaint-chant scores adapted to Iroquois—the only instance of the liturgical use of the vernacular sanctioned by the Church.

if in a good humor, politely assent to everything the Jesuits said. But they had little ability to comprehend an abstract proposition or any terms in which to express it. The doctrine of the Trinity itself had to be made a concrete expression of belief in *Our* Father and *His* Son and *Their* Holy Spirit. As the notion of a Supreme Being could hardly be conveyed, the Black Robes fell back on analogy. The Indians maintained that every animal had its type in the spirit world. "Very well: if that be true of animals," the Black Robes argued, "it must also be true of man." The Indians admitted the force of the logic, but as Jogues had sadly to exclaim, "If only they believed as easily as they are convinced!"

The Indians had, by way of compensation, most tenacious memories. Our brains are largely compounded of paper and ink; the savages had no more than the mnemonic device of the wampum belt. Therefore what they heard they never forgot. It was easy to teach such people the catechism, even if it was not quite so easy to make them grasp it. Then too there was the richness of their language—or rather, languages—of which many Jesuits made themselves complete masters. As Father Talbot writes in his life of Isaac Jogues: "The verbs were conjugated in tenses and numbers in as many ways as in Greek; more than that, there was a double conjugation, at least in some persons. The more they learned of the native tongue, the more the Fathers realized that this was no barbarous language but one of regular constructions, richer than the French in its complex shades of meaning."[2] What Parkman said of the greatest of the tribes would apply almost equally as well to the Hurons and the Algonquins: "The Iroquois was the Indian of Indians. A thorough savage, yet a finished and developed savage, he is perhaps an example of the highest elevation which man can reach without emerging from his primitive condition of the hunter."

It is impossible here to do more than indicate a little of what these Jesuits accomplished and suffered. Nor is it easy to draw a very definite line between their work in Canada and the offshoot of it in upper New York state. I shall have to set on one side, at all events for the moment, any account of the Illinois and Louisiana missions. As for those in the Northwest, partly because they are at first largely matters of the exploration by Marquette and the Franciscan Hennepin, but

[2] *Saint among Savages*, pp. 89–90.

also because afterwards they come into the eighteenth century, I shall have to dismiss them with a passing reference. They contain much privation; only seldom is the story one of martyrdom. Père Ribourde indeed, while with Tonty's expedition, was tomahawked; otherwise what has to be set down is a chronicle of dogged labor, performed upon filthy ill-cooked food, amid appalling stenches, and with the lack of the most elementary privacy. Yet its fruitfulness is shown by the fact that when Allouez died in August, 1689, among the Miamis of Michigan, he had preached to a hundred thousand souls, of whom he had baptized ten thousand.[3] For the sake of convenience I confine myself to the Jesuit missionaries and to that group who worked with Canada as their center. Their labors have a special unity and also a unique splendor.

What these missionaries knew they would probably have to face sooner or later was hideous and protracted torture. They knew moreover that, unless they wanted to disgrace themselves and their religion in the eyes of their torturers—even in the eyes of the youngest child who gazed greedily at the spectacle—they must not flinch or allow the least sigh to escape. The Indians from youth schooled themselves in this sort of disdainful courage, on which they put an exaggerated value. They were helped by the simplicity of a nervous system that had not been overwrought by civilized life. By nature stolid, by training impassive, it was their pride to bear all that was put upon them. The Jesuits, on the other hand, were men of studious and refined habits. That great ox, Brébeuf—or Frémin, the "apostle of the babies," with his fierce air of a colonel of dragoons—might be fitted to endure much. At all events they had the physique for it. But the wonder is that the sensitive Garnier could support his trials. Parkman, however, was able to write, "Brébeuf was the lion of the Huron missions, and Garnier the lamb; but the lamb was as fearless as the lion." In the distinctive Indian courage they excelled the Indians themselves. The only explanation is that their faith, hope and charity were such as completely to conquer the impulses of their nature. Writing with mangled hands, from which blood still flowed, to the General of his order, Bressani could say, "I could not have believed a man was so hard to kill." And Jerome Lalemant wrote in 1646, "We shall be taken;

[3] Father Campbell says truly that though these were not so tragic as the Huron missions, they were just as heroic. (*Pioneer Priests of North America*, Vol. III, p. xxi.)

we shall be burned; we shall be massacred. But that is a trifle. One's bed is not always the best place to die in."

In the South and South-west there had been martyrs long before this period, but there the martyrs had to taste only a swift death—an arrow, a club, an axe. That was sometimes how it all ended in the North-east too, but before the last hour arrived there were almost invariably days and sometimes weeks of suffering, skilfully prolonged. By temperament these men were among those worst constituted to stand it. Said Noel Chabanel—one of the few martyrs to escape torture—"Mine will be a martyrdom in the gloom." To the torment of his melancholy no more needed to be added. Perhaps almost as much to be pitied was Père Millet, who was made an Oneida chief by adoption—a chief in chains.

It would be tedious to recount the tortures inflicted on each of the martyrs; for ingenious as these were, they were constantly repeated. But the following may be taken as an example of what each man, with slight modifications, had to go through. He was stripped naked and made to run the gauntlet —as priest coming at the end of the procession so that he might receive the hardest blows. That was merely a little preliminary. The next thing was that a child would saw off a finger with an oyster shell or—better still—that a woman captive, if a Christian, would be compelled to saw it off. The martyr was lucky if he escaped having to eat it afterwards.

But still this was only a preliminary. After the feast the chief would assemble his people—men, women and children— to "caress" their captives. The victims, standing on a platform, would have strips torn from their arms and legs, be burnt with pine torches under the arm-pits, and have their nails pulled out. Meanwhile perhaps another finger or two would go. After several hours of this amusement, during which the chiefs would look on gravely smoking and the children were encouraged to learn their first lessons in making a captive suffer, the Jesuit would be fastened to pegs in the ground for the night. By way of saying good-by, the boys of the encampment would throw live coals upon his naked flesh.

Sometimes a bit of cloth might be provided against the cold; more often, not. The next day the food of the dogs would perhaps be spread on the captive's body, so that they might lacerate it with their fangs. Then would come another night at the fire, at which variants were likely to be introduced—for instance, boiling water thrown over the priest's head as a mockery of baptism. This happened to Brébeuf. Through it all there were constant taunts, in the vein of Indian humor. Torture was a kind of game which was won by the savages if their captive showed any fear or writhed in pain. If he did not, why then he was admired as victor, and might even be spared. Or, by way of posthumous compliment, as with Brébeuf, his heart would be eaten for the acquiring of valor.

Often the captive was taken the rounds of several villages in order that everybody might have an opportunity to torture him. If that did not happen, there was sometimes a cessation of torture for a while, so that it could be repeated when he had sufficiently recovered. Before the end came there was not much left whole in his body. Usually the death stroke was not administered until after some major disfigurement—such as the slicing off of the nose—had been inflicted.

The keenest pangs of the Jesuits were mental. As Jogues wrote after witnessing the torture of a group of Huron captives, "While each one suffered his own pain, I suffered that of all. I was afflicted with a great anguish, great as one may believe the heart of a loving parent is afflicted when he sees the sufferings of his own children. For, with the exception of the few older Christians, I had borne all these in Christ through their recent baptism." The opportunity now and then occurred of baptizing a savage while he was actually on the scaffold. Garnier, stricken with the death stroke and with blood pouring from his wounds, tried even then to crawl to baptize a dying man.

Sometimes it fell out, however, as with Jogues, that in admiration of his fortitude a captive would be "adopted." To try to escape was death but—again as with Jogues—an escape was sometimes possible. We have the dramatic incident of how, after being smuggled on board a Dutch ship in the Hudson and taken to France, he made his way to the Jesuit house at Rennes. There the superior asked the shabby visitor from America, "Did you know any of the Fathers there? Did you know Father Isaac Jogues?"

"I knew him very well," came the reply.

"We heard he had been captured by the Iroquois. Is he alive or dead?"

"He is alive: it is he who speaks to you."

Another story, unfortunately apocryphal, is that when he was presented to the Dowager Queen of France, who had the boy King Louis XIV at her side, she kissed his mangled hands.

What *is* true is that Pope Urban VIII gave him special permission to say Mass despite his mutilations with the words, "It would be shameful that a martyr of Christ should not be allowed to drink the Blood of Christ."

Jogues returned, eagerly, to the missions, to drink what remained of his chalice. This time there was no torture but the sudden blow of a tomahawk. Along with René Goupil, who had once been a Jesuit novice and then a doctor before joining the Fathers as a lay assistant, and Jean la Lande,[4] another *donné*—both of whom died on the soil of the United States —he was canonized in 1930. His murderer, who was captured by the French in September, 1647, received the name of Isaac Jogues in baptism before execution.[5]

One may call the missions among the Hurons a failure if one chooses. But this is only because the Hurons were exterminated by their inveterate enemies, the Iroquois. And the efforts to evangelize the fierce Iroquois snatched no more than a few individual souls for salvation. Nevertheless, as Father Campbell asks by way of conclusion to the first volume of his *Pioneer Priests of America,* "May not the marvellous growth of the Church in New York State have some connection with the heroism of its first priests?" The failure was only that of the cross.

St. Isaac Jogues may be taken as representative of the Jesuit missionaries in America. There were among them men probably more gifted than he was, but there was none greater—not even Garnier, not even Brébeuf, not even Marquette. Fortunately for everybody, the world rests upon the shoulders of commonplace men—or of men who seem to be commonplace. Father Talbot, the latest and best of his biographers, makes no attempt to represent him as brilliant. But he does show him to be in his unassuming way a saint, in his matter-of-fact way a hero. The story of this typical son of a typical French

[4] The first of these died on St. Isaac's first trip; the second on his second. Goupil was allowed to make his religious vows before he died.

[5] As for the Indian who had tried to ward off the blow that cracked Jogues' skull, he went to France—or was sent there by the authorities, who did not fully trust him—and became a Christian on his death-bed. Yet he was a savage who had in his time, as Lalemant wrote of him, "perhaps eaten his share of more than fifty men." His conversion was attributed to the prayers of the dead Jogues.

bourgeois family is one that will always thrill the world. I have laid emphasis upon it here for the reason that Jogues summed up in his own career the careers of many Jesuits who came to our shores. In his place they would have behaved as he did, as all did who had to meet his fiery struggles. Their greatness was not of natural talents—though such talents were frequent among them—but of grace.

One must reflect sadly upon the possibility, so nearly brought into actuality, that all the Indians of the North American continent might have been won for Christ. This is what would have happened had not the Protestant settlements undone the work of the Spanish and French missionaries. It is, however, useless to repine over the fate of the red man. He need not have been treated so badly, and yet it is difficult to see how he could have held his ground against an energy of which he had no conception. Nobody is now less American than the first inhabitant of this land, though he too might have found a place in American life had we been more wise and generous. As things turned out, he was swept away by a torrent too strong for him to withstand. Even Catholicism, though not of design, because of this took a course in America it had never taken before. Elsewhere it converted the native. Here the native himself was snatched from the Church's hands.

CHAPTER FIVE

LORD BALTIMORE'S SANCTUARY

Contrary to the usual belief, the reign of Elizabeth was not one of exploration and colonization. Only faintly were the sea-dogs (or the Queen) interested in anything except immediate cash returns. It was while they were in search of these—to be made by selling slaves in defiance of the humane Spanish regulations—that Hawkins and Drake were chased from San Juan de Ulloa in 1567. It was in search of plunder that Drake attacked Nombre de Dios and Cartagena. Though it is true that Martin Frobisher did make some effort in 1576 to discover the Northwest Passage, what got him his financial backing was that he brought back samples, from his first voyage, of what was thought to be gold. When it was proved by the assayers to be worthless, the Northwest Passage was forgotten—or regarded as less remunerative than piracy. Before Frobisher had returned from his third and last voyage to North America, Drake had set out to sail around the world. He too had instructions to look for the Northwest Passage. Yet his search for it was so perfunctory that off Vancouver Island he decided that the "arctic" conditions and the icebergs made further exploration impossible! Why should he bother about such trifles when his hold was stuffed with loot? He did land at Point Reyes in California—completely missing the superb harbor of San Francisco—and he made the gesture of taking possession of the country. It was, however, only a gesture; there was no way for England to establish a settlement there. The thing that really matters is that there was hardly any serious project at this time on the part of the English to establish colonies even in places in America which would have been within their reach. All that we can say of the freebooters is that they familiarized men of another type with the idea of America: in that sense alone did they prepare the way.

The first actual attempt at an English colony in America was a Catholic one. This occurred in 1584, when Sir Humphrey Gilbert carried two hundred and sixty recusants across the Atlantic to dump them on the coast of Maine. So desperate was their situation at home that even the bleak shores of

"Norumbega" seemed a desirable refuge. The scheme was a fiasco. The largest ship went down with most of the stores, and on their way back to England Gilbert and many of his Catholic colonists were lost off the Azores.

Sir Walter Raleigh was the one man of his time who seems to have had a genuine ambition to establish an American settlement. He took over the plans of Sir Humphrey (who was his half-brother), at the same time dropping the Catholic part of them, as papists would only hamper the Virginian enterprise. Moreover, Sir Richard Grenville, whom he induced to take charge of the hundred and eighty settlers at Roanoke Island in 1585, was a notorious anti-Catholic.

Grenville was also an incompetent administrator. Under him the plight of the colonists became so pitiful that Drake had to remove them the following year, after he had finished sacking St. Augustine. But another hundred and seventeen people went to Virginia in 1587 and Virginia Dare, the first English child of America, was born. This group in its turn dismally failed. When they were looked for three years later they had all disappeared—either massacred by the Indians or absorbed into savagery. The succeeding years were too turbulent to permit any further attempt at colonization.

Not until peace had been signed with Spain in the reign of James I did such projects get underway again. And again the project was a Catholic one—backed this time by Lord Arundel of Wardour and the Earl of Southampton. The two noblemen themselves went out for a while to this settlement in Maine on the Kennebec, and with them went a couple of priests. It is worthy of note that we have here, long before Maryland, a foreshadowing of the Maryland idea: the Catholics and the Protestants used the same church and agreed to respect one another's religion.[1] It was because of the arguments of the famous Jesuit, Father Robert Persons,[2] that Arundel decided to abandon a plan which could not hope to receive official recognition.

About the same time Sir Walter Raleigh's old dream of Virginia at last became a reality. Sir Walter himself was under sentence of death for high treason—but was living comfortably

[1] See Shea, *History of the Catholic Church in the United States*, Vol. I, p. 28.

[2] His written presentation of them is to be found in Hughes, *History of the Society of Jesus in North America*, Vol. I of the *Documents*, pp. 3–5.

with his wife in the Tower—when a patent for two colonies
was signed by James I. Now Michael Drayton produced his
magnificent Ode "To the Virginia Voyage":

> And cheerfully at sea,
> Success will you entice,
>   To get the pearl and gold,
>   And ours to hold,
> Virginia,
> Earth's only paradise.

Even with that inducement, however, only gentlemen thirst-
ing for adventure or criminals who wished to escape the gallows could be persuaded to go. Still, it was the beginning.

The story of this settlement, and of the others that were
made soon afterwards, need not detain us long. Suffice it to
say that a body of Separatists, the "Pilgrim Fathers," landed
at Plymouth in 1620 and that nine years later a larger group
took possession of Massachusetts Bay. Their history will impinge to some extent upon that of the Maryland foundation.
Otherwise it does not belong to this book.

But perhaps the difference between the religious sentiments
of the two earliest Protestant New England settlements might
be indicated at this point. Puritans were at first quite distinct
from Separatists, although the distinction gradually faded until "Puritan" came to serve well enough as a generic term for
both. Originally, however, Puritans were a party within the
Church of England. Their American leader, John Endicott,
was a bigoted fool, as he showed by his exploit of cutting the
"Popish" cross out of the English flag. Yet he expressed strictly
Puritan sentiment when, in his farewell to his native shores,
he exclaimed, "We will not say as the Separatists, 'Farewell,
Babylon! Farewell, Rome!' But we will say, 'Farewell, dear
England! Farewell, the Church of God in England!' " Nevertheless, as time went on, the distinction between them tended
to disappear. If it comes to that, Plymouth was perhaps a
shade or two less intolerant than Massachusetts Bay—for the
Separatists knew what it meant to profess a proscribed faith.
Then, too, after 1640, when the Puritan party began to gain
political control at home, Puritans had less incentive to leave
England—a circumstance which tended to make those who
were in the colonies draw nearer to the Separatists. Eventually
the Puritans became Separatists for all practical purposes, independent of the Anglican establishment and refusing the

jurisdiction of any bishop. Whatever religious liberty the men of either group sought for themselves, they were not prepared to extend it to those who disagreed with them. Baptists and Quakers in turn found the Puritan hand heavy. As for Catholics, there was of course absolutely no place for them in any part of New England.

It was natural that Catholics should think once more of establishing a religious sanctuary across the Atlantic. They had, in fact, originated the idea which the Puritans and Separatists borrowed, though we must not press this too far. The religious motive was only one among many in the foundation both of the New England and the Maryland settlements. In each case it has been stressed altogether too much: an asylum was indeed provided for those who sought liberty of conscience; many others—perhaps the majority—went out mainly in the expectation of bettering their material conditions.

Just as those who promoted the colonizing schemes looked to make money, so also the English government encouraged these schemes because it was by now aware of the political advantages in colonization. England had to hurry, or be too late. The French were established in Canada and Nova Scotia, as the Spaniards had been for a long while in Florida, Mexico and the South-west. And the Dutch, for whom an English captain, Henry Hudson, had explored the river that bears his name, had already set up a trading station on Manhattan Island. Nor were the Swedes much behind them in establishing Fort Christiana on the Delaware. The opportunities for trade were increasingly evident to all the seafaring nations, and none of the settlements neglected such opportunities. But it was the Catholics who first thought of America—even in their abortive experiment in Maine in 1607—as a place where Protestants and Catholics alike could enjoy religious liberty.

The credit for carrying this concept into execution must be given to Sir George Calvert. In 1620 he bought from Sir William Vaughan the patent he possessed for part of Newfoundland. Two years later he sent a body of colonists there to a place he named Avalon. He was as yet not a Catholic though, as he was born in Yorkshire, the most strongly Catholic part of England, we may surmise that, like so many men of that age, he had a vague sympathy for the "Old Religion" long before he openly accepted it.[3] Even in Avalon he tried to provide for religious freedom.

[3] We must not make too much of this, however: his parents were Protestant Flemings.

His adhesion to Catholicism in 1625 necessitated his resignation of the position of Secretary of State. But King James, while perforce accepting it, created his friend Baron Baltimore and continued to further his colonization schemes. The new Baron retained enough political influence to prevent the Virginia Company from taking over the territory south of the James River. In his official capacity he had had a good deal to do with the drawing up of the charters for the New England colonies. He therefore understood in what terms best to frame his own charter.

Avalon seemed to be promising enough for him to visit it in 1627 and then to take his second wife and their children there. His sons Cecil and Leonard, by a previous marriage, were already grown men. They never saw the country which the first reports described as a paradise—or the mermaid whom others caught sight of in the harbor. Their father, meeting difficulties —on the one hand from the French who regarded him as an intruder, and, on the other, from some of his colonists who objected to his toleration of Popery—decided to abandon Avalon. In any event the northern winter was too severe. It was in search of a better climate that George Calvert sailed for the south. He reached Jamestown on October 1, 1629.

One would have supposed that the Atlantic seaboard would have been large enough for many settlements. Those in possession did not think so; and Lord Baltimore was, to make things worse, a Catholic. To get rid of him the Virginia authorities insisted that he take the Oath of Supremacy, though the King had already so far stretched a point as to give him a special exemption in this regard. Perhaps they remembered against him that it was he who had estopped their spreading southwards. They were certainly anything but friendly to him.

But Calvert had seen the Chesapeake Bay region and was now determined to settle there if he could. In search of the concession he sailed for England, leaving his wife and children behind. It may be his grief at their perishing at sea when they followed him a little later that was responsible for his death at the age of fifty-two. Before dying, however, he had obtained the charter for Maryland. It was this that he bequeathed to his son Cecil.

Some people have suggested that George Calvert's concept of religious liberty was instilled into his mind by the Utopian's descendant, Henry More, who was at this period Provincial of the English Jesuits. It may be so, though we have to remember that this concept is a good deal older than More's

Utopia, and that Calvert had already put it into practice at Avalon, before he became a Catholic.[4] So also it is possible that the design of reduplicating in the New World the palatine powers of the bishopric of Durham may have been inspired by Sir Toby Matthew, the convert son of the Bishop of Durham, who had received George Calvert into the Church. It was, at all events, those powers that Calvert actually obtained. Under them he was to be virtually autonomous and could rule his territories as a prince. The charter he received gave him rights such as were never accorded to any other proprietary. They extended not only over the present Maryland but also Delaware and part of Pennsylvania.

James understood clearly enough that it was Calvert's intention to offer a refuge for Catholics. As this could not be explicitly stated, the charter was so drawn as to indicate merely that the laws of the colony were to conform to the ecclesiastical laws of England. To have left out this proviso would have raised such a tempest as to ruin everything. At the same time the proviso was capable of a wide interpretation—one amply sufficient for Calvert's purpose.

An exclusively Catholic colony was never in the Baron's mind. Had he attempted to establish one there can be no doubt that the English authorities would have forbidden it. His intention was to prove that it was possible to have Catholics and Protestants living in amity side by side on a perfect equality, and so provide a model that others might copy. In this he was perfectly disinterested. His harder-headed son, Cecil, though loyal to his father's principles, realized that, if Maryland was to be made to pay—and he was very keen on his profits—he must offer inducements to Protestant settlers, as he could not get a sufficient number of Catholics to go out. That is why (as we know from an entry in Winthrop's Journal for 1643) Massachusetts Bay was invited to send any people it could spare. They were assured of a welcome and of religious freedom.

One of the ironies of history is that George Calvert named his son after his university friend, Robert Cecil, the son of Queen Elizabeth's crafty persecutor of Catholics, the gentle-faced and vindictive Lord Burghley. Cecil Calvert, however,

[4] It might be worth noting that one of the main backers of the New England colonies was Robert Rich, Earl of Warwick, the grandson of that Richard Rich whose perjury sent St. Thomas More to the block and secured for himself the Lord Chancellorship.

changed the name to "Caecilius" at his confirmation. It was he who was appointed Proprietary when the Maryland charter was finally drawn up, his father having died before the document was signed. To George Calvert must go the credit of its central idea; to Cecil, the credit for putting it in operation. But the son probably would never have obtained his concession had it not been for the father's friendship with James I and the new king.

Nor must Charles I be denied some credit. Without his sympathetic interest the Maryland scheme would have come to nothing. He was known to have a personal fondness for Catholics, though he had repudiated the terms in his marriage contract calling for toleration of Catholicism. If this action is far from being praiseworthy, it may be said in his extenuation that he had a Puritan Parliament to contend with and had to placate bigots who were suspicious of his well-known "Anglo-Catholicism." This being the case, what he did for the Calverts must be acknowledged to have been a great deal.

Certain things should be noted about the actual application of Cecil Calvert's palatine prerogatives. One is that under them he was able to send Jesuits to Maryland when the settlement was made in 1634. Another is that he and the King ventured upon a name of definitely Catholic connotation. For though it was prudently given out that Maryland was called after Queen Henrietta Maria, everybody understood that a kind of pious *double entendre* was involved.[5] Finally—and here we come to the explanation of Maryland's early history —a thorough-going exercise of the palatine powers given to the Proprietary by the charter did not prove feasible. From the beginning an assembly was established, in which all freemen, irrespective of property qualifications, had the right, and indeed the obligation, to vote. Although the Proprietary looked upon this assembly as having merely advisory functions, it soon began to act as though it had the right of initiat-

---

[5] *Mariana* was first proposed, until it was remembered that this was the name of a Jesuit controversialist who had argued in favor of regicide, under certain conditions. That would have been going too far. *Maryland* might pass. Dilhet, who published his account of the Church in the United States in 1810, fell into the error of saying that Maryland was named for the Blessed Virgin. That he did so at all shows that such a belief must have been prevalent. Even those who knew what was the official explanation rejoiced at the name of Mary.

ing legislation. The air of America went to the head like wine.

It was on this account that some friction arose between Calvert and the Marylanders, though never enough to cause open conflict. There was always at hand Leonard Calvert, the Proprietary's brother, who had been appointed Governor, and he was usually able to smooth over threatening difficulties. But the point to remember is that neither side ever gave in: Lord Baltimore continued to assert his palatine privileges, while the colonists considered that, as they were on the spot, they should be free to direct their own affairs. The result was that a *modus agendi* came about. The colony was in fact largely self-governing; at the same time it made a theoretical acknowledgment of the palatine prerogatives—on condition that Lord Baltimore was careful not to exercise them in important matters. Because of this, Maryland was, of all the English colonies, the most independent. For whereas the others were ruled by governors appointed directly by the Crown (though they, too, were inclined to assert democratic rights), Maryland had a Governor appointed by the Proprietary who, in his turn, depended on the Crown. Ultimate authority being placed at a further remove meant greater liberty for Maryland.

Cecil Calvert was in some respects a driver of hard bargains—a cold, cautious, efficient man, with an eye always open to his own profit. His father having lost rather heavily in the "Norumbega" venture, he was careful to invest little actual money in his palatinate. It is probable that the founding of Maryland cost him hardly more than the *Ark* and the *Dove*, the ships which brought his colonists over. The "gentlemen" of the community came at their own expense, and they also paid the expenses of their servants and indentured men. They were recouped by being given additional land—of which there was plenty to spare. It was all for Lord Baltimore's benefit: the more settlers, the more rent for the Proprietary. Although these quitrents were not onerous, in the aggregate they brought in a tidy sum.

Whatever else Cecil Calvert was, he was not an idealist with his head in the clouds. Had he been one, his colony in all likelihood would not have been a success. This does not mean of course that he was without ideals, but that they were balanced and controlled by his business instincts and his aptitude for politics. There is no need to be sentimental about the second Lord Baltimore. He was just and honest and he did, after all, carry out his finer-grained father's ideas. At the same time, he never forgot his own interests.

On the question of his treatment of the Jesuits, Father Thomas Hughes, in his monumental study of the history of the colony, assails him with considerable rancor, which is not altogether alleviated by the occasional brilliance of his literary style. It seems to be useless, after the event, to complain that no provision was made for the support of the clergy. The Jesuits had gone to Maryland on the definite understanding that they were to be on the same footing as the gentlemen adventurers. Obviously no part of the colonial revenue could be assigned to their use without bringing about an accusation that the Catholic Church was established and endowed, an accusation that might easily have ruined the whole enterprise. That this was hard on the Jesuits need not be denied. The condition was, in fact, so hard that no Protestant minister would accept it, which is the reason why none went, though any would have been welcome. Calvert, however, cannot justly be blamed for taking the position that all ministers of religion should remain private persons without official standing.

He may, nevertheless, merit some blame with regard to the land the "Emperor" of Piscataway (as they called him) donated to the missionaries. From the Jesuits' point of view this was a free gift, one that the Indians had a right to make. Baltimore's point of view was quite different. All the land in Maryland he considered to be his own under the terms of the royal charter. Therefore the Emperor had no competence to give what he did not own—an argument technically sound. All the same, Calvert would have been generous to have waived his prerogatives in view of the handicap a priest was under in exercising his sacred office while burdened with the necessity of getting a livelihood as a planter. Instead Calvert put an exceedingly strict interpretation upon the Statute of Mortmain: no gifts of land to the clergy were to be made without his express consent. After a long dispute the Provincial of the Jesuits in England referred the problem to the General at Rome and he, without going into the abstract rights or wrongs of the case, decided against his Maryland subjects "for the sake of peace." The solution was not satisfactory to either side and created ill will between Baltimore and the priests.

It was unfortunate that Cecil Calvert was served in this matter by John Lewger, who arrived in the colony as secretary in 1537. Leonard Calvert was an easy-going man who operated on the principle of live and let live. Had he been allowed to follow his own devices no trouble would have arisen. But he was only the Governor, subordinate to that sternly unbending man his brother, the Proprietary in England. It was Lewger who had most of the business details in his hands, and he was fussy and consequential.

What may be said in his defence is that he was employed to look after Calvert's interests and that he was being conscientious. Father Hughes, however, charges him with Erastianism, and even if we acquit Lewger, on the ground that he had to carry out instructions, it seems likely that Calvert himself was tinged with that heresy. Or if this is too much to assert positively, it is at least true that his delicate position obliged him to proceed in what may be described as an Erastian manner. His acts were being suspiciously watched. His charter could be revoked at the King's pleasure. And however well disposed the King might be, he was not anxious to embroil himself further with a bigoted Parliament.

A fact of even greater importance should be taken into consideration. It is that during Elizabeth's reign the Jesuits and a section of the secular priests on the English mission—known as the Appellants—got at loggerheads. How this happened does not concern this book, and would in any event take too long to explain. What does bear upon the present story is that, though the Jesuits had devoted adherents, they also created implacable enemies among some of the English Catholics, and that this hatred took a long time to die down. That Cecil Calvert did not originally share the anti-Jesuitical sentiments is shown by his choosing Jesuits to go to Maryland. That he came to share them, is shown by the treatment the Jesuits received from him after he had quarrelled with them.[6] He eventually carried things so far as to refuse to exempt the clergy from militia duty and threatened them, if they did not obey, with the penal laws of England. Perhaps it was intended to be no more than a threat; that he made it reveals a good deal as to the inflamed state of his mind. Bitterly did he regret that he had ever invited Jesuits to go to Maryland. As he could not very well get rid of them—since on his own

[6] It is a curious fact that Lewger, who became a Catholic while at the university, applied, after he had returned to England, for admission to the Society of Jesus. Upon being refused, he became a secular priest.

showing they were merely private persons—he thought to bring in other priests in the hope that the Jesuits would retire of their own accord. Wires were therefore pulled at Propaganda, and in 1642 two seculars went out, to be followed in 1673 by a few Franciscans.[7] But the Jesuits hung on. They hung on even after their suppression as a corporate body. The spiritual work in the colony remained a Jesuit affair. By the time the Revolution occurred every priest then in the Colonies had been a Jesuit and was still dreaming of the Society's restoration. Though in canon law there was no such person recognized as a Jesuit, and though under civil law no priests had any rights, it may nevertheless be said that the Jesuit missions of America were almost the only part of Calvert's institution that survived.

There was, however, one other part—the great idea of religious liberty. This remains the chief glory of Maryland, and is not to be dimmed by the squabbles between the Proprietary and the clergy. Even though it seemed to have been destroyed before the seventeenth century was out—with the passage of penal laws against Catholics in the very colony they had founded—the Maryland concept lived on, to be taken up again after the Revolution. And although religious liberty would doubtless have been established as a natural concomitant of the political liberty won at that time, it was Maryland after all, that had provided a working model. Here already was the American Church; here already were Catholics living as Americans.

The toleration attempted, and for a while achieved, in Lord Baltimore's colony did not begin with the famous act of 1649. That act merely framed as positive law what had existed, in undefined fashion, from the outset. We might go still further: the Toleration Act of 1649 marks the beginning of the decline of toleration. For it limited toleration to Christians, at least in theory. Further, certain provisions of the Act—for instance, those concerning the keeping of the Sabbath—strongly suggest that they were inserted to placate the growing Protestant element. It is therefore very unjust to argue, as some have done, that Maryland's toleration was imperfect—or even spurious—merely because of the way the law was drawn up. We all know how crochets are often given legal effect to humor a

---

[7] We hear little about their activities. The last Franciscan in Maryland died in 1720. (Hughes, *op. cit.*, Vol. II, pp. 85–87.)

particular group or some influential person. In such cases the legislators, while passing a law of this kind, know perfectly well that, in some of its details, it will be inoperative. It was so in Maryland: such few Jews as were there suffered no disabilities, in spite of toleration being legally extended only to Christians.

The real test of Maryland toleration lies in the circumstance that, until trouble-makers appeared on the scene, there was no need for a law at all. A dogma is defined only when it is challenged; a law is made to clarify a situation. So scrupulous were the Catholic authorities—and all the twenty gentlemen who arrived in 1634, along with an undetermined proportion of the servants, were Catholics—that they enjoined the saying of Mass with as little ostentation as possible so as to avoid wounding Protestant susceptibilities. So far from there being any flaunting of the Faith, the magistrates leaned backwards in the matter. Thus we hear of a Mr. Lewis being hauled into court by a couple of his servants because he had reproved them for reading aloud—making sure that he should hear—a scurrilous anti-Catholic sermon. He was justifiably annoyed about their deliberate offensiveness. Nevertheless a Catholic magistrate fined him five hundred pounds of tobacco leaf—to be contributed towards the building of a Protestant church when a minister should arrive. It was not merely tolerant but good humored, and not merely good humored but humorous. In such a society there was no need of any law except for the keeping of the peace.

The establishment of toleration[8]—in so far as it was established—was of course something that could only now and then have occupied the minds of those responsible for directing the affairs of the colony. The majority of settlers, we may safely assume, took it for granted—and dismissed it from their thoughts. In the beginning all the leading men were Catholics, and they had no inclination for persecution. Even when

[8] A more accurate term than "toleration" would be "religious liberty." For toleration implies that one religion is official, which was not the case in Maryland. However, in so far as the Catholics were in the beginning the dominant religious group, at that time capable of making things uncomfortable for Protestants, we may permissibly speak of toleration, as people spoke then. Theoretically Maryland was under the ecclesiastical laws of England (whatever that meant). Therefore it would have been inadvisable to have explicitly affirmed religious liberty.

the indentured servants (many of whom were Protestants)
emerged from their term of servitude and acquired property
and standing in the community, they were not as a rule interested in raising the religious question. Had they been bigoted
Protestants, they would hardly have gone to a colony which,
as they well knew, would be under Catholic control. Instead
of abstract considerations, therefore, we may be sure that they
—as well as their Catholic fellows—were mainly engrossed by
the material problems created by the need of adjusting themselves to a new mode of life.

In so far as that life could be like English life, it was like
it. The same thing was true of life in New England. But in
Maryland, as in Virginia, the colonists had to discover means
of livelihood of a kind unknown before. They could of course
raise the familiar crops; and they could plant orchards. These,
however, were incidental to the great source of profit—the
raising of tobacco. For this reason all the shores of the Chesapeake, and all the mouths of the rivers running into it, were
utilized as wharfs to which ships could be drawn up for the
loading of tobacco, which was rolled down to the waiting vessels in barrels. These wharfs were also necessary for the
unloading of the supplies brought from other American
colonies or from England.

During the first year or two the mode of existence must
have been primitive. But the Maryland climate was not severe, however trying it can be on account of its changeable-
ness. In their log cabins the colonists were snugly warm in
winter and sufficiently cool in summer. Game of all sorts
abounded—deer and 'possum and wild turkey and canvas-back
duck and terrapin. And all a man had to do to get all the
shell-fish he could eat was to spend half an hour on the Chesapeake.

The gentlemen among the settlers brought over with them
—or soon sent for—good plate and pewter and glassware. Nor
were they long in building substantial houses of brick. The
oldest of these, which was erected in 1640, may still be seen.
It is plain and unpretentious but comfortable and commodious. Already the English settler was departing from the English mode by having a porch running the entire length of both
stories.

Enough domestic utensils and furniture of seventeenth century Maryland remain to attest to the spacious manorial style
which was soon adopted by the gentry. Although the accounts

left of the manner of life of the colonists are meager, as compared with those for Virginia and New England, we can piece them together well enough to obtain a fairly coherent picture. Father Spalding, in his *Colonial Catholic Maryland*, draws upon these and his memories of a still somewhat primitive Kentucky that was settled by people from the Chesapeake region. His descriptions of cooking and soap- and candle-making are detailed and, we must suppose, accurate. The Englishman can be depended upon to be adaptable when forced to it. It is only at home that he sinks into that helplessness which William Cobbett, after his American experiences, sought to remove by writing his *Cottage Economy*. He wrote in vain. Even the maize offered as "Cobbett's corn" was rejected in England as unfit for human food. The Marylander at once discovered how good it was.

In the South the settlers had an advantage over those in New England. The sour-faced saints among the Puritans and Separatists at first regarded hunting, and even fishing with a line, as "ungodly," because they partook of the nature of sports. The consequence of this was that—in the early days of the settlement, until they had learned better—they nearly starved to death in the midst of plenty. Benjamin Franklin was to say that no man who could bait a hook or pull a trigger need ever lack for food in America. The Marylander, unlike the newly-arrived Pilgrim Father, had no scruples about having a little fun while getting his provisions, but bowled over his turkey or pulled in soft-shell crabs by the pail-full, and thanked God for His bounty.

It was fortunate for the colony that the settlers of 1634 numbered only twenty gentlemen as against three hundred servants, among whom must have been many farmers and artisans. The Spanish *hidalgos* often found themselves at a loss in an emergency, their one trade being that of war. In the same way, the first colonists of Virginia had perished because they did not know how to adapt themselves to unaccustomed conditions. Maryland, on the other hand, was well supplied with men skilled with their hands. It was they who constructed the houses and mills and forges and fishing-boats; therefore they thrived from the start. In bringing over so many servants Lord Baltimore had shown his wisdom, as in other matters.

These servants were for the most part indentured men who paid their passage by binding themselves for a term of four or five years to work for the more affluent of the settlers.

When their indentures expired they were provided with land and at once given the suffrage. This explains how it soon came about that the majority of the Maryland freemen were of the Protestant persuasion. Although their religion was not very deep—they did not get a minister until 1650, and then only a hard-drinking, loose-living cleric of the type already common in Virginia—the large and growing non-Catholic body provided a fertile field for the bigots to work upon when they intruded, as they speedily did, into Calvert's domain. With the emergence of the indentured men as landowners and planters it became necessary to look for negro slaves to do the rough work. These facts contributed to make the new citizens assertive, and the sphere of religion was the easiest one in which they could make themselves felt.

But before coming to the internal troubles of Maryland, I should glance for a moment at the efforts made by the Jesuits to evangelize the Indians. If their efforts were not as successful as they might have been, the partial failure was due to opposition raised by a Proprietary who stood too stubbornly on his prerogatives and to the circumstance that the Jesuits were few and had about as much as they could do to administer to the spiritual needs of the English colonists. Even to this religious work only a portion of their time could be devoted: as they had no other means of support, they had to develop their plantations or engage in trade. So far as possible this work was left to the lay-brothers; but the Fathers were not quite free.

Yet an effort to convert the Indians was made. Several chiefs and their wives were baptized, and the young "Empress of Piscataway" was taken under the wing of the redoubtable Margaret Brent—"the first American suffragette," as she has been called—to be educated. An Indian reserve was formed, so anticipating (in some respects) later American policy. And Andrew White compiled the first Indian grammar made by an Englishman, which may still be seen in manuscript in Rome. If the Indians of Maryland have almost totally disappeared, this is not because they were (as elsewhere) exterminated of set purpose but rather because many were absorbed by marriage with the settlers or drifted westwards. They were never very numerous in Maryland. There is, however, to this day in southern Maryland an Indian group (all of them Catholics) who have lost all record of their origin, their native culture, and of their language itself. These are now known as "Wesorts." The name is imagined to indicate their wish to declare their racial difference from both white and colored. Without making any pretense to Indian philology, I throw out the suggestion for what it is worth that the name derives from "witchotts," which was what the Maryland Indians called their oval houses of bark.[9] It was just such a house that Father White used as his first chapel among them. The "Wesorts"—whatever may be the derivation of the word—are certainly the descendants of his converts.

Another factor that impeded missionary work among the Indians was the animosity of some of the Virginia settlers—particularly of William Claiborne. His is usually accused by Catholic historians—and by some historians not Catholics—of being actuated solely by bigotry. And there can be no doubt that he was bigoted—or at least found in the "Papistry" of Maryland an additional cause for grievance. In justice to the man, however, it should be remembered—as Channing points out[10]—that Claiborne had, after all, set up a post on Kent Island by 1629, and possibly even by 1625, and that this settlement had been represented in the Virginia Assembly in 1631. The Privy Council, moreover, had assured Virginia that no private rights were to be affected by the Calvert charter. In view of all this, Claiborne had a case and could regard himself as a defrauded man striking for his just dues. His methods are another story, and cannot be defended. Smarting under his wrongs (real or imaginary) he allied himself with one Ingle, a Puritan pirate of the school of Drake, and, kidnapping Fathers Copley and White, sent them in chains to England to be tried under the English penal code.[11] There it was only

[9] In the same way *Port Tobacco* is simply a corruption of the Indian *Portopaco*.

[10] *History of the United States*, Vol. II, p. 256.

[11] Some of the Maryland Jesuits, because of the necessity they had been under of dodging pursuivants in England, had adopted assumed names, which they used indifferently with their real ones. Thus Copley was also known as Fisher, and Gravenor as Altham. The fact indicates that they thought it advisable to refrain from too open a display of their priestly character even in Maryland. As for the kidnapping, Father Hughes points out (Vol. I, 487) that Lord Baltimore himself had pointedly suggested to his brother in 1642 that Father Copley be kidnapped and sent out of the province. There is no possible excuse for this pretty scheme, though it may be explained by the comment of More, the English Jesuit

by pleading that they had been forcibly brought into the country that they escaped the penalties to which a priest entering England was liable. Even so, they were in danger. Father White's jailer used to tell him with grim humor that he had so little flesh on his bones that there would not be enough for Tyburn.

This kidnapping was in 1645. Warned by the religious passions now being aroused, Lord Baltimore sent over the provisions of the Toleration Act of 1649, which was passed by the Maryland Assembly. Further to lessen the fury of bigotry, he appointed the Protestant William Stone as governor, to succeed Leonard Calvert, who had died in 1647. It would be a totally false inference that this proves that Lord Baltimore was frightened into granting toleration. Toleration (or more correctly, religious freedom) had existed from the beginning of Maryland. The true statement of the case is rather that Baltimore, upon whom it was now brought home that freedom of conscience was being menaced both from without and from within, was seeking to insure, by means of legal enactments, which had hitherto been superfluous, that religious liberty would be perpetuated in a colony where Protestants already constituted a majority. But as a law was necessary, it had to be carefully drawn so as not to arouse too much alarm. In other words, the limiting clauses embodied in the law of 1649 were a concession to those who—unless there had been some such limitation—might have refused to ratify the Act of Toleration.

Even so, Baltimore was unable to prevent disorders—disorders which, in Maryland, reflected the Civil War in England. After Charles I had been executed at the end of January, 1649, and the news had reached the colonies, Bennett and Claiborne, who were commissioners in Virginia, discovered an excellent pretext: Baltimore's government was disloyal to the new Commonwealth. With this as their justification, they invaded Maryland, summoned an Assembly from which all Catholics were excluded, and repealed the Act of 1649. When Governor Stone tried to assert his rightful authority he was defeated at the Battle of the Severn on March 24, 1655; and despite promises of quarter to those who surrendered, four of Stone's adherents, including three Catholics, were hanged.

Provincial, that Copley was "deficient in judgment and prudence," in spite of other good parts. Worthy men are not always ingratiating.

The priests in Maryland fled to Virginia, where they lived for some time "in a mean hut, sunk in the ground like a cistern or a tomb." All practice of Catholicism was proscribed by the ascendant party.

Lord Baltimore's cause now seemed lost. He had, however, played his cards in England very dextrously—too dextrously indeed for the credit of his honor or his gratitude to the King to whom he owed so much. Never had he committed himself so deeply to Charles as to be unable to make terms with Cromwell. So great was the distrust for him felt by the Royalists, that Charles' widow, Henrietta Maria (for whom Maryland had been named), acting for her young son, authorized Sir William Davenant to proceed to the colony to take over its administration. This was on the ground that Cecil Calvert "doth visibly adhere to the rebels of England and admit all kinds of schismatics and sectaries and other ill-affected persons into the said plantation of Maryland." It would have added a picturesque element to our history if this Catholic poet, who was reputed to be Shakespeare's natural son,[12] had ever reached American shores. Instead he was captured at sea by a Commonwealth ship, carried back to England, and kept in an easy custody, during which he wrote his heroic poem *Gondibert*. He was to live into the Restoration, when he had something to do with getting the life of Milton spared. But also, he was never to be Governor of Maryland.

Cecil Calvert now got his reward. The rights conferred upon him by the King were confirmed by the Protector, and the laws passed by the rebels were repealed, leaving the old Act of Toleration in force. It is curious that his political salvation came from Cromwell. But political "deals" often are very strange affairs. In the next generation a mitigation of the persecution initiated by the local bigots was effected by the direct intervention of William and Mary and (afterwards) by Queen Anne, whereas the Catholic James allowed his coreligionists in Maryland to stew in their own juice.

The second Lord Baltimore died in 1675, without having visited the colony of which he was made Proprietary in 1632. During that long and troubled period he had managed to steer it through shoals beyond the skill of his successors. Though it is not possible to think of him as a great man—for he was

[12] Davenant complacently allowed the imputation to pass. His Shakespearian blood nevertheless is now believed to be a myth.

grasping and a time-server and showed bad faith in minor matters—allowances should be made for the difficulties he had to surmount or circumvent. He must therefore be acknowledged as being among the most successful architects of colonial enterprise. His line was to weaken in capacity and lost, in the person of Charles Calvert, its palatine charter. The greatest grief of the aged Baron, of whom we have a charming and amusing portrait as a child with his father, was to see his son, Benedict Leonard, apostatize in 1713 in the hope of recovering the abrogated powers of the house of Baltimore. His son Charles visited Maryland and showed enough decent respect for his ancestors to do what he could to restrain the persecution of Catholics. The last of the Baltimores was the sixth, Frederick, who died in 1771. His sole distinction was that he was eminent for profligacy in a profligate society.

The ending was inglorious. Yet George and Cecil Calvert had initiated an experiment that was to bear fruit a century and a half later. I do not suggest for a moment that the religious liberty established after the Revolution was due solely to the Maryland idea. On the contrary I believe it to be an inescapable corollary of political liberty. But what Maryland did was to confer religious freedom in an age when intolerance was almost universally assumed to be axiomatic. That is the Baltimore achievement; it is achievement enough.

CHAPTER SIX

THE PENAL AGE

If Maryland was the only colony to come into actual being under a Catholic Proprietary it was not the only one projected. About the same time that Calvert received his charter, King Charles I granted similar palatine powers to the recusant Sir Edmund Plowden—son of the earlier Sir Edmund, the celebrated Elizabethan lawyer whose arguments were of such weight that, after he had delivered them, there was nothing to say except "The case is altered!" (Which was the origin of that proverbial expression.) Plowden sent over a Captain Yong, who established a fort on the Jersey bank of the Delaware, and came himself in 1642 to take possession of his province of "New Albion." As the Swedes naturally regarded him as an intruder he could make little headway, and though he apparently had much the same general plans as Lord Baltimore, few Catholics could be induced to join him; nor is there any record of a priest going to his colony.

New Albion having failed to prosper, James II gave part of Plowden's original territory to a group of noblemen, among whom was the Earl of Perth, a Catholic. By now there seems to have been no such plan of sanctuary as George Calvert had conceived and his son had put into execution. It was thought to be unnecessary: the English Catholics had high hopes of a Catholic restoration—or at least the cessation of persecution. There was therefore no point in their seeking a refuge abroad. The policy of James was instead, to give a certain number of important colonial appointments to Catholics. Thus Anthony Brockholls was made second in command to Governor Andros, and Colonel Thomas Dongan (afterwards Earl of Limerick) obtained the governorship of New York. With the usurpation of William of Orange and James' precious daughter Mary of course all Catholic influence came to an abrupt end. It had always been fiercely resented.

But before we come to a survey of the general colonial situation, it might be as well to observe how the ground was cleared by the dispossession of the Swedes and the Dutch. Petrus Stuyvesant unwittingly worked for England by ejecting the Swedes from Delaware. They had been there since 1638 and in 1642 obtained, in Johann Printz, one who was an exceedingly capable governor in spite of his four hundred pounds and his fabulous thirst. These Swedes were Lutheran "high church," priding themselves upon the elaborate liturgy and the gorgeous vestments which so sharply differentiated them from all varieties of Dutch and English Protestants. But in 1655 Petrus Stuyvesant annexed New Sweden, only to fall himself nine years later. He went around on his wooden leg swearing most luridly that he would defend New Amsterdam to the end, until the other officials convinced him that resistance to the British was useless. Then the brother of Charles II, the Duke of York, after whom the town was renamed, became its governor, with jurisdiction over New England. The whole Atlantic seaboard was now English from Maine to Florida.

The very fact that it was all English united it in its old suspicion of the Stuarts. James I was known to have dallied, before his accession, with the thought of becoming a Catholic. His son Charles I was openly high Anglican, and was suspected of Catholic leanings. As for Charles II and James II, both did become Catholics—the one upon his death-bed in 1685, the other, while Duke of York, in 1670. All of which has a considerable bearing upon American as well as English history.

We should remember, too, that the execution of Charles I and the ousting of James II weakened the whole principle of monarchy and created the notion that, unless that principle was opposed, it would result in the encroachments of tyranny. Linked with this idea was another: that royal tyranny—and, indeed, tyranny of every kind—was inherent in Catholicism. That nothing could have been more nonsensical is beside the point: it is not always what is true that matters in history, but what people believe to be true. Even more than the English themselves, the American colonists were convinced of this —including those learned Puritan ministers who, having read their Aquinas, should have known better.[1]

In spite of superficial differences between the colonies of the South and those of New England, their political uniformity was remarkable. The Virginians, among whom there already seems to have been developing the Southern romanti-

[1] Concerning their study of the Scholastics, see Perry Miller's *New England Mind*. Its documentation puts this beyond question.

cism which so soon became overblown, liked to call themselves "cavaliers." It was merely a sentimental fancy. Few of the Southern families—only about three of the important ones—had an aristocratic derivation. And even if we understand the term "cavalier" in the more general sense of a royal adherent against Parliament, the term still has no validity. We have seen how the Virginia commissioners invaded Maryland on the pretext that Lord Baltimore's government was disloyal to the Protectorate. But to think of themselves as cavaliers accorded with the spacious, gracious, somewhat indolent life already characteristic of the wealthier planters.[2] They looked with disdain upon the strait-laced saints of New England, with their interminable sermons and the theocratic domination of dour ministers, and for this very reason were indulgent towards their own cock-fighting, bibulous clergymen. Anything was better than being suspected of Puritanism, of which, it must be admitted, nobody has ever accused them. At the same time they were not a whit less Protestant than their northern brethren, and hardly less bigoted. Above all, they were no less inclined to stand upon what they considered their rights as against what was supposed to be a secretly papist royal house.

There was, however, during this period a good deal less general culture in the South than in New England. Nothing came of the project, put forward as early as 1620 by the enlightened Sir Edwin Sandys—whose American Catholic descendants are still among us[3]—for the establishment of a college in Virginia.

[2] Actually the first New England settlers came, upon the whole, of more substantial stock than those of the South. However, this superiority did not ultimately weigh very heavily, as all the colonies were largely recruited by poor men who sold themselves into a term of servitude in order to pay their passage to the New World, or of felons who were transported thither.

[3] Collateral descendants, however. Sir Edwin Sandys himself never came to America, though his brother George, the poet, did and was Treasurer of the Jamestown colony. Around 1621 another Sandys arrived with the Puritan group in Massachusetts and had part in the founding of Boston. One of his young kinsmen, James Sands, followed Anne Hutchinson to Rhode Island, but eventually settled at Sands Point, Long Island. The graveyard there is full of people of this name, among them twin sisters, both spinsters, charmingly christened "Silence" and "Submit." In 1685 we find a William Sandys settled in St. Mary's City, Maryland. There is no record of when he came: however, there is a Sands house in Annapolis that was built in 1681. The family was a large one and stemmed from

Even in 1691, when a charter was asked for the College of William and Mary, which was to be a Southern balance to the Puritan Harvard, Edward Seymour, the Lord of the Treasury, was anything but enthusiastic. Dr. Blair, who had gone to England in Virginia's behalf, explained that it was necessary to have a seminary for the training of ministers and that Virginians as well as Englishmen had souls to save. "Souls!" Seymour snapped. "Damn your souls! Make tobacco."

The Southern planters eventually got their college and Virginia produced its full share of cultivated and able men; but intellectual interests were never so widely diffused there as in New England. But there is, in this connection, an important factor to notice. Though William and Mary—like Harvard and afterwards Yale and Princeton—had as its main function the manufacture of ministers, the passion for theology never took root in the South to the extent that it did in the North. It was a circumstance that proved fortunate for Catholics. The more mundane interests of Virginia promoted political speculation, and this by degrees worked in favor of religious toleration.

This is not to say that the New Englander was ever without a shrewd business sense. The economic motive was admitted by William Bradford. The dourness generated by Puritanism was a valuable economic asset in a land where, the soil being so stubborn, no staple crops could be produced. The consequence was a turn to manufacturing (especially of rum) and shipbuilding and the establishment of commercial towns.

In the case of the Puritans, however, the economic motive was itself sanctified. Prosperity was considered a sign of heaven's approbation and of the soul's election. Only hard-working and sober people could expect to prosper. The love of money

Queen Elizabeth's apostate Archbishop of York. But some of them remained faithful to the "Old Religion"; one of these, John Sandys, a seminary priest, was hanged, drawn and quartered at Worcester, after being sentenced by a court of which Miles Sands, a Puritan, was a judge. After the introduction of the penal laws into the Maryland colony, most of the Sands there conformed or emigrated. Some, however, did not, but remained in the Faith, practicing it as best they could, without benefit of clergy, the father baptizing the son, until such time as a priest was encountered, when conditional baptism was received. Their marriages they recorded in the nearest Protestant church. This custom of crypto-Catholicism was rather general during the dark days of persecution.

with them was not the root of all evil; rather the lack of it indicated reprobation. With great learning this ingenious formula was advanced for the justification of worldliness. Although it was admitted that, in individual cases, adversity might be sent for the trying of a chosen spirit, the principle was of absolute force with regard to society as a whole. God had made a covenant to bless New England.

At the same time we must not suppose that by any means all the inhabitants of the northern colonies were church members. Many, on the contrary, were indifferent to religion; many others made a profession of religion for secular advantage. Nor was there always a close correspondence between theory and things as they actually were. Even among the elect drunkenness was prevalent. Any social gathering was a sufficient excuse for rum-bibbing, and the ordination of a minister was considered a privileged occasion. Then, too, despite the supposititious Puritan strictness about sexual lapses, fornication was generally looked upon as a very venial sin. At Harvard in 1722 the question was publicly argued—as among the stock commonplaces of a debating-society—"Whether it be fornication to lye with ones sweetheart (after contraction) before marriage." Though the practice of "bundling" was probably fairly innocent as a rule, it can scarcely be described as seemly. Jonathan Edwards was ousted from his charge at Northampton not so much on account of his stringent theology as because of his stand against the popular *mores*. Yet after having made all due deductions, it must be admitted that the Puritans did give a distinctive tone of austerity to New England. Their ideals were lofty, if narrow, and their practice of their beliefs sincere. They strike us now as a queer historical aberration. But it is only just to acknowledge that America owes much to them.

What I am mainly concerned with, however, is not so much their antiquated theology as their attitude towards religious liberty. That they served it, after their fashion, by coming to the New World, is perfectly true. They served it by showing that it was something for which it was worth making sacrifices. Yet what cannot be denied is that, while seeking liberty of conscience for themselves, they had little inclination to grant it to others. Nathaniel Ward—a jovial and humorous sort of a man, as many Puritans were—put the issue uncompromisingly in his *Simple Cobbler of Aggawam*: "He that is willing to tolerate any religion, or discrepant way of religion, beside his own, unless it be in matters merely indifferent, either doubts of his own, or is not sincere in it." Nothing could be clearer: the doctrine was taken as axiomatic. And if a quotation bearing more directly upon Catholics is concerned, here it is, from John Cotton: "The Holy Ghost puts no difference between Popish Pagancie and Heathenish Pagancie. . . . Popery is but Pagancie refined; and the estate of Popish people dying in Popery is more dangerous than the estate of Pagans dying in their Ignorance." This new twist to *extra ecclesia nulla salus* is also admirable in its forthrightness. In neither instance is anything like toleration shown.

Faced with these awkward and undeniable facts, those who still cling to the naïve belief that religious liberty in America sprang from Protestantism, make a great play of the Rhode Island colony. Unluckily Roger Williams and Anne Hutchinson cannot be correctly called apostles of toleration. Cotton Mather described Mrs. Hutchinson in his *Magnalia Christi Americana* as a "gentlewoman of haughty carriage, a busy spirit, competent wit, and a voluble tongue." Her speciality was a claim that her private (or as some would say, eccentric) religious views were directly imparted to her by divine revelation. Brave she certainly was; equally certainly she was arrogant. The ministers upon whom she used her sharp tongue so unsparingly cannot be blamed for driving her out to Rhode Island. In any community she would have been an impossible person.

As for the tolerance of Roger Williams, this is largely a myth. He was a contentious fellow, never happy except when he was quarrelling with somebody. When Massachusetts ejected him, he made a proclamation of toleration, though mainly, one must suspect, in the hope that the Quakers (whom he had in mind) would go to Rhode Island and give him somebody with whom he could argue.[4] His mode of dealing with them, so far from being conciliatory, was acrimonious, insulting and even (according to modern notions) obscene. The very title of *George Fox, Digged Out of His Burrows* contrives to hit at once at the founder of the sect and at George Burrows his disciple. The controversial tone of the period is indicated by the fact that when John Cotton replied to Williams' *Bloody Tenant of Persecution for the Sake of Conscience* with *The Bloody Tenant Washed and*

---

[4] See the provocative article, "Roger Williams, Apostle of Religious Bigotry," in *Thought*, Vol. VI (1931), pp. 478–492.

Made White in the Blood of the Lamb, Williams promptly
came back with a still more truculent pamphlet, *The Bloody
Tenant Yet More Bloody through Mr. Cotton's Endeavour to
Wash it White in the Blood of the Lamb.* As if that were not
sufficiently disagreeable, Williams refused to join his wife and
children in family prayers because they found themselves unable to subscribe to all his queer opinions.

We must give the man credit for the courage of his convictions. Perhaps, too, his affirmation of them did in the long
run make for religious liberty. But to regard him as an apostle
of toleration is absurd. His denunciations of "the Romish
wolf" who was gorged with "huge bowls of the blood of the
saints" was not exactly an inducement to Catholics to trust
that they would be less molested in Rhode Island than elsewhere in New England. They carefully avoided the apostle of
toleration; well they might.

What emerges from all this is that nowhere in New England was any freedom given to dissent. One would think that
Massachusetts would have been content with having got rid
of its religious malcontents. Yet when in 1651 three Rhode
Island Baptists went to pay an innocent visit to a friend in
their former colony, they were imprisoned, fined and flogged.
One of them, Obadiah Holmes, the minister of Seekonk, on
hearing his sentence cried, "I bless God that I am worthy to
suffer for the sake of Jesus!" upon which John Wilson, a
Massachusetts minister, hit him in the face with "The curse
of Jesus go with you!" The best that can be said of Rhode
Island is that the jail and the pillory were not its instruments
of persecution. But the furious tongue-lashings prevalent in
the Baptist colony cannot very aptly be described as an illustrious instance of tolerance. It is only necessary to compare
this state of affairs with early Maryland, where all derisive
terms regarding religion were absolutely forbidden.

In all the colonies there was but one Protestant sect which
was really tolerant. This was that of the Quakers, whose persecution is such a blot upon the Puritans. Their doctrine of
the "Inner Light" was, of course, highly obnoxious, since it
virtually means that each man may make up his own creed
and alter it, if he chooses, every day, as the Inner Light shines
upon him. A Catholic must disagree with their central theories
more strongly than even with the doctrines of the Puritans.
Nevertheless the Quakers were, in their behavior, a harmless
set of people. The fullest acknowledgment is due that it was

only where they had power—in Pennsylvania—that Catholicism can be said to have been tolerated at all.

This being the situation, such Catholics as entered the Northern colonies did not dare proclaim their faith, nor did they have any opportunity for the practice of their religion. Irish men, women and children were sent in droves to American soil, especially during the Cromwellian regime, but they arrived as indentured servants or temporary slaves. The first generation of them made some attempt to say what prayers they knew; the second or third generation were always lost to the Church, for there were no priests to say Mass for them or to administer the sacraments. Social pressure brought about the conformity of the children, even when the parents stubbornly held out.[5] Their principal effect upon America is that, when the Revolution occurred, they were eager to settle scores with England. Since many of them had been hedge-school masters in Ireland, they practiced their calling in the new land, and therefore were able to influence the young in political matters. Their Catholicism, however, had to be kept concealed. In the sphere of religion they had no influence whatever. And what was true of New England, was almost as true of the South.

How weak and helpless the Catholics were is revealed by Cotton Mather's telling in his *Magnalia* of a Goody Glover, "one of the wild Irish," who was executed as a witch in 1688 and who "profest herself a Roman Catholick and could recite her Paternoster in Latin very readily." Why, in view of the fewness of Catholics, and their complete impotence, there should have been such excitement about them will have to be explained. Surely old women like Goody Glover did not imperil what Mather, in the same book, said was the purpose of the settlements in New England—"to raise up a bulwarke against the Kingdome of Antichrist which the Jesuits labour to build up in all parts of the world." The explanation can best come from an examination of the nature of anti-Catholic feeling itself.

This feeling existed everywhere in the colonies, including (after a short happy day) Maryland. It is important to stress its existence because it has kept cropping up—though with

[5] Bishop Shaughnessy estimates these losses at 125,000, though his book in general inclines to minimize Irish Catholic defections. These losses were more numerous in the southern than in the northern colonies. More Irish went to the South.

gradually diminishing force—all through American history. As
verse can always put a point more succinctly than prose, let
us turn to the stanza attributed to John Rogers, one of the
Marian martyrs. It appeared hundreds of times in colonial
pamphlets and almanacs. No New England child but knew
the gory lines:

> Abhor that arrant whore of Rome,
>   And all her blasphemies
> And drink not of her cursed cup,
>   Obey not her decrees.

As that was what they thought of the Church, the colonists
introduced penal laws designed to make the practice of Catholicism impossible. These laws were not uniform and were
more severe in some places than others. But their purpose was
invariable—that of suppressing Catholics and their abominations. Perhaps the worst instance was that of Lord Bellomont
who, after the Revolution of 1688, got a law passed for New
York imposing the death penalty on priests and induced Massachusetts to pass a similar law. He even tried to bribe the
Indians in upper New York state to kidnap their Black Robes
and hand them over to him for the execution of justice. As no
genuine priest was ever caught a bogus one was offered up to
appease the lust of bigotry. The unlucky man was John Ury,
a non-juring Anglican clergyman who, because he inoffensively
minded his own business, was brought under suspicion. With
some Spanish negroes who were accused of sabotage—and who
were confessedly Catholics—he was hanged on August 15, 1741
in New York City. Except for Pennsylvania, I repeat, there
was no colony in which Catholics could live in comfort—not
until after the American Revolution.

The explanation is, in part, that the American colonists had
inherited the English penal code with its ferocious anti-Catholic laws. In part, it is that from time to time things happened
which made the colonists dreadfully afraid.

Fear is nearly always the spring of cruelty. When terrified,
even kindly men are quite likely to do horrible things. And the
colonists were afraid—afraid of the Indians, afraid of the
French in Canada (whom they believed were egging the Indians on to massacre), afraid of the Spaniards in Florida,
afraid of the Stuarts, and—when the Stuarts had gone—afraid
of a Jacobite uprising. They knew that the professed Catholics
in their midst were an insignificant handful, even in Penn-

sylvania and Maryland. But they also knew that many Irishmen were scattered throughout the colonies. These they supposed to be crypto-Catholics, if not actually Jesuits in disguise,
and imagined them to be biding their time. It was a perpetual
"fifth-columnist" scare, as we should now call it. The signal
would be given; then from all sides their enemies would burst
upon them with fire and knife and tomahawk, while the
wicked Catholics seized their chance of cutting the throats of
Protestant Englishmen.

There was just this much foundation for the fear: France
in Canada was powerful, and the Indians now and then perpetrated an atrocity—which was usually imagined to have been
instigated by the French. However this may be, there was no
solid foundation for the distrust of the Stuarts. Even James
II, though his methods were often tactless, was the most
statesmanlike of his house and the worst used by history. Shea
does him tardy justice in saying that he was "the first to appre-
hend the future greatness of America."[6] His offence was that
he displayed the atrocious tyranny of desiring to bring about
toleration in England. That he showed his sincerity by granting this toleration to dissenters as well as to Catholics did him
no good: the move was called a wily Jesuit trick, whereas the
truth is that he lost his throne because he was so lacking in
guile as to trust those who were plotting to betray him.

Everything a Catholic king did was of course wrong. When
James appointed Governor Andros he had in mind a unification of the colonies for the sake of their defence. But as the
Anglican Andros happened to be rather overbearing, the
King's projects were sourly regarded as the kind of tyranny to
be expected from a papist. Why, the man was actually ordered
to decree toleration "to all persons of what religion whatsoever"! This simply could not be borne. James had introduced
a Catholic bishop into England—one with jurisdiction over
the papists in Maryland and Pennsylvania. The next thing
would be that he would set up the Inquisition!

It is not for me to defend James here. I merely remark that
this Catholic head of the Church of England acted very
straightforwardly in his ambiguous position. Thus we find him
writing in 1688 to the Catholic Governor Dongan: "You shall
take care that God Almighty be devoutly and duly served
throughout your government, the Book of Common Prayer

[6] *Op. cit.*, Vol. I, p. 344.

read every Sunday and holyday, and the Blessed Sacrament be administered according to the rites of the Church of England." James was here upholding Protestantism in his official capacity while, as a private person, he was practicing Catholicism. Nobody could be more loyal to what was expected of him as king; nobody has got less credit for his loyalty.

I am going to quote Sanford Hoadley Cobb, the author of *The Rise of Religious Liberty in America*, upon the maligned monarch. His judgment carries all the more weight because it is that of a Protestant who, though in his character of historian, fair to Catholics, dislikes them enough to keep alluding to them, a little insultingly, as "Romanists." This is what he says of James II: "What he did and said in the matter [of toleration] was altogether honorable, and far in advance of the toleration accorded by his son-in-law, William, the idol of seventeenth-century Protestants." On those who dispossessed James let me quote Father Hughes, and so ease my soul. "Bancroft says, that by deposing their King, they annihilated his right; that by disenfranchising a dynasty for its Catholicism, they had a right to disenfranchise it; that by breaking a contract, they had a perfect right to break it; and, by establishing new conditions, they had a right to go back upon a contract and reform it *ex post facto*. In all this the historian finds not the slightest inkling of a latent consciousness that possibly there is some obligation imposed by allegiance, truth, fidelity, or solemn oaths. The breaking of all these obligations is a general dispensation from them. It is the philosophy of the accomplished fact. The end justifies the means."[7]

That judgment, though severe, is deserved. At the same time we must in justice allow for the sincere belief prevalent in many minds that toleration could not be extended towards Catholics—whoever else might be tolerated—because Catholicism was the foe of all freedom. This was the position taken up by John Milton and John Locke in the seventeenth century and by Samuel Adams in the eighteenth. Minds less liberal rejected the principle of toleration altogether. All types of minds agreed that, when a Catholic king proposed it, it was a case of Greeks bearing gifts. Even the wise steps taken by James towards the unification of the colonies was regarded as the first move to effect their religious subjugation.

The hatred of James persisted long after his deposition, and

7 *Op. cit.*, Vol. I, pp. 114–115.

has, for that matter, created a tradition which has persisted up to our own times. Well into the eighteenth century there was the fear of a Stuart restoration. It was in many ways unfortunate that the appointment of English Catholic bishops remained in the hands of the Cardinal of York (1725–1807), the brother of Prince Charles Edward, the "Young Pretender." After "Bonnie Charlie's" death, the Cardinal was himself regarded by the Jacobites as their true King—Henry IX.[8] We can therefore hardly wonder that Protestants were convinced that Catholicism was synonymous with an attachment to the Stuart cause.

In religious matters the colonies were only following England's example. The blame for intolerance should therefore be laid where it really belongs—on the English government itself. If during the eighteenth century there was in England (though not in Ireland) some relaxation in the enforcement of the laws directed against Catholics, the laws remained unrepealed. As late as 1767 a priest was condemned to life imprisonment for saying Mass, and spent four years in prison. And in 1782 the fines imposed upon recusants for non-attendance at the parish church were collected from two poor farm laborers in Yorkshire. What can be said of the American colonies is that they were upon the whole more lenient than the Mother Country. They might have been more lenient still had it not been for England's example.

The toleration that obtained during the Jacobean interlude quickly passed. Governor Dongan had brought priests to New York, where they established a school. But Leisler, upon the fall of James, stamped out all vestiges of Catholicism, and throughout the colonies Protestantism settled itself more firmly than ever in the saddle. It was not that there was any ferocious persecution. This was not necessary: the hard smooth surface of social disapproval was itself sufficient to discourage Catholicism which, so far from making headway, steadily lost ground. The remarkable thing is that, by the time the Revolution broke out, any Catholics at all were to be found in America to provide a nucleus for ecclesiastical reorganization.

The treatment given the Acadians is a case in point. They had been deported from their homes, separated from their

8 It was remembered that in 1745 he had come to England to support his brother's rising.

families, and dumped on American soil. Though they made pathetic efforts to hold on to their Faith—the first regular saying of Mass in Baltimore was for their benefit—as a rule no provision could be made for their religious needs, so that they, like so many of the Irish, were eventually lost to the Church. The best they could do in most places was to meet on Sundays for prayers, to appoint one of their number to administer baptism, and to be content with marriages which consisted of a public exchange of consent. It was as much as these hapless people could do to survive even physically, since no support from the public funds was offered and private charity was discountenanced. Thus the *Maryland Gazette* for February 10, 1757, petitions with a comical smugness: "As it is no easy task for a Christian to withstand the unfortunate cravings of their [*sic*] distressed fellow citizens, those among us who especially possess the greatest degree of humanity must, of course, be the greatest sufferers." That is really a harrowing state of affairs: how unfair that a good Christian should have to suffer because of his sensitiveness! But the writer finds additional reasons for not helping his "fellow citizens": "Their religious principles in a Protestant country, being dangerous, particularly at this juncture, and their attachment to their mother-country, added to their natural resentment of the treatment they have met with, render it unsafe to harbour them. . . . We therefore pray you to have this pest removed from among us, after the example of the people of Virginia and Carolina." The final ingenious argument is that "since they so earnestly desire to quit his Majesty's protection, in a manner renouncing it, they enfeeble their claim to the restitution and restoration they contend for." In short, the very misfortunes of the Acadians were excellent reasons for letting them starve to death.

These quotations represent, it is to be feared, the official Maryland attitude. As that colony was—with the exception of Pennsylvania[9]—the one in which Catholics were allowed most liberty, it would be instructive to inquire how far this liberty extended.

Under the law they hardly had any liberty at all, though positive persecution had lessened since the time when John

[9] William Penn was suspected, because of his tolerance, of being a Jesuit in disguise. Actually, however, he had a low opinion of Catholicism. But because Catholics and Quakers had been fellow-sufferers from persecution, he gave a practical sort of toleration to all religious beliefs. Only atheists were technically excluded.

Coode[10]—in turn Catholic, pirate and Anglican minister—led the attack. The saying of Mass was proscribed. The making of converts became a capital offence. Heavy fines were imposed for educating children in the Catholic religion, even if it were done in the quietest way by employing a private tutor. And children who apostatized to Protestantism might take possession of everything their parents owned. All of which was justified, in the memorial sent to William III, on the ground of "the injustice and tyranny under which we groan" —the Act of Toleration of 1649.

Nor did the matter end with the passage of anti-Catholic laws: an effort was, from time to time, made to enforce them, although William and Mary modified their full rigor. Thus the chapel at St. Mary's City was closed and we hear of Governor Seymour's having a couple of "Mass-mongers" haled before him in 1704. If he let them off with a warning, he made, among other pleasant remarks, the following: "Gentlemen, it is the unhappy temper of you and all your tribe to grow insolent under civility. . . . Yet of all people, you have the least reason for considering that if the necessary laws that are made were let loose to crush you . . . you would need to dread. I assure you the next occasion you give me, you shall find the truth of what I say. . . . If you intend to live here let me have no more of these things, for if I do, and they are made against you, be assured I'll chastise you. . . . Pray take notice that I am an English Protestant Gentleman, and can never equivocate."

Queen Anne, however, who had succeeded to the throne in 1702, came to the rescue. Governor Seymour's penal laws were suspended for eighteen months, and were in fact never allowed to become operative by the Crown. Yet the suspension could at any moment be withdrawn. Though Mass was permitted, it could only be in private houses. So long as Catholics were so obliging as to keep themselves out of sight, it would be pretended that they did not exist. There was a sound motive for not pushing persecution too far: if things got too hot for them, Catholics might emigrate to the French or Spanish dominions and build up a rival tobacco trade there. They

10 In 1699 he was indicted and convicted of atheism and blasphemy. His religion had probably never been anything but a hatred of the Catholic Church—in which he was like so many other people of his time.

were therefore persecuted just enough to keep them in subjection, but not enough to completely alienate them.

But even a little persecution is more than enough for most people. When the fourth Lord Baltimore apostatized, many leading Marylanders did the same, in which they were followed by the majority of their dependents. These losses were permanent, for even the appearance of proselytism had to be avoided and the utmost discretion exercised in the administration of the sacraments. The priests were unmolested only on condition that they lived as private gentlemen on their lands, which they and the Jesuit lay-brothers (aided by negro slaves) managed as farms. If anyone wanted to go to Mass, he could go to the priest's residence. It was unsafe for the priest to go to him. Especially was it perilous to reconcile any lapsed Catholic, even on his death-bed.

Nor was it anything but difficult to get any sort of Catholic schooling. The Jesuits, almost from the moment of landing, formed such grandiose educational schemes, that some enthusiasts would like to regard 1634 as the ideal date for the founding of Georgetown. Father Hughes writes: "This plan would have given us a St. Mary's College, Maryland, within a few years after Quebec College, New France, and within still fewer years after Harvard College, Massachusetts (1637)." So to be sure it would—had anything come of it. But although that goal could not yet be attained—even had Lord Baltimore not been opposed to so rash a proceeding as the establishment of a Jesuit seminary in his palatinate—a school was founded at Newtown in 1639 by Brother Ralph Crouch. It was a good school, but Father Phelan would have been well advised not to claim that "it ranks as the second college within the present limits of the republic, being antedated only by Harvard."[11] It is true that Harvard was at the outset hardly more than an academy—as Georgetown was for some time hardly more than an academy; but both Georgetown and Harvard developed into universities, whereas Newtown (in spite of improving its curriculum in 1677) did not last long even as a school. The law of 1704—"An Act to Prevent the Growth of Popery"— passed by the Maryland Assembly brought about its suppression.

Catholics who wanted their children to be well educated were obliged to send them abroad, to St. Omer's. This was

11 *Catholics in Colonial Days*, p. 60.

forbidden by existing statute but winked at—since rich people can usually contrive to break the law with impunity. Those who could not afford this luxury had to fall back upon the use of Irish indentured servants who had been hedge-school masters. As even that was possible only to a few, the majority grew up more or less illiterate.

The years 1715–1751 brought relative freedom to Maryland Catholics. The Jesuits opened a school again—that of Bohemia Manor, which the Carrolls were to attend. But persecution was soon renewed and though some of the bills introduced in the Assembly failed to pass, the one of 1756, which doubled the taxation for Catholics, did become law. It could have been little more than an annoyance; yet in the eyes of the elder Charles Carroll it seemed so outrageous that he wrote to his son, the future signer of the Declaration of Independence, saying wrathfully that if only he were younger he would leave Maryland. He went so far as to sound the authorities in the West Indies and Arkansas in turn asking for land on which to settle, but as he asked too much of them, his overtures were declined. We need not be very sorry for him. He was the wealthiest man in Maryland, and perhaps in all America. During the worst days of the persecution he was able, as factor for the Proprietary, to maintain a private chapel in Annapolis—to which Protestant town the capital had been shifted from St. Mary's. And he was in the position to educate his sons abroad without fear of having to pay the fines, which, in any event, would have been easy for him to pay. Instead we should be glad that the Carrolls remained rooted in Maryland—to play their great part during and after the Revolution.

In general the eighteenth century may be described as a period of pressure rather than of positive persecution for Maryland Catholics. The laws against them were as a rule held *in terrorem* instead of being strictly enforced. For that matter, even during Elizabeth's reign, the ferocious anti-Catholic legislation was much too ferocious to be strictly applied. Only a few hundreds suffered the extreme penalty, whereas hundreds of thousands were liable to have torture and death inflicted upon them. No Catholic ever suffered to that extent in Maryland nor in any of the American colonies. It is true that the authorities supposed they were hanging a priest in New York when they hanged John Ury. And it may be that one or two of the New England "witches" lost their lives quite as much for being able to say the Hail Mary as for their imagined relations with Beelzebub. But these instances hardly count. The American martyrs were killed by savages not by fellow-Christians. It is something upon which America may congratulate itself.

There is, however, one case which may seem to disprove this statement—that of Father Râle in Maine. I shall come to it in a moment, and pause now merely to remark that I believe this must be considered as an instance of that partly political, partly racial, conflict which had already begun on the continent and—though its forms have varied—has never completely ended. Deplore such violence as we must, we must try to understand its true significance. Religion played a minor part in the matter.

First let me dispose of events in Louisiana, as these come first in time. Those who regarded the French possessions as of immense potential wealth were of course perfectly accurate in their estimate. France, however, though it held the Mississippi, had failed to exploit its possibilities as fully as it exploited the St. Lawrence gateway to the sea. It needed the canny Scot, John Law (1671–1729) to persuade the French that they were not utilizing their opportunities. In 1716 this ill-starred financial genius organized the Banque Général and in the following year the Compagnie de la Louisiane. He was at first so successful in his financial operations that he was almost rated a wizard. Unfortunately he was too successful. The fever of uncontrolled speculation brought about the blowing of an enormous bubble, which burst in 1720 with an enormous bang. It was not Law's fault; he was an honest man. But Louisiana needed a development it never received before the shares of its company could be worth much. Its settlements were few and badly managed. New Orleans itself was hardly more than a collection of miserable huts and rotting warehouses. The result was that France lost interest in its American province. In 1763 it was ceded to Spain.

As for the ecclesiastical administration of the vast sparsely settled territory, this had once had a great history in the north; but lower down the river a long period of conflict between Franciscans and Jesuits—or, more accurately the resentment of either order to the administration of a Vicar-General of the other, under the jurisdiction of distant Quebec—was anything but conducive to active missionary work or the edification of souls. Anyone who wants to pursue the matter can best do so in two doctoral dissertations that have come from the Catholic University of America. In the one, Father Claude Vogel argues the case for his fellow-Capuchins; in the other, Father Jean Delanglez argues in favor of the Jesuits. He does so at great length and with notable thoroughness. He must be said to have put the controversial issues involved beyond debate.

The question was not the simple one of jealousy between rival religious orders. There was continuous misunderstanding also between the ecclesiastical and secular authorities, which were seeking very different aims. The officials wanted to gallicize the Indians; the missionaries, to Catholicize them. But to Catholicize them it was necessary to keep the two races apart as far as possible, since the red man acquired the white man's vices more readily than his culture. This separation, not being very easy to effect, the Indians were, for the most part, merely exploited and exasperated and corrupted. As one of the Jesuits had to write, "If our missions are not so flourishing as others on account of the great number of conversions, they are at least precious and beneficial *to us*, on account of the labors and hardships inseparable from them."[12] The pious reflection did the good Father credit; but, after all, the missions were for the saving of the souls of the Indians; only incidentally were they for the spiritual benefit of the missionaries. They must be said to have been, upon the whole, a failure— like the material development of Louisiana.

The end of an age that had opened gloriously was at hand. The Jansenists of France were not only a religious but a political party, and one very dextrous in pulling strings. They had old scores to settle with the Jesuits. Even before the papal Bull ordering the suppression of the Society had been issued, the French government acted. Indeed, the local administration in Louisiana did not wait for formal instructions from France. The Jesuits were thrown out, neck and crop, as soon as it was known that their suppression had been decided upon. With that came the virtual collapse of the French missions. Ten years before the Bull of Clement XIV, France had been forced to relinquish Canada to England. In Louisiana a few friars lingered on under the new Spanish regime, some of whom gave scandal to their flocks and trouble to John Carroll when, after the Louisiana Purchase in 1803, he was obliged

12 Delanglez, p. 380.

to saddle himself with the administration of a territory as large as that of the original thirteen states.

Up to the time of the Revolution the French (or Spaniards) in Louisiana were too far away from the English colonies to cause any problem. English settlers and traders were, however, already crossing the Appalachians, though they had not begun to think of pressing on to the Mississippi. Louisiana, after the bursting of "Jessamy" John Law's bubble was not regarded as of much use to anybody. Ceded to Spain in 1763, in 1801 it was receded to France.

In the case of foreign settlements nearer at hand the situation was altogether different. South Carolina invaded Florida in 1702 and burnt St. Augustine, though without being able to capture the fort. A few years later the Spaniards retaliated with a fruitless siege of Charleston. The English did not feel at all comfortable with papistical Spaniards on their borders. When war with Spain broke out in 1739, General Oglethorpe (who had founded his colony for the relief of debtors and with the high ideals of the prohibition of slavery and rum, but of all his ideals was able to preserve only intolerance towards the Catholic Church) tried once again to eject the Spaniards. If he failed to do that, the Spaniards—as in the case of Charleston—failed in their attempt to dislodge the English.

But the real menace to the English colonies was not in the South but in New England. Now and then the Indians swooped down upon a settlement and perpetrated a massacre, such as that of Deerfield. When these attacks occurred, it generally happened that captive children were taken to New France, where they grew up happily as Catholics, while their Puritan relatives regarded their fate as worse than death.[13] War was more or less sporadic between the French and English colonists, even when war was not going on between England and France. From the beginning there had been at the back of the minds of the New England settlers, as we know from John Winthrop's own statement, the idea that unless they acted with decision the French and the Jesuits would soon come into possession of the Atlantic seaboard as far south as New Amsterdam. In these clashes the Jesuits were believed

---

[13] Some of them even became nuns. But it must be added that in almost every known instance of a returned captive, a reversion to Protestantism occurred. Nobody could for long hold out as a Catholic in New England. The cases are examined in some detail in Father Riley's *Catholicism in New England*.

to be the tools of the French authorities (when those authorities were not the tools of the Jesuits). As for the Indians, they were supposedly egged on by the Canadians, while the Jesuits blessed their tomahawks and scalping knives.

The idea was fantastic—at any rate as far as the Jesuits were concerned. Being Frenchmen, they naturally had an interest in the development of the French colonies, but so far from their being hand-in-glove with the officials, they were frequently at loggerheads with them. No doubt some Frenchmen stooped to base means in their contest for the continent; so too did some equally unscrupulous Englishmen. Both sides were at times willing to pay for their scalps of their enemies. In all this, however, the French missionaries had absolutely no part. They wished for peace because they knew only too well what demons were unleashed by war. Only during peace could they hope to convert the Indians.

It was nevertheless hard to eradicate so deeply set, so fiercely inflamed a Puritan obsession. Even such moderate men as refused to give credence to the notion that the Jesuits sought to murder them could see that the influence the Jesuits had over the Indians worked for the advantage of France. Yet now and then friendly relations obtained, especially in the beginning, between the Puritans and the French missionaries. For example, Père Gabriel Druillettes, when he visited Boston in 1650 on diplomatic business, was courteously entertained by Governor Dudley, and went on to Plymouth, where Governor Bradford was so kind as to serve him fish on Friday. Major-General Gibbons actually went so far as to give him a key to a room in which he could offer Mass without being disturbed. Endicott—even the bigoted Endicott—was affable; and John Eliot at "Rogsbray" invited the priest to spend the winter there. All the saints at "Pleimout" and "Marbletz" were charmed with the agreeable Jesuit. A special friendship had already been formed between him and the younger Winthrop. The Devil's horns were not visible when seen at close quarters. Nothing, however, came of the negotiations. The political alliance sought against the Iroquois did not eventuate. All that was accomplished was to show that a few personal meetings of this kind would have dissipated much prejudice.

A century later it became clear that there was to be a life and death struggle between England and France. It was perhaps inevitable that to such a struggle a religious complexion should have been imparted. "Dear Parson Moody," striding along with his axe for the demolition of the "idols" at Louis-burg in 1745, may be laughed at. What is not quite so funny is the fate of Sebastian Râle in 1724.

The best version of this affair, in my estimation, is that given by Father Arthur J. Riley. He presents his facts dispassionately and is able to see what was really involved. And that, quite simply, was the frontier between the French and English claims in America. It was then undetermined and was, indeed, not settled until some time after the Revolution. On the basis of that settlement—though England got a good deal more than she was entitled to in establishing her border so far south of the St. Lawrence—it is at least arguable that France never had any solid claim to Maine. At the time of the Râle affair it was not so much that France was making specific claims—which in any event she was not prepared to support by arms—as that claims were likely to be made later on the ground that the Maine Indians were being evangelized by French missionaries. On the other hand, one could not expect the missionaries to withdraw merely to oblige the English. Their first duty was to their flock.

Further, however fully one may admit that the English claim to Maine seems to have been well founded, it cannot be denied that there was a strong French case too. Long before the English had come to New England—if we except the abortive colonization attempts of 1584 and 1607—Madame Guercheville, unable to induce Pourtrincourt to see eye to eye with her, had sent three Jesuits named Masse and Biard and Quentin, and a lay-brother, to open a new missionary field in the colony she founded. This was in 1613, at Mount Desert Island at the mouth of the Penobscot. There they might have remained had not Samuel Argal sailed north from Virginia to bundle them out.

There was, however, no renunciation by France of her claim. Therefore when the series of eighteenth-century wars opened, the English settlers first tried to buy the Indians, promising to build them commodious churches and send them ministers. The Abenaki were not to be hoodwinked. Already they understood the difference between a Black Robe and a Protestant divine. Already their Catholicism was so deeply ingrained that, when occasion demanded it, they were willing to go all the way to New France to fulfill their Easter duties. As the Puritans could not seduce the Indians on the Kennebec, they determined to punish them.

An expedition was sent against the Abenaki in 1705. As it failed to accomplish anything, the Massachusetts authorities fell back on flattery, bribery and propaganda, though not without omitting to try, when opportunity served, what force could accomplish. Thus when four of the Abenaki went to Boston to discuss matters with the Governor, they were clapped into jail and held as hostages. This was the sort of thing the Indians could not understand. Père Râle, who understood it much better, advised the abandonment of the country to the English, as they were evidently determined to get it. As the Indians could not see why they should do that, he of course would not desert them. For their part, they scornfully rejected a really handsome offer the Puritans made for the saintly priest's head.

Some of the English settlers were opposed to what came to be called "Father Râle's War." Samuel Sewall found, as usual, an amusing reason for his stand: he disapproved of attacking the Indians because he was sure they constituted the lost ten tribes of Israel! Others were not so squeamish as the sentimental Judge. On August 23, 1724, after five previous attempts to capture Râle, a force of 170 men surprised him at Norridgewock. He was alone, except for a few braves. These put up what resistance they could; in the scuffle the Black Robe was killed.

There are two accounts of the incident. The one written by Père de la Chasse depicts Râle as going unaccompanied to meet the advancing English, in the hope of saving his people. The other, by Governor Thomas Hutchinson, represents Râle as shot by an officer named Jacques because he was about to murder an English boy, a captive. Neither version can be accepted. The French Father wrote only from hearsay; Hutchinson's story is preposterous. Father Riley decides that "it would be reasonable to conclude that Râle was slain by Lieutenant Jacques in violation of orders." Râle's body nevertheless was treated with indignity and his scalp carried in procession through the streets of Boston.

"Father Râle's War" was a kind of unofficial skirmish in the great series of wars that ended in the French loss of Canada and India. Just as in America the War of the Spanish Succession was known as "Queen Anne's War," so that of the Austrian Succession, which opened in 1744, was known as "King George's War," and the culminating phase of 1755–

1762, the Seven Years' War, was viewed by American eyes as "The French and Indian War."

It was a period of excited political passions, when of course patriotism and anti-Popery tended to become identified. The frame of the public mind was revealed when the Justices of Bucks County wrote to Governor Morris of Pennsylvania concerning the notoriously dangerous principles of Catholics. "And we have reason to fear, just at this time," they added, "that the Roman Catholics in Cussahopen [Goshenhoppen] —where they have a magnificent chapel, and lately have had long processions—have bad designs." What the long processions had to do with the case it is hard to imagine, but it is not at all hard to catch the hint about the magnificent chapel. For when Braddock suffered his defeat, the Philadelphia mob was with difficulty prevented by the authorities from destroying the Catholic churches. Everybody felt sure that, in some way, the wicked papists were responsible. It is this frame of mind that must be reckoned with when we come to the next stage of our story.

CHAPTER SEVEN

THE CAUSES OF THE REVOLUTION

Obviously a general discussion of the causes of the American Revolution has no need to appear in this book. My concern must be to indicate specifically Catholic causes, if such exist. I believe they do, though I make no claim that they were the only causes or even of decisive importance. But as their importance has, until recently, been commonly ignored, and is still not fully recognized, they demand examination.

There were at least two such causes—one positive, the other negative. The positive cause was the close affinity between scholastic political philosophy and the American concept; the negative cause was the Quebec Act, or rather the violent resentment aroused in the Colonies by England's extension of religious liberty to her newly acquired possessions in Canada. They may seem to cancel one another; actually the anti-Catholic emotions stirred up in the Colonies by the Quebec Act precipitated the raising of those theoretical questions which had so long before been propounded by Catholic thinkers, and which had become part of the thought of Americans, although they were ignorant of their origin. Even with regard to the practical issue of taxation, Maryland was the only colony able to point to a provision in its charter under which the King renounced for himself and his successors all right to levy taxes.[1] When Franklin attempted to claim the same thing for Pennsylvania and was challenged to point out the clause granting it, he found he had to fall back upon the less convincing argument that the rights of Englishmen as defined by Magna Carta were being violated. In any event such charters were part of the medieval (and Catholic) tradition and were based upon the idea, not so much of special privileges, as of inalienable rights, which charters merely confirmed.

It is a little difficult for some modern men—including many Americans, though their formally defined liberties are of so recent a date—to believe very strongly in "rights" or any abstract propositions. The Marxian formula is that the economic is

[1] See Ives, *The Ark and the Dove*, p. 86.

the determining factor, and the materialistic historians of the Beard school are hardly prepared to admit any other. I do not intend to enter into controversy with them: all that I do is to express my conviction that they misunderstand the nature of man. He lives by bread; so much is true. He does not live by bread alone.

But so as not to ignore material considerations, I had better briefly set down once more what it was that brought American discontent to the point of rebellion. The various taxes—on stamps, glass, sugar, tea and the like—were irritants rather than precipitatives. Nobody likes paying taxes, and the colonists resented them as a novelty. That they resisted them as they did, however, was due to their political philosophy. Unless you believe you are born free, you accept tyranny, even while you groan under it. The colonists had so keen a sense of their rights that they thought it tyranny when the Mother Country taxed them without their consent. It cannot be called a very extreme instance of tyranny; to the American mind it was nevertheless intolerable.

The real issue went very much deeper than the taxes that brought it to the fore. But as there was hardly time to sit down and debate all the questions of political philosophy involved— though of course this was done too—a slogan was discovered. It was one so simple as to be capable of comprehension by everybody. The slogan was: No taxation without representation. When it was asked upon what principle it reposed, the answer came pat—"On Magna Carta." That, like the slogan itself, was beautifully satisfactory.

The argument did not strike the British government as particularly impressive. As for taxation, it was coldly explained, the Americans ought to pay their share of the war against France, which was so very much for their benefit and in which they had left most of the fighting to the British regulars. As for representation, they *were* represented in Parliament. In England there were only 160,000 voters out of a population of eight millions. Yet everybody was represented in Parliament, or at least every "interest" had a group there committed to its support. Why must Americans alone seek direct representation?

There were of course several sophistries in the English rejoinder. Yet as Samuel Adams said, "There is nothing that the colonies would more dread" than to send members to the Parliament at Westminster. There they could always be outvoted. And to travel back and forth between America and England was not feasible. What the colonies wanted was local autonomy.

From the English point of view, the Americans had their heads full of a subversive opposition to the theory of "omnicompetence" of Parliament that had been first advanced in the seventeenth century. Blackstone had devastatingly laid down in 1758: "What Parliament doth, no power on earth can do." These strange colonials, unimpressed in their turn, affirmed this to be a denial of fundamental law, a throwing overboard of Magna Carta. Magna Carta! Magna Carta!—this was their shibboleth. They quoted Locke, "A government is not free to do as it pleases. . . . The law of nature stands as an eternal rule to all men, legislators as well as others." This was the result of giving the Americans charters! They had turned them into constitutions—though England had got along very well without a written constitution. Van Tyne sums it up, "The absolutism of Parliament was to Otis and Adams as hateful as the absolutism of the King."[2] They looked upon an oligarchy as being as tyrannical as a monarchy.

To the English the American attitude was most unreasonable. The taxes, after all, were not very heavy, and the British government had shown its willingness to withdraw obnoxious duties and to put others, less objectionable, in their place. It was clear that the colonists did not want to be taxed at all, though it was a small price to pay for British protection.

The taxation issue was not, in itself, insoluble. Even Benjamin Franklin had at first raised no protest against the excise duties. And Richard Henry Lee had applied for the position of Stamp Commissioner for Virginia. That it was largely a manufactured grievance is shown by the fact that, after Parliament had humored the Colonies, they remained unappeased.

The truth is of course that the Colonies were by now suspicious. They might have been willing to pay what England considered a fair share for America to shoulder of the cost of the war with France, had they not believed that England merely meant to exploit them. Trade restrictions could be—and had been—accepted with no more than a little grumbling. It was well known that these were much less severe in the case of the English colonies than in that of the other powers. And the English connection was worth something to Amer-

[2] *Causes of the American Revolution*, p. 232.

ica. But the British government was no longer content with the general principle, or willing to look the other way when smuggling went on. The defeat of France and the acquisition of Canada and an Indian empire had made England insufferably arrogant. And the new mercantile policy involved an efficiency as unpopular as it was unfamiliar.

Furthermore, there was the allied question of debt. The Colonies, which had never had much specie, were for this reason always in debt to London bankers and merchants. If England had allowed them to print paper money for their immediate relief, it would have made a great deal of difference. This, however, was peremptorily forbidden—with the consequence that the financial situation grew daily more desperate. There was some truth in Tom Moore's gibe at the colonists:

> Who could their monarch in their purse forget
> And break allegiance but to cancel debt.

But it was England's obstinacy that had made a revolution seem less of a financial burden than the settlement of debts. A war would bring a moratorium; it might even bring cancellation.

The question of the western lands was also an important material motive. Nearly all the colonies had vast claims that stretched away, more or less indefinitely, beyond the Alleghenies. Many of these claims overlapped and were not, in fact, adjusted until after the Revolution. All of them, however, were denied by the British government on the ground that, if the fur trade were to be preserved, the Indians must be protected from the encroachments of the settlers who were already pressing westwards across the mountains. To the land-hungry this denial of their right to land seemed insufferable.

Yet the British land policy, from our vantage-point in time, now seems sound. The government took up the position that the question of the western lands was an imperial one and that individual colonies could not be permitted to take it into their own hands. Its solution of the problem—broadly speaking —had ultimately to be adopted by the Federal government after the war, when the various claims were surrendered to it by the new states. But as tension mounted between England and the Colonies, such a solution was unacceptable to Americans. They held that the tyrannical British were robbing them of their rights, in this as in other matters. They could not be brought to believe that the attempt of Lord Shelburne, the "Jesuit of Berkeley Square," to make the Alleghenies the frontier was regarded by him merely as a temporary measure, pending final settlement after full investigation. To minds inflamed with many grievances, the restriction appeared highhanded and unjust. Order *was* needed; unluckily it was arbitrarily imposed from above.

Worst of all, the colonists' resentment at the British attitude towards their western claims was acerbated by the fact that the government extended the application of the Quebec Act to the banks of the Ohio. As this meant toleration for Catholics living in those territories, Protestant prejudice discovered another reason for resisting the Mother Country. They were being defrauded to endow the Whore of Babylon! Even those who cared nothing about religion could now use it for political purposes. Even those who had no personal concern in the western lands (but who were stoutly Protestant) were outraged by the spiritual injustice of tolerating Catholics. The most powerful of all combinations was effected—that between material interest and religious passion.

All the same, we need not attach—like the English historian, Cardinal Gasquet—an undue weight to the effect of the Quebec Act. No doubt the Revolution would in any case have broken out. And it should be recorded that, as soon as the Revolution occurred, the wise minds in control of the American cause did all they could to quench the flames of bigotry, if only in order to placate Catholic Canada and to secure assistance from Catholic France. But as the Quebec Act certainly helped to precipitate the Revolution, a word should be said about it here.

When, at the treaty of 1763, France ceded to England everything east of the Mississippi and Iberville rivers, along with Canada—everything west going to Spain—there was enormous joy in America. Guns were fired, bells rung, bonfires lit; and General Winslow of Plymouth got so drunk in an excess of patriotic enthusiasm as to jump on the dinner table, where his prancings broke a large number of punch-bowls and glasses. The joy faded only when it was learned that the western lands were not only to be closed to settlers but that the detested religion of Canada was to be tolerated there. Land speculators considered themselves robbed. Fanatics bellowed with rage. And politicians found it decidedly to their advantage to have so lofty an issue with which to appeal to bigots.

They used it for all that it was worth, and all the ancient suspicion of the colonists that there was some dark connection between the monarchy and popery was instantly revived. The King was not merely a tyrant; he was the protector of Catholics.

This notion had died down since the deposition of James II. Now people began to wonder once more whether there was not a natural affinity between Pope and King. Hundreds of violent sermons were delivered, scores of pamphlets were printed. Echoes of these ravings reached Canada, where some of the pamphlets also found their way. And Catholic Canada, then under the firm rule of Bishop Briand, was appalled at the outburst. It was remembered a little later, when the war began, against the *Bostonnais*. It eventuated in Canada's adhesion to the side of England.

In view of these circumstances the question arises why American Catholics supported the Revolution. That they could not openly oppose it is easily understandable—they were too few in numbers to dare that. But why did they not take up a position of neutrality? In spite of what John Gilmary Shea says—he tries to maintain that there were no Catholic loyalists at all—they were, like other American groups, divided in their sympathy. Yet it is true enough that there was a higher degree of unanimity among them in favor of independence than anywhere else. Practically all the prominent men among them took the side of the Revolution. Unlike the Episcopalians—many of whose ministers were so active as Tories as to find it advisable to leave the country—not a single Catholic priest got himself into difficulties on this account.

It may perhaps be supposed that the Catholics for the most part supported the Revolution because they were, as Irishmen, opposed to England. This no doubt operated in some cases. But of the laity, relatively few were of Irish descent, and, with the exception of a few German Fathers working in Pennsylvania among their fellow-countrymen, practically the whole body of priests were English either in blood or actual birth.[8] The country was, indeed, full of Irishmen; but the vast majority of these were either Presbyterian "Scotch-Irish" from Ulster or those who should have been Catholics, but who had

[8] Shea gives in a footnote on pages 259–260 of the second volume of his history, the names and locations of all the priests in America in 1785. There were twenty-four of them, and there could have been little change since 1776.

long since lost the Faith. And whereas the Scotch-Irish formed a rather solid anti-British bloc, some of the Catholic Irish served as Tory volunteers. So that explanation will not hold. In Pennsylvania there were many German Catholics, but they were without any political antipathy to England. The bulk of the Catholic population in the Colonies was still of English origin. Even those who, like the Carrolls, were partly Irish in blood, as a rule had strong personal English attachments. Nevertheless they came down on the American side.

How did this happen? In Maryland they had every right to feel aggrieved at the treatment they had received from their Protestant fellow-citizens. It was, on the other hand, the English Crown that had given them the brief freedom they had enjoyed. It was the English Crown that had restrained the persecuting frenzy of the Maryland Assembly. One would naturally have expected that the English Crown would have received their support in the struggle.

The only possible answer is that they were Americans. They loved their country. They saw, more clearly than anybody else, that despite the screaming denunciations of the Quebec Act, the winning of political liberty would also mean the winning of religious liberty. They understood the genius of America and its destiny. Without hesitation—though let me repeat, without quite the degree of unanimity claimed by Shea—they threw in their lot with Congress.

They did so because the principles of the Revolution were so closely consonant with Catholic political philosophy.

As this statement is likely to sound paradoxical it had better be expanded. A great many people have the curious notion that absolutism and Catholicism go together. They even vaguely suppose that the doctrine of the "divine right of Kings" is of Catholic origin. The fact is, however, that that monstrous and ridiculous notion came to flower only with the Renaissance and represents the weakening of the medieval Catholic tradition. If it was advanced, in a modified form, by some Catholic monarchs—to a great extent because they believed that only by an absolute rule could they preserve, in troubled times, what remained of national and Catholic unity —its most extreme presentation was among Protestants. As far as English and American history is concerned, we think of the "divine right of Kings" in association with the pretensions of James I. We are also only too likely to think that resistance to the doctrine came solely from the Puritans.

That the Puritan oligarchy in England opposed it is true; they opposed it because it conflicted with the domination they were attempting to establish. To find intellectual weapons for doing so, however, they were obliged to go to the armory of scholastic philosophy. This was perfectly understood and was pointed out by their opponents. As Sir Robert Filmer put it in his *Patriarcha,* "Cardinal Bellarmine and Calvin both look asquint this way."

This is not to affirm that the fate of the Catholic Church is inextricably bound up with the political system of democracy. The Church has, in the course of its history, accommodated itself to many systems, and will always do so whenever such accommodation is possible. But the Church has always maintained that, whatever may be the accidental inequality in gift and station between man and man, they are all essentially equal in the sight of God. It is only upon such a doctrine that democracy can repose. It is only democratic institutions that put that doctrine into visible practice. For despite the Declaration of Independence, with its "self-evident" truth that all men are created equal, the thing is not self-evident at all. On the contrary, it seems to be at variance with self-evident facts. It is really a mystical dogma, and the one institution we can be perfectly certain will never renounce that dogma is the Catholic Church.

Where then did Jefferson find it? That what he wrote in the Declaration of Independence was regarded as anything but original is shown by John Adams' gratuitous sneer that it contained nothing but what had been constantly said before. All that Jefferson and the other Founding Fathers did was to state, with superb lucidity and concision, ideas which, because they were so completely accepted, had come to be regarded as axiomatic.

Concerning the source of Jefferson's ideas there has been much controversy. The supposition—which once found some acceptance, but was a mere guess—that he was influenced by Rousseau has been thoroughly disproved. The latest theory, advanced by Professor Gilbert Chinard, is that Jefferson drew his inspiration from Anglo-Saxon law. That he was very interested in Anglo-Saxon law is evident in his *Commonplace Book,* which Chinard has edited. But the entries there are drawn from a number of very disparate sources, and indicate that Jefferson was glad to find corroboration for his ideas wherever it existed. Jefferson rides his Anglo-Saxon hobby horse often enough to enable Chinard to say that "Jeffersonian democracy was born under the sign of Hengist and Horsa, not of the Goddess reason."[4] Jefferson did indeed write in his boyish enthusiasm that it would have been better had England developed under its unwritten Anglo-Saxon law instead of under the feudalism which was introduced at the time of the Norman Conquest. But the professor also gives full rein to his hobby. The thesis is, however, so fanciful that he is obliged to admit in the end that "the Declaration of Independence is essentially of Lockian origin, but it does not ensue that Jefferson had memorized Locke, nor even that he was conscious, when he wrote the document, that he was using a Lockian phraseology."[5] Jefferson's consciousness of what he was doing is immaterial; Chinard's admission surrenders his entire thesis. We have to come back to Locke's *Two Treatises on Government* as the Bible of the Revolution.

Locke wrote to refute Filmer, whose *Patriarcha*, though written thirty years before, was not published until 1680. Those who read Locke, when serious students, had also to read Filmer. We know that Jefferson read him, because his copy of the *Patriarcha* is preserved in the Congressional Library. That he read Locke (it is not necessary that he "memorized" his work) is patent in the very phrasing of the Declaration of Independence.

Now Locke's thought was formed by Hooker, and Hooker's thought was formed by St. Thomas Aquinas. As for Filmer, he was an honest enough controversialist to present the gist of his opponent's arguments faithfully. That opponent was Cardinal Bellarmine. And while Filmer signally failed to establish his own position, those who read him got, at secondhand, a sufficiently adequate acquaintance with Bellarmine. In the same way, those who read Locke, got—also at secondhand—the scholastic political doctrine.

It might also be pointed out, as Dr. James J. Walsh conclusively shows in his book, *The Education of the Founding Fathers*, that the system of the public defence of a list of theses (framed in Latin) by the graduating students in American colleges of the period was purely scholastic in form, and generally in content, and that a good half of the members of the Continental Congress were college men whose minds had

[4] *Thomas Jefferson, the Apostle of Americanism* (2nd. ed. revised, Boston, 1939), p. 87.
[5] *Ibid.*, p. 72.

been moulded by this system. Had any of them ever read Suarez—who wrote, "The civil power, whenever it is found in a man or a prince, has emanated according to usual and legitimate law from the people and community, either directly or remotely, and cannot otherwise be justly possessed"—they would have found in him a political philosophy that accorded with their own.

Catholic writers have perhaps sometimes made excessive claims in this matter. Thus I have heard it argued by some Dominicans that their Constitutions must have been on the table when the Constitution of the United States was being formulated. On the face of it such a claim must be rejected. The framers almost certainly had never heard of the *Constitutiones Sacri Ordinis Predicatorum*, and would not have known where to lay their hands on a copy had they known of it. But what is quite certain is that, however unconsciously, the Founding Fathers went to the same body of political thought that had inspired the "democratic" system of government set up by the Dominican order. Hence the similarities between the two documents. The Jesuit Father, Moorhouse F. X. Millar, is on safe ground when he writes that the American denial of the omnicompetence of Parliament is no more than a reassertion of the denial of the divine right of kings.[6] Without being aware of it, the leaders of the Revolution might almost be called scholastics themselves.[7] John Quincy Adams said that the American theory of government was something that "had been working itself into the mind of man for many ages." The American originality does not consist in the theory itself—for that was European in inception—but in

[6] Ryan and Millar, *The State and the Church*, pp. 177–178.

[7] We must, however, guard against the supposition that the scholastic theory about sovereignty being resident in the people is the official doctrine of the Church. Since the publication of Leo XIII's *Diuturnum* most Catholic political scientists are inclined to follow him in holding that the popular power is merely that of designating the recipient of authority. Consequently it is implied that the power of sovereignty does not reside in the people pending a nomination, but rather the power of designation, upon which God confers authority, not mediately through the people, but immediately. However, this in turn is not precisely the official doctrine, in the sense of excluding all other theories. And in any case it offers no difficulty to the proposition of a close general consonance between the American and the Catholic concepts.

the fact that a nation now tried, for the first time, to provide it with the machinery for putting it into operation.

All this was recognized at the time. Thus the loyalist Chief Justice William Smith could say afterwards, "I trace the late revolt . . . to a remoter cause than that to which it is ordinarily ascribed. The truth is that this country had outgrown its government and wanted the true remedy for more than half a century before the rupture commenced." Or as John Adams put it, "The Revolution was effected before the war commenced. The Revolution was in the minds and hearts of the people." In other words, the thing had happened before anyone was aware of it. Even the wisest English statesmanship therefore would have been severely taxed to keep people duly submissive who had so long enjoyed liberty. But English statesmanship was far from being wise. A policy of easy-going drift might perhaps have kept the Colonies loyal for another generation or so, though sooner or later the demand for independence would have been heard. Instead the imperial government decided to tighten and restrict by methods which were not in themselves particularly oppressive, but made its decision at the worst possible moment and tried to enforce it in the worst possible way.

Other factors should be remembered. The war with France had brought Englishmen and Americans to serve together in the army. This had the result of making the English professional soldier contemptuous of the American volunteer, because of his lack of discipline, and of making the American volunteer contemptuous of the British regular because of his stupidity. Braddock took his disastrous defeat from his refusal to listen to the Americans who could have told him how to fight in a forest. Instead he and his officers rode about disdaining cover—and had to accept the consequences. It was Braddock's defeat, as Franklin said, that "gave us Americans the first suspicion that our exalted ideas of the prowess of British regulars had not been well founded." In spite of this, the English—rubbing it in that it was they who had performed the exploit of capturing Quebec and that it was they who had had the main hand in suppressing the conspiracy of Pontiac—said openly that the colonists were of little use in military service and could never face redcoats.

But if this made many Americans itch for a chance of showing what they could do against the boastful British, it was not the cause of the war. The Revolution sprang from a passion for liberty. The Americans desired it for the excellent reason that they already possessed it; they were the freest of all colonies in the world, so that there is a sense in which the winning of American independence is among the most illustrious events in English history. It was from England that the Colonies had obtained their charters. It was from England that they had derived—though at several removes—the political ideas that animated them. Under the wide skies of the New World they lived a life which was, in some respects, more English than that of the English themselves. For at the time of their coming to America, England still had many local administrative bodies that were destined to disappear in the eighteenth century. In America these were preserved.

Perhaps it is never quite possible to extinguish the hunger for liberty in the human heart. But it is possible to come close to doing so—a psychological fact which totalitarianism exploits. Instead English rule—at any rate as compared with the absolutism of France and Spain—had encouraged liberty. "The freest of all peoples," says Van Tyne, "were the first to revolt."[8] They revolted, because being free, the slightest shadow of oppression was intolerable to them. Their Americanism did not begin as a mere theory but as a way of life. But, having enjoyed that life, they turned to the theory to whet their appetite still further and to rationalize their emotions.

In nothing was America more fortunate than in the fact that when the outburst occurred it was without fury, that, instead of seeking to tear down, its main concern was how to build most enduringly upon foundations already securely laid. To direct matters there was at hand as admirable a set of men as ever were available for such a task—thinkers as well as men of action, scholars as well as soldiers, conservatives as well as revolutionists. Among them the Revolution had been a slow natural growth. The tyranny against which they fought was no more than an attempted restriction of what they believed to be their constitutional rights; the tyranny was not, as it had been in so many other cases, a bloody oppression which could only end in as bloody an uprising.

All this was fortunate for the Catholic Church in America as well as for America itself. Catholics, if one may put it so, were able to be revolutionists without wearing the red cap. They could join their compatriots in a national movement so

8 *The Causes of the War of Independence*, p. 18.

eminently reasonable and moderate. The only possible ground for controversy was not concerning principles—for these were professedly accepted by both sides—but as to whether or not this or that specific act of the British government was a cause sufficient to warrant a demand for independence. No attack on property or morals was involved. This was not the delirium of desperate men who would stick at nothing, but an orderly adjustment of affairs which manifestly called for some adjustment. In such a revolution Catholics could take part with a clear conscience. The Revolution was only an application of commonplaces in their own philosophy.

It therefore mattered very little to American Catholics that the leaders of the Revolution were unaware as to the derivation of their ideas. No harm was done by the "noble Roman" color given to the affair. If Plutarch corroborated the schoolmen, so much the better. The Carrolls knew that the American inspiration did not really come from Plutarch but from Aquinas. It was the reaffirmation of an ancient doctrine upon the sound basis of practical needs. As such they could wholeheartedly accept it. The American Catholic was not only able to be an American; he knew that it was he who had the deepest understanding of the American idea.

CHAPTER EIGHT

CATHOLICS IN THE REVOLUTION

The date 1774 is one of great importance both to America and to the American Catholic Church. The clouds of revolution were already heavy on the horizon—that much everybody could see. What perhaps nobody had the discernment to recognize was that the return of a sedate middle-aged ex-Jesuit from abroad the same year was destined to be of immense consequence to the Church.

John Carroll had left his native Maryland in 1748, after attending the Jesuit school at Bohemia Manor with his cousin Charles, now known as Carroll of Carrollton. Both boys—John was only thirteen, Charles two years younger—entered St. Omer's. But Charles left his Jesuit college when he was eighteen to study law at Paris and afterwards at London,[1] whereas John joined the Jesuit order soon after his arrival in France. At this college and then at Liège John Carroll became a professor in due course, varying this occupation for a while as travelling tutor to the son of Lord Stourton. His last year in Europe was spent in England, where he acted as chaplain to Lord Arundel of Wardour, who seems to have been a classmate of his at St. Omer's. The rigorous Jesuit training, like his travels and his contacts with the best circles of English Catholicism, did much to broaden and deepen John Carroll's mind. Though he did not know it, he was being prepared for a life work he never envisaged.

Equally was he strengthened by the shocks he had to undergo. In 1762 the Jesuits were expelled from France. If that was sufficiently painful it must have been less so than Carroll's discovering, when in 1772 he visited Rome, that, as a Jesuit, he was to be cold-shouldered by the ecclesiastical authorities who had already decided upon the suppression of his Order. In charge of all English ecclesiastical appointments was the Cardinal of York, whom the Jacobites regarded as King Henry IX; and the Cardinal was an open enemy of the Jesuits, as was also Marefoschi, the Cardinal-Secretary of the Congregation

---

[1] Carroll of Carrollton returned to Maryland in 1765.

de Propaganda Fide. His experiences at this time created in Carroll a distrust of the Congregation, which was to bear bitter fruit; for as Dr. Guilday says, "The complaisance of the authorities of the Church towards the Bourbon intriguers burned a remembrance into Carroll's mind which was not forgotten when he came in later years to treat with the same officials." In 1773 Pope Clement XIV issued his Bull entirely suppressing the Society of Jesus.

In the ordinary course of events Carroll would probably have remained in England, where he had many friends who wanted to keep him there. This was what Father Nicholas Sewall, another Marylander, did. After the restoration of the Jesuits he became their Provincial in that country. But already the gathering troubles at home made Carroll feel that it was his duty to return. In the end, therefore, the blow directed against the Jesuits which had, at the time, seemed the destruction of all his hopes, turned out to be providential. The country about to come into being was given precisely the ecclesiastical leader it needed.

Yet Carroll's return did not awaken any great enthusiasm. The Maryland Jesuits, after their downfall, had formed themselves into an association for the protection of their property, and they showed no willingness to extend financial support to this former member of their order. Therefore, because he had already renounced all claim upon his dead father's estate, he lived unattached in his mother's house at Rock Creek, near Georgetown. The influence that he gradually built up was due to sheer force of character and ability. Though among the Maryland priests were men of some intellectual distinction, most of them were old and far from energetic. The long years during which they had lived under the penal laws—even if those laws were not strictly enforced—had engendered in them excessive caution, a sloth which tended to consider itself humility, and what would now be described as an inferiority complex. A rash young man—John Carroll was thought of as such by his elders who remembered him only as a boy—setting out to achieve reform at a stroke would have accomplished nothing. So he kept himself aloof and made no attempt to interfere in their affairs. Only the pressure of his unobtrusive zeal came by degrees to mark him out as the natural leader of American Catholics.

We have an account written by him in 1790 of the situation of the Church in America at the time of his return. Attempts, he says, were then still being made to introduce the whole penal code of England; "And it seemed to depend more on the temper of the courts of justice than on avowed and acknowledged principles of justice that these laws were not generally executed, as partially they were sometimes." The consequence was that many Catholics were apostatizing. Those who remained faithful were, for the most part, shut out from all lucrative employment and were "poor and dejected." Nevertheless, he says that their numbers had increased, though the congregations were scattered and not always visited regularly by a priest. The majority were either illiterate or lacking in books, and while the native-born among the Catholics were as a rule well-behaved, "great licentiousness" prevailed among the new Irish elements. As no support was given by the people to the clergy, who were expected to subsist on the proceeds of their not very valuable estates, Carroll foresaw in this fact a decided handicap to the progress of religion. He estimated that there were sixteen thousand Catholics in Maryland and between six and seven thousand in Pennsylvania, with a few on the borders of Virginia and New Jersey. It was disturbing to him to note that only about half the Maryland Catholics approached the sacraments, and presumably the same was true of Pennsylvania. In short, he gives us anything but a rosy picture, though it was not in his make-up to be downcast over it. We must conclude that the Church in America was now almost at its lowest ebb and that, had it not been for the galvanizing effects of the Revolution and the religious freedom that followed it, American Catholicism would soon have become virtually extinct. It was this situation that Carroll had to overcome.

That he was the cousin of Charles Carroll, owner of sixty thousand acres and, as he was called, "the Duke of Norfolk of Maryland," was to be to his advantage, though there was no close intimacy between the two men. In the Revolution about to occur, Charles' wealth and social position had much to do with gaining the general adhesion of the Catholic body to the American cause. As Leonard, his biographer, puts it, "He was the richest man that signed the Declaration of Independence, the first man that signed, the only Roman Catholic that signed, and the last man to die of those that signed it." John's sympathies also were well known, though, as a priest, he was careful not to be too openly a political partisan. It is probably due to him that the American clergy, many of whom had been born in England, acted as they did during the years that followed.

As has already been remarked, there was no very obvious inducement offered that they should support the Revolution. Though I believe it can be shown that there was at least a general consonance between the principles upon which the new nation was to be built and those of scholastic philosophy, this may then have been far from evident. For as yet there was no definite enunciation of American principles. On the contrary, up and down the land orators were wandering, some of them giving vent—as always happens during periods of political excitement—to wild and absurd sentiments. If one clear note could be caught above the din of these hoarse voices, if one opinion might be said to be common to all, it was that the Catholic Church was a menace to be opposed and crushed. The mere granting of religious toleration under the Quebec Act had so enraged the masses that, for them, it seemed to be the chief spur into war. If that was not a sufficient deterrent to Catholics, there was the fact that they were, as ever, inclined to hesitate before resisting legally constituted civil authority, except as a last resource.

St. Bartholomew's Day, 1772, was popularly supposed to have been selected as the appropriate occasion for a general massacre of Protestants. Nobody of course explained how this was to be carried out by a subdued handful of papists. But though so preposterous a prediction was smiled at by sensible men, the fact that the prediction was made reveals the prevailing hysteria. When the Quebec Act was passed, George III was accused of being a disguised Jesuit and his statue was adorned with a rosary. Scurrilous engravings appeared of His Majesty and his ministers depicting them in their most lurid papistical colors—Paul Revere being specially prominent in the production of such caricatures. Catholics could hardly do other than gaze with horror at the lowering skies.

Nor was the bigotry confined to the ignorant. John Adams, Samuel Chase, the violent red-headed orator Patrick Henry, Alexander Hamilton, Samuel Adams, and Richard Henry Lee, among others, united in denouncing the Quebec Act, Hamilton declaring, "If [Parliament] had any regard to the freedom and happiness of mankind they would not have done it. If they had been friends to the Protestant cause, they would never have provided such a nursery for its greatest enemy. . . . They may as well establish Popery in New York and the

other colonies as they did in Canada!" Men like these, it need
not be said, were much too intelligent and well informed to
give countenance to the sillier sort of accusations against
Catholics; they were not, however, unwilling to make use of
religious prejudice for their political ends. With them the
Quebec Act was rather a pretext for revolution than a true
motive. They were, nevertheless, ready to use bigotry to in-
flame the unthinking,[2] whose view of the issue found perfect
expression in the doggerel stanza of Bob Jingle, the self-styled
Poet Laureate of Congress:

> If Gallic Papists have a right
> To worship their own way,
> Then farewell to the liberties
> Of poor America!

Nothing could have been more wrong-headed; nothing could
have made its point more clearly.

It was precisely because such opinions were widespread that
both sides, after the outbreak of the war, appealed to them,
each side to turn them to its own advantage. When the
French fleet was on its way, *Rivington's Royal Gazetteer*, the
Tory Paper, announced to a shuddering public (or one that
it hoped to make shudder), that the ships were carrying "tons
of holy water, and casks of consecrated oil, reliques, beads,
crucifixes, rosaries, consecrated wafers, and Mass books, as well
as bales of indulgences."[3] To add to the full beauty of the
comic representation, France was also said to be sending,
along with an army of "priests, confessors and mendicants,"
a complete equipment of instruments for the Inquisition it intended to set up. Samuel Adams, it seems, was already converted and planning to take holy orders; and the Boston
meeting houses were to be turned into cathedrals and convents! The editor of the same paper, in its issue of July 26,
1779, wrote darkly, "I could name a member of the rebel
Council in one of the New England colonies, who was for-

---

[2] Cardinal Gasquet, however, affirms in an article in the London
Tablet (see bibliography) that "the Taxation Acts were only a
minor cause, or rather occasion, and the dispute would have been
settled by constitutional agitation but for the Puritan fire-brands
and the bigotry of the people." It is a judgment that calls for
considerable qualification.

[3] It is curious how a Miltonic echo appears here. See *Paradise
Lost*, Book III, line 491.

merly considered as a zealous Protestant dissenter, who not long since harangued a large assembly of people on some of the points disputed between Protestants and Papists, such as the invocation of saints, purgatory, transubstantiation, etc. After palliating each of them, straining the sense to put the most favourable and least offensive construction on them, and softening them with as much art as the most subtle disciple of Loyola could use, he finally declared that he saw nothing amiss or erroneous in them; and his audience seemed to be wonderfully pleased and edified."

The attack on the Church was to some extent offset by the circumstance that both Patriots and Loyalists used anti-Catholic propaganda when it suited their book. It was, in a way, reassuring to Catholics that no one party could be considered to possess all the virtues of bigotry. When Tories took up the tune discarded by the Revolutionists, papists could smile, and almost sigh with relief. It did not, however, remove the fact that bigotry existed among the leaders of the American cause. Nor was it an inducement to Catholics to throw in their lot with that cause.

Moreover, the matter did not always end with mere words. In 1776, for instance, a number of Catholic Highlanders were driven from the Mohawk valley and had to take refuge in Canada. They had settled around the fortified mansion of Sir William Johnson. These fierce, proud, quick-tempered men, all armed with dirk and broadsword and nearly all McDonalds, had taken an oath after Culloden never again to bear arms against the King. Now because the little transplanted clan proposed to honor their oath—and the same fidelity must be recorded of the Scotch Presbyterians who had taken the same pledge—they were driven out as traitorous Tories with their priest, the Irishman John McKenna. In Montreal they became a living witness to American intolerance.

The most damning fact of all is that between October 21 and October 26, 1774, three addresses were drawn up in Congress. These are, in part, arranged in parallel columns, with telling effect, by Dr. Guilday in his life of John Carroll. The Address to the People of England (dated October 21, and written by John Jay, a man brought up in the intensely anti-Catholic Huguenot settlement of New Rochelle) expresses "our astonishment that a British Parliament should ever consent to establish in that country [Canada] a religion that has deluged your island in blood, and disbursed impiety, bigotry, persecution, murder and rebellion through every part of the world." Yet five days later Congress concocted a cajoling address to the Canadians asking, "What is offered to you by the late Parliament? . . . Liberty of conscience in your religion? No. God gave it to you; and the powers with which you have been and are connected, firmly stipulated for your enjoyment of it. . . . We are all too well acquainted with the liberality of sentiment distinguishing your nation, to imagine, that difference of religion will prejudice you against a hearty amity with us." And on the same day the Petition to the King complains that "great numbers of English freemen" are subject to French laws under the Quebec Act which establishes "an absolute government and the Roman Catholic religion throughout those vast regions."

Congress was evidently capable of facing not only two ways but three ways at once. It is possible to make allowances for politicians seeking support in any quarter where it may be found, but this hypocrisy passes all ordinary bounds. The Canadians were no fools. Even had the Address to the People of England not fallen into their hands, they knew the *Bostonnais* well enough not to be suspicious of all professions of liberality coming from such a source. When the anti-Catholic Address reached them—it was of course at once translated and given wide circulation—there could be only contempt for the trick Congress had tried to play.

Had it not been for this, it is quite probable that Canada would have joined the rebelling Colonies. England was not greatly loved there. As it was, a couple of regiments of Canadian volunteers did join the Americans under the name of "Congress' Own," despite all the fulminations of Briand, the Bishop of Quebec. A few priests also defied excommunication in order to help the Americans. But Briand himself was not to be moved. He had taken an oath of allegiance and he intended to keep it. By keeping it he saved Canada for England. At the same time it must be added that not even his firmness and fidelity would have sufficed had it not been for the astonishing stupidity of that ill-fated Address to the People of England. If ever the chickens of bigotry came home to roost, it was now. And this time to bigotry was added duplicity.

There was, however, some positive good that eventuated to American Catholics from the incident. Congress soon came to see that it had made an egregious blunder and therefore swung away from its anti-Catholic attitude. A mission was sent to

Canada from America to see whether anything could be done. Benjamin Franklin, who already enjoyed enormous prestige in France (to which country he was soon to go as American minister), was its leading member. Samuel Chase was another, and Charles Carroll of Carrollton (as a Catholic educated in France) also went along. Congress, attempting belatedly to undo its havoc, resolved that "Mr. Carroll be requested to prevail on Mr. John Carroll to accompany the Committee to Canada." It was thought that a priest would be useful to explain to Canadians the true objects of the Revolution. We do not know—though we can guess—how Congress explained away its actions to the Carrolls. We can, however, be reasonably sure that the Carrolls, without this, had already divined that religious frenzy was merely incidental to the excitement of the times and was destined to pass. Probably, too, they were glad of a chance to prove that Catholics were patriotic.

Yet John Carroll had no belief that any good could be accomplished. He understood what an affront had been given Canada and that there was there no incentive to rebellion. Already two military expeditions—under Philip Schuyler, Richard Montgomery and Benedict Arnold—had been driven out, Montgomery being killed in action. But Father Carroll accepted his appointment as a duty and hoped against hope that perhaps persuasion would succeed where force had failed.

Persuasion failed as completely. It was impossible to gloss over that outrageous Address to the People of England. And awaiting the committee in Montreal was Father John McKenna, the priest of the Mohawk valley. What could one say in face of that fact and the double-dealing documents! When Floquet, who had been superior of the Canadian Jesuits before their suppression, allowed Carroll to say Mass in his house he was suspended by the enraged Bishop Briand. The Carrolls and Chase and Franklin had to go home. The sole useful result of the mission was that Franklin struck up a friendship with the priest in his party. Later on, when Carroll's appointment as bishop was pending, Franklin was able to offer his diplomatic services in a situation that was somewhat delicate. But Canada was not conciliated. Before the year was out twelve Canadians, who had taken arms against the King and were now prisoners of the British, were freed only after making the *amende honorable* in prison and after asking, with ropes around their necks, pardon in the cathedral for the scandal they had given, with the further necessity of doing public pen-ance, each in his parish church.[4] Not until then would the Bishop remove their excommunication.

This Canadian episode reflects little credit on Congress. The best that one can say of the men who drew up the addresses is that politicians often attempt impossible distinctions when caught in tight corners. In 1775 the Congress was still acknowledging "our rightful sovereign George III," and still later the King's health was regularly drunk in Washington's mess. The convenient subterfuge was employed that resistance was being made not to the King but to his ministers.[5] It was because America was very far from being solidly united in a common purpose that diverse groups had to be placated and black called white and white black as the occasion demanded. It was not so much deliberate hypocrisy as a confusion that sprang from the issues involved.

By now it is a commonplace that the success of the Revolution was ensured by a determined minority. Though John Adams claimed that, in its later stages, it had the support of two-thirds of the American people, it is now believed likely that the number of outright American partisans were hardly more than a third of the whole population, with an equal number definitely opposed, and the rest either indifferent or sitting on the fence. If the number of avowed Revolutionists steadily increased, this was due to their growing success and to the fact that England, by using German mercenaries—and still more by using Indian auxiliaries—forced many neutrals into active opposition. Until then the affair had been regarded by many on both sides as a gentlemanly kind of civil war which would end in a reasonable compromise. If Congress blundered badly over Canada, the British government blundered even worse by bringing in Hessians and savages to thwart the liberties of colonial Englishmen.

But what of American Catholic loyalists? John Gilmary Shea roundly declares that they were "spontaneously, universally, and energetically" united in support of the Revolution

[4] Griffin, *Catholics in the American Revolution*, Vol. I, p. 99.

[5] Afterwards historians—especially English historians—tried hard to throw all the blame upon the King. The truth is, however, that the war was always supported by large majorities in Parliament, and though men like Burke and Pitt made their protest, they were not listened to. The number of American sympathizers in England was never large enough to do more than slightly hamper the prosecution of the war.

and that "in the list of Tories and Loyalists, in the volumes since written about them, you cannot find the name of a single Catholic. There were no Catholic Tories." This he said in an address delivered in 1884,[6] but is of course nonsense. In the second volume of his *History* (published in 1888) he lists some of their names himself. There were not many of them, it is true, but they existed, and, as Dr. Guilday remarks, "the wonder is that the Catholic body, after a century of persecution by the colonial leaders, did not remain entirely neutral."

Well, I have tried to explain how it happened. But it must be admitted that three Catholic Tory regiments were recruited—if we count the one raised by Lord Rawdon in New York, which though Irish and not exclusively Catholic, must have included some Catholics. The two recruited in Philadelphia, however, could only muster together 668 men and never appear to have been an effective force.[7] Dr. Guilday accounts for their loyalty to King George on the ground that in Pennsylvania, alone among the Colonies, Catholics had enjoyed religious liberty. I can hardly see that this really solves the mystery: one would rather suppose that toleration there would have attracted the inhabitants to the American cause, just as the lack of toleration elsewhere should have had the effect of dampening their enthusiasm. We would be nearer the truth, I fancy, if we remembered that Philadelphia was a main center of Toryism and that Catholics living in that city were affected by the sentiments prevailing in their environment. Yet the same parish—St. Mary's—that supplied Colonel Clinton of a Tory regiment also supplied John Barry and Thomas Fitzsimmons and General Moylan and George Meade and Captains Roger Kean and John Walsh to the American side. Even there it would seem that Catholics usually discounted the anti-Popery issue as something artificially stirred up for the sake of rabble-rousing and saw true Americanism to be something very different.

The question arises as to what proportion of Catholics served in the American armies. John Carroll's sober sentence is, "Their blood flowed as freely, in proportion to their numbers, to cement the fabric of independence as that of their fellow citizens. They concurred with perhaps greater unanimity than any other body of men in recommending and promoting that government from whose influence America antici-

[6] Quoted in Guilday's *Carroll*, Vol. I, pp. 81–82.
[7] Griffin, *op. cit.*, Vol. I, p. 315.

pates all the blessings of justice, peace, plenty, good order, and civil and religious liberty." But we have no statistics as to how many bore arms in the struggle, and all the criteria upon which estimates might be based are uncertain if not fallacious.

Michael O'Brien in *A Hidden Phase of American History* makes an eloquent claim that the official historians have minimized what the Irish contributed towards the winning of American liberty, that when they come across an Irish name they always say it is that of a Scotch-Irishman. But even if Mr. O'Brien's thesis could be substantiated it would merely prove —what hardly needs to be proved—that the Irish are born soldiers and that they were glad to seize an opportunity of settling their scores with England. If there were as many Irishmen in the army as he contends, they must have been apostates or the sons of apostates. There is the typical case of General John Sullivan. His grandfather, Major Philip O'Sullivan, fought in the siege of Limerick; and his father, a schoolmaster, came to New England but ceased to practice—no doubt he was unable to practice—his religion after his arrival. In addition to the General this Sullivan was the father of three other revolutionary officers, of a governor of New Hampshire and a governor of Massachusetts and a judge. Among his grandchildren were a governor of Maine, a United States senator from New Hampshire and an attorney-general of that state and another judge. All these, so far from being Catholics, were conspicuous for their animosity towards the Church. Unfortunately the same thing was true of thousands of other families less distinguished than the Sullivans.

Some of Mr. O'Brien's facts would, I suspect, if investigated further, tend to destroy much of the force of his argument. For instance, he lists variant spellings of the same name as though each were really distinct. But "O'Brian, O'Bryan, O'Brien, O'Brion, O'Brine, O'Byrne, O'Briant, O'Bryant, o'brient, obriant, obriam, obrian, obrien, obryan" obviously indicate the deficient education of their officers. The same man probably often appeared with his name spelled in several different ways—or, for that matter, in the same way—serving for a time and dropping out, then joining again, perhaps each time in a different regiment. Yet each name on the list is counted as that of a separate person. We know how it was, not only with Irishmen but with all the men in the American forces: they flocked to the colors when a fight was impending and, after the battle, drifted home; the difficulty before Congress was to keep an army in being. I do not doubt that at any given moment a large proportion of the American soldiers were Irish or even—if the admission will give Mr. O'Brien any pleasure—that they were mainly from the south of Ireland. But how many of these Irishmen were Catholics nobody can say. We have to fall back upon John Carroll's cautiously worded statement and be content to believe that American Catholics—whether or not of Irish blood—did their duty towards their country.

A final word might be said about the appeal of the American mode of thought for the Catholic mind. I have already suggested that the American idea was largely (though unconsciously) inspired by the scholastic political philosophers. It was therefore only natural that American Catholics should respond to Americanism, recognizing in it familiar features. The Revolution, though it soon proceeded to a demand for national independence, began as—and to a considerable extent remained—a demand for those large local liberties which had been accorded in innumerable medieval charters. The Colonies had all been founded on some sort of written agreement, and any infringement of such an agreement made them indignant, just as any infringement of a charter was liable to stir a medieval mob to riot. Both Catholic and non-Catholic Americans attached a special sacredness to the Magna Carta, which Englishmen also professed to venerate but which the precedents of English law had so whittled down as to leave virtually without force. The British Constitution was therefore by now something that was at the mercy of lawyers. It had never been put into writing, as it is still not in writing. And the American appetite was for definitely defined rights. In other words, the American radical was really an English conservative, in so far as he wished to retain in undiminished vigor all that Magna Carta had granted.

We may go still further: the American thought of his constitutional rights as something indeed defined by a document but as also inherent in the law of nature. An elastic constitution and a haphazard assortment of laws—many of which were obsolete and unenforced—seemed plainly to contradict that concept of fundamental and immutable law so dear to the American mind. Flux and confusion were intolerable to him, and he saw how in such a state of indefiniteness tyranny could very easily appear under the guise of law—even under the guise of a constitution which, precisely because it was unwritten, could be made to bear almost any interpretation. Thus the phrase "No taxation without representation" meant to him something altogether different from its meaning to English parliamentary lawyers. And in this matter he found a natural ally in the Catholic who was accustomed in the legal code of his Church to definite privileges and definite restrictions. It cannot be determined how far this operated in practice. But it is certain that both the Catholic habit of precise dogmatic definition and a Catholic life under canon law prepared, however unconsciously, the Catholic mind for the acceptance of what we think of as the American theory of government. It is a point that I do not recall anybody having made; it is, for that very reason, a point worth making. Catholic support for the Revolution was therefore perhaps not quite the desperate gamble that Dr. Guilday describes it as being.[8]

The war itself, however, was very much of a gamble, and one that might not have been undertaken at all had the leaders of the Revolution foreseen all the difficulties ahead of them. The British ought to have won decisively, and fully expected to do so. The initial plan of marching down the line of the lakes and the Hudson, thus cutting the colonial forces in two, should have succeeded, and would have succeeded had not an official in London gone off for a long week-end in the country instead of sending Howe his instructions to march north to join hands with Burgoyne. Even after the disaster of Saratoga, the English might still have won had operations not been entrusted to Howe (who owed his command mainly to his descent from an illegitimate union of an English king), or had Howe been an energetic soldier. But he happened to combine a sneaking sympathy for the American cause with an excessive liking for wine, women and song. So he did nothing. And when finally Cornwallis acted, it was to crown all the blunders of the other British generals by allowing himself to be trapped at the peninsula of the James River at Yorktown. It was near there that the first permanent English settlement had been made; it was there that English domination ended.

Yet even with all the incompetence of most of the British commanders, Washington could hardly have won the war without the French alliance. He had first to obtain enough success to decide a hesitating France to give him aid. That much was accomplished at Saratoga. Without the French

[8] *Carroll*, Vol. I, p. 87.

navy, and a considerable French military support—and above all French money[9]—the most that he could have hoped for was the wringing of concessions short of independence.

The French alliance also had a very considerable effect upon the fortunes of the American Catholic Church. When the sending of an emissary to France was first proposed, both Washington and Franklin were in favor of appointing Charles Carroll of Carrollton. With great wisdom Carroll declined the mission. "I am the one man," he pleaded, "who must be kept entirely in the background." There was already dislike enough of an alliance with the Catholic French—against whom Americans had so recently fought—to make it inadvisable to entrust the negotiations to a Catholic. The amusing and artful Franklin therefore took Carroll's place and proved to be the perfect ambassador. It was Carroll, however, working behind the scenes, who prepared the way for Franklin's mission.

One of the first effects of this was an immediate choking off of all anti-Catholic demonstrations. Washington issued strict orders in 1775 that "Pope's Day," the colonial equivalent of Guy Fawkes' Day, was not to be celebrated, lest the susceptibilities of the French should be offended. The thing was already harmless enough and had degenerated into nothing but a yearly opportunity for gangs of rowdy youths to indulge in horseplay and to collect money to be spent at the tavern. But even this foolish "racket" was forbidden.

Consequences much more important than that to American Catholics immediately resulted. For instance, when the French fleet appeared at Newport, Rhode Island made haste to repeal its act of 1664 that refused citizenship to Catholics. And though the Tories were now able to represent themselves as the true-blue defenders of Protestant liberties, not only the American but the Catholic cause everywhere benefited from the French alliance. It was in vain that Benedict Arnold tried to justify his treason on the ground that he had seen with his own eyes "your mean and profligate Congress at Mass for the soul of a Roman Catholic in purgatory and participating in the rites of a Church against whose anti-Christian corruption

[9] Though the importance of this French aid is admitted by all historians, few of them seem to know where the French money came from. It was a gift from the clergy—ostensibly a free one, but actually more or less compulsory. See Sister M. Celsas Normand's article in *Historical Records and Studies*, Vol. XXV (1935), pp. 167, 168, 200, 201, 203.

your pious ancestors would bear witness with their blood."
Americans did not forgive his treason—nor forget the patriotism of Catholics. Arnold was correct in his statement: Congress *had* attended a requiem Mass on May 8, 1780, at St.
Joseph's Church, Philadelphia, for Miralles, the Spanish
Ambassador. Dr. Rush declined to be present because of his
"Protestant principles";[10] but official America as a whole
thought it was worth while showing some courtesy towards
Catholics. If a few defections from the American cause arose
from the national entanglement with Catholic allies, they
were more than compensated for in other directions. It is
doubtful if anything worse eventuated than a virulent Tory
editorial or two.

We need not ascribe the virtual toleration that existed during the war solely to the new spirit that had been born in
America. Such a spirit had, indeed, come into being, so that
after the war there could be no thought of going back to the
old penal system. But the toleration was merely a general tacit
consent; it was not as yet legally sanctioned, but was largely
a matter of diplomacy. France and Spain had to be persuaded
that Americans were not such black Protestants as they had
been painted.

Moreover, Catholic priests could now be useful to Congress.
John Carroll had already been employed, and an occasion
might arise to necessitate his employment again. Massachusetts meanwhile was glad to welcome a chaplain of the French
fleet and to send him as a missionary to the Catholic Indians
of Maine. He served to cement the adhesion of those Indians
to the Revolution. And although Count d'Estaing, when he
issued an address to the Canadians in the name of the French
King, did not succeed in detaching them from their loyalty
to Great Britain, he at least weakened the loyalty of many individuals. Friendship towards the Catholic Church had become a very good card for Congress to play.

The trend of events made it increasingly evident that American Catholics also had played their cards well—or had had
great luck. However, they could not have calculated upon this.
Nor had they thrown in their lot with the Revolution merely
to get something out of it. Of all the patriots they were the
most disinterested. Yet there was no group of Americans who
actually profited more by the winning of independence. Where

[10] His card of invitation, with his annotation, may be seen in
the Ridgeway branch of the Philadelphia Library.

others obtained political liberty, they obtained religious liberty as well.

It was not obtained without their deserving it. Though they had taken up arms not as Catholics but as Americans, it would be as well to indicate briefly the part that some of them played. Fitzsimmons was Washington's secretary and aide-de-camp. Moylan was quartermaster-general and afterwards in command of a cavalry regiment. Barry, in spite of limited opportunities, is rightly regarded as the father of the American navy. To these names should be added those of Meade, Lloyd, Doyle and McGuire. Nor should Orono, the blue-eyed half-breed chief of the Penobscot Indians be forgotten. If the positive aid he supplied was perhaps not very great in itself, his defection would have been serious.[11]

The foreign officers who served, either as soldiers of fortune in the American army or with the French allies, also put the Revolution in debt to Catholics. Of the one sort there were Pulaski and Kosciuszko; of the other, De Grasse, Rochambeau, d'Estaing and Lafayette—not all of them conspicuously devout but all definitely sons of the Church. As such they not only helped to establish the independence of the United States but to win religious freedom for America. Their faith is now often overlooked; it was not overlooked at the time. Nor was it possible, when peace came, for the nobler type of American mind to be so ungrateful as to return to persecution.

Of all the priests who played an active part in historical events the one who did most was Pierre Gibault. Those who were working in the missions of Maryland and Pennsylvania of course stayed quietly with their flocks. It was not for them to engage in politics. At the same time their unobtrusive influence probably counted for much more than we shall ever know. But Gibault—despite the fact that he was Bishop Briand's vicar-general—was to a great extent responsible for the winning of the old North-west. Vincennes was taken largely because of him, as George Rogers Clark afterwards handsomely acknowledged. It is true (or would seem to be true) that his personal character was not of the best, and his difficulties with his bishop were not altogether due to insub-

---

[11] The biographies of the more notable Catholic officers are to be found in Griffin's *Catholics and the American Revolution*, a rambling work that is in some sections hardly more than a collection of odds and ends, but one that contains valuable and interesting information not readily accessible elsewhere.

ordination in a political matter. It is certainly true that in later years, while smarting under a sense of being badly treated by the Americans he had helped, and in the hope of reinstating himself in the good graces of Briand, he wrote to his bishop denying (one fears a little disingenuously) that he had had any hand in the capture of Vincennes. He rubbed off some of his gilding as an American hero by adding, "I always regretted and do regret every day the loss of the mildness of British rule." But the fact remains that he did have a good deal to do with the success of Clark's campaign. As Americans we should be grateful to him; as Catholics we need not boast about him too loudly.

Another Catholic—but one rather lax in his religious practice—who had a share in the taking of Vincennes was Colonel Vigo, an Italian. He went as a spy to the settlement where, upon being taken, he would have been hanged by its British commander, Hamilton, had he not been able to prove that he had served with the Spanish army in Louisiana and therefore had to be counted as a Spanish subject. In the same gallery must be placed Bernardo de Galvez, the young Governor of Louisiana, who prevented its seizure by the British. Had it not been for him England would have been in a position to retain the west bank of the Mississippi after the peace and perhaps would even have been able to keep a grip on a large portion of the intervening western lands. He, too, served the American cause, however little he may have cared about it.

In listing these things I do not wish to make any extravagant claims for Catholics. Some of the men mentioned were naval or military officers who merely carried out orders. Those who served in the French forces were thinking primarily about the interest of France, not of that of America or of the Catholic Church. But even of those who acted only as a matter of routine duty, the majority were soon filled with a genuine enthusiasm for American liberty. Therefore Catholics need not be less grateful than are other Americans for the services they rendered. Rather they should be more grateful than other Americans because of the vastly improved relations brought about between the hitherto proscribed Catholics and their fellow-citizens.

When the news of the surrender of Cornwallis at Yorktown reached Philadelphia a Mass of thanksgiving was offered at St. Mary's Church. According to Shea, both Washington and Lafayette were present. A pleasant legend even has it that they celebrated the occasion by a ceremonial crossing of swords in front of the altar. The story is unfortunately baseless: the two men on the day of the Mass—November 4, 1781—were still at Yorktown. There is, nevertheless, a kind of symbolical truth in the legend. With the end of the war, Catholic France and Protestant America pledged undying friendship. From that friendship was to come something that was much more than mere toleration for Catholics. What resulted was an absolute religious equality for all faiths and, with it, a new opportunity for the dispirited American Church. Instead of being confined to Maryland and Pennsylvania, it now found the whole United States an open field.

CHAPTER NINE

RELIGIOUS LIBERTY IS WON

The English Colonies—which had gone to war with the Mother Country because of the toleration extended to Canada (at least as a minor motive), and had lost Canada's support because of their own intolerance—nearly won that vast territory after all, at the peace conference. At the first meetings of the Commissioners Lord Shelburne was inclined to accept Franklin's suggestion that the former French possessions be ceded. It was only Jay's insistence that Richard Oswald, Shelburne's agent, return to London for more strictly worded credentials that prevented this from going through. His pedantry lost America one of the greatest prizes of the peace. It is appropriate that this should have happened because of him; he was the author of the bigoted Address to the People of England. An instance of poetic justice may be seen in his second huge blunder.

Choiseul, twenty years before, when France had ceded Canada to England, had said that England would have been wiser to have left Canada in French hands. His reason was that, with a powerful France at their northern borders, the attachment of the Colonies would be forever ensured. To this Franklin made the rejoinder that a better way for England to secure the attachment of the Colonies would be to treat them fairly. Choiseul was more clever than profound. The Revolution probably would not have occurred when it did had France still been in possession of Canada. But the only thing likely to have averted it at some later date would have been the granting of dominion status to the Colonies—and that was something for which English public opinion was not ripe.

Canada, instead of serving to keep refractory colonials under control, was for a long time a temptation to the new Republic. Hungry American eyes were often cast in its direction, and the true (though not the avowed) *casus belli* in 1812 was that it might be annexed.[1] Yet it was in several ways fortunate that nothing came of these designs. For one thing, it is never

[1] Nor has this idea yet completely ended, as witness a recent speech by Charles Lindbergh.

good for any country to be too large or too powerful, any more than it is good for a man to be too rich. For another thing—the matter that most concerns this book—it was a blessing for the Catholic Church in the United States that there was no union of the countries, however that union were affected. A chance was given to Catholicism to develop upon American lines. Suspicion and hatred would have been engendered had Catholicism worn a too distinctively Gallic garb. Even on the supposition that the Colonies had remained loyal to the King, or had been defeated, nothing could have kept the colonists out of the western lands; and there they would have found the Quebec Act in force. There, too, the religion tolerated would have been considered foreign. French priests might have made their way into the English settlements, where their presence would certainly have been resented; a French bishop might have been given jurisdiction over the Catholics in Maryland and Pennsylvania. As it was, all these dangers were averted. The American Church was destined to have a history and a character of its own.

Yet both the Church and the Republic soon found that they had many difficulties to solve. The glaring inconsistency of slavery with the Declaration of Independence and the spirit of American institutions was not for some time to provoke internal strife. But it was from the outset felt to be a weakness. Jefferson, contemplating what the South was to describe euphemistically as its "peculiar institution," trembled when he remembered that God was just and that His wrath did not sleep forever. And Patrick Henry was troubled in conscience that he was the owner of slaves. Unable to justify it, all he could say was, "I am drawn along by the general inconvenience of doing without them." Therefore he somewhat lamely proposed, "Let us transmit to our descendants, together with our slaves, a pity for their unhappy lot, and an abhorrence of slavery." It was the same attitude that Charles Carroll took when drawing up his will, bequeathing his slaves (under some restrictions) to his children. Unfortunately the abhorrence was (as we know) to diminish in exact proportion to the growing "inconvenience" of doing without them. As a later generation could not afford to condemn human bondage—however airily and in the abstract—they came to glorify it as the ordinance of God. No such idea was in the minds of the Founding Fathers. It being impossible to reconcile their ownership of slaves with the doctrine that all men were equal, they wryly accepted the inconsistency—and passed on a bloody legacy to their heirs.

The more immediately pressing secular problem was of another sort. The Republic had been founded upon the basis of democracy; yet many of the Founders were afraid of drawing all the logical conclusions. They affirmed equality and—even apart from the negro question—were anxious to set up every possible safeguard to prevent democratic sovereignty from fully functioning. In this they were not unwise, when we bear in mind the fierce cross-currents of the time. The very safeguards, though largely designed for the protection of the propertied classes, proved to be of inestimable value as a barrier against the radicalism the Revolution had let loose. A period of restraint was necessary until the country had settled down. But unrest (and alarm) gradually disappeared as the general prosperity increased. In the end America came to accept all the implications of the Declaration of Independence and the Constitution. Even the word "democratic" ceased in the course of time to be obnoxious.[2] Luckily the foundations of reconciliation between the conservatism of South Carolina and the radicalism of Pennsylvania were already to a considerable extent laid down before the storm of the French Revolution broke.

During all this period Catholics would of course have been among the first to deny that they were "democratic." Their natural caution made them averse to anything savoring of political excess. Though as a body they were not notably active in politics, two Catholics—Daniel Carroll (the brother of the future Archbishop) and Thomas Fitzsimmons—were members

---

[2] Too much may easily of course be made of this matter, though some people still assert that what was established was a republic, not a democracy. This, however, seems to be only a question of terms. The word "democracy" happened at the moment to be in bad odor, but John Locke had explained clearly enough in the opening of the tenth chapter—"Of the Forms of a Commonwealth"—in his *Second Treatise of Government:* "The majority having, as has been showed, upon men's first uniting into society, the power of the community naturally in them, may employ all that power in making laws for the community from time to time, and executing those laws by officers of their own appointing, and then the form of the government is a perfect democracy." His concept was fully taken over by the Constitution, though it borrowed at the same time the idea of Montesquieu of checks and balances in dividing the functions of government between the executive, the legislative and the judiciary departments.

of the Constitutional Convention that met in Philadelphia in 1787. In so far as they had influence—and Catholics were at least represented out of proportion to their very meagre numbers—their influence was thrown on the side of moderation. They, like the other conservatives, were sufficiently democratic, but they feared a word which, because of its misuse by extremists, had come to have a bad connotation.

It is not necessary here to retell the history of the framing of the Constitution except to remark that its ratification was a slow process and that the adhesion of several states was only with great difficulty secured. A vast amount of political discretion and diplomatic finesse was called for to persuade many people that the framers were not thinking mainly of their own interest as owners of property. If they did eventually accept the Constitution this was because Washington assured them that it was not submitted as something free of all imperfections but that "as a constitutional door is opened for future amendments and alterations, I think it would be wise in the people to accept what is offered them." Without much enthusiasm, the people did. Though many dangers still lay ahead, the first dangerous corner had been turned. America now had its Federal Constitution.

The part of it that concerns this book is the one dealing with religion. Charles Pinckney of South Carolina laid before the Convention his "Draft of a Federal Government" in which was the clause, "The legislature of the United States shall pass no law on the subject of religion." Although it was not accepted as it stood, it was incorporated in the First Amendment which reads: "Congress shall make no law respecting an establishment of religion, or prohibiting the free exercise thereof; or abridging the freedom of speech, or of the press; or of the right of the people peaceably to assemble, and to petition the Government for a redress of grievances." In that form it became even more comprehensive as well as more specific. At the same time an indication was given of the absolute secularity of the Federal government. As Washington was to say, the United States was not founded on the Christian religion. As such, it was neither religious nor irreligious, but impartial. If a religious complexion has been admitted in practice, none has been admitted in strict theory.

The last clause of the Sixth Article concludes, after binding all senators and representatives both of the national Congress and of the various state legislatures, as well as all judicial and executive officers, to an oath supporting the Constitution: "But no religious Test shall ever be required as a Qualification to any Office or Public Trust under the United States." Again there is no clause standing by itself. And again nothing is done by way of restraint upon any state legislature or constitution. But it was enough for the purpose: there could be no established religion for the United States—whatever the individual states might do—and no Federal office required a religious test oath.

If these provisions have been a charter of freedom for the Catholic Church—as for every other religious body in the country—one thing should be frankly said. The basis decided upon has never been considered by the Catholic Church as being, absolutely considered, the best basis, though American Catholics will not wish any change so long as our society is constituted as it is. According to Catholic doctrine, however, the union of Church and State is still affirmed to be the most perfect solution, in itself. As the statement is likely to be misunderstood, it should be added that this union is thought of only in a society so predominantly Catholic as to be able to be described as Catholic *sans phrase*, one in which government and people are in full accord in the matter of religion. For only where such unity exists is it possible for ecclesiastical and secular authority to act freely, each in its own field, and to coöperate. Elsewhere there is no chance of putting the principle into operation at all. Under prevailing conditions, therefore, the Church is quite content with the guarantee of sufficient freedom to exercise its functions unhampered. Things being as they are, the Church does not contemplate putting her preferred principle into execution. Before that were done a homogeneity, which would seem to have been permanently destroyed, would first have to be regained.

I point this out for two reasons. One is that American Catholics, in legitimate satisfaction over the religious freedom they enjoy, and in their awareness that the American system prevents that domination by the civil power which has been only too often the practical result of the union of Church and State, have far too often spoken as though the American system is, of all possible systems, the best. That most positively it is not; it is merely the best—by far the best—that could be devised for a country like the United States, where Catholics form a decided minority, but where the nation's fundamental laws ensure them freedom for the practice of their religious life.

Therefore not only do they not wish to change it; they would dread any change.

The other fact that should be pointed out is that some non-Catholics commonly imagine that the moment Catholics find themselves in the ascendency in America—if that event should ever occur—they would immediately amend the Constitution so as to set up an official church. They need not be alarmed over this hypothetical prospect. Much more than ascendency would be necessary to make the union of Church and State workable; it would demand a virtual unanimity of religious belief, which is almost unthinkable. Almost as unthinkable is that, even under such conditions, Catholics would seek this union. For a constitution, once amended in their favor, might afterwards—should wide defections occur—be amended again to their disadvantage. The Constitution, as it exists, stands as their protection; no group may be depended upon to defend it more strongly than Catholics.[3]

It must be noted that the solution adopted is nothing else than the one previously put into effect in Maryland, but which was operative there only during the short period when there was a Catholic Proprietary and an Assembly predominantly Catholic. When the Protestants came into power in that colony, the Church of England was established and Catholics put under penal law. And though not all the colonies had an established church, most of them had; and, except for Pennsylvania, all of them had discriminatory laws against Catholics. This is a fact that American Catholics will never forget. It was, therefore, with joy that they recognized that the United States had taken over the old Maryland idea.

We should bear in mind that what was involved was not "toleration." There can be toleration only when one religion is officially established yet the secular government approves a policy of allowing each man to worship according to the dictates of his own conscience. What the Constitution of the United States, following first the undefined practice of Maryland and then the Toleration Act of 1649, guaranteed to all its citizens was, so far as Federal concerns went, an absolute

[3] So also with individual states, in one or two of which they are in a majority. Theoretically they might find themselves in a position to establish Catholicism there, as others are theoretically in a position to establish Protestantism—or even atheism. It is quite certain that no such attempt will be made by any religious majority, however great its ascendency.

religious equality. A free field and no favor was accorded; and Catholics were more than content. It gave them their opportunity.

We should note, however, that despite the lead taken by the Federal Constitution, not all the states at once fell into line. Indeed, there is to this day in the constitution of one state—that of New Hampshire—an official recognition of the Protestant religion. It is of no practical consequence, as it is left so vague as to be inoperative. But it should be said that for some time after 1787—or rather 1791, when the Constitution went into effect—attempts were made in a number of states to maintain the Protestant ascendency, if only by means of religious tests that excluded Catholics from office. Yet even in these cases, the discrimination was generally theoretical rather than actual. Where it was clearly defined —as in New York—it broke down when challenged. Americans everywhere soon came to see that it was highly anomalous to insist upon political liberty and to refuse religious liberty. Therefore the discrimination proved unworkable and was abolished under state constitutional law.

A rather comical instance of this is provided by the constitution of North Carolina, passed in 1776. Section XXXII provided that "No person who shall deny . . . the truths of the Protestant religion . . . shall be capable of holding any Office or Place of Trust or Profit in the civil department within this state." Nevertheless the Catholic Dr. Thomas Burke represented North Carolina in the Continental Congress and in 1781 became its governor, while his cousin, Aedanus Burke, who had studied at St. Omer's, was appointed Chief Justice of South Carolina. In all this there was for once a happy confusion between thought and sentiment. Apparently people believed that there were Catholics *and* Catholics —the ones they happened to know being decent, the rest being put beyond the pale.

Still more amusing was the case of William Gaston. His father was a Presbyterian, but he had been brought up as a Catholic by his English mother and was the first student to be enrolled at Georgetown College, whose auditorium now bears his name. In 1800 he was elected to the Senate and afterwards became a justice of the Supreme Court of North Carolina. His eligibility to hold office being questioned on constitutional grounds, he took up the position that he did not deny the truths of the Protestant religion at all. Only, he pertinently asked, just what were these truths? The question was so ingenious as to be flabbergasting. No Catholic, it need hardly be said—now that Gaston has said it for us—denies any of the truths of Protestantism, for they are also the truths of Catholicism. In so far as Protestantism has positive content, it is a Catholic content—though in truncated form.[4] The one feasible method remaining, of excluding Catholics from political office, was the old-fashioned one of abjuration of some specifically Catholic doctrine. As that was not done, clever Gastons could, and did, easily break through the meshes of an ill defined law.

It would be tedious to indicate here the precise legal provisions on the subject of religion in the several states, or to give the history of the changes that occurred. The important thing to seize on is that throughout the country there was a new spirit from which Catholics benefited. Bigotry did not expire at once, to be sure, but at least it was no longer able to act in its former fashion. The Scotch-Irish, though bitterly antagonistic to Catholicism, were still more antagonistic to the Anglican establishment, as this was part and parcel of the government they had thrown off.[5] In short, the very diversities of religious opinion and sentiment in the new nation worked in favor of religious liberty, for no one sect was able, except locally and briefly, to dominate others. Where none could rule, it was tacitly agreed, none should rule.

As for the Puritans, their theocratic dream had long been over. The Great Awakening had affected for the most part only the lower orders and had spent its force. Revivalism was coldly regarded by the intellectual leaders of New England, who were already turning from the Calvinistic tradition to Unitarianism and Universalism. In Jonathan Edwards they had produced a powerful and original thinker. But his thought had ceased to have much influence. And though the Congregationalist church in Massachusetts was still constitutionally established and endowed, the appointment of ministers had become a prerogative of the town-meeting, not of the church-

---

[4] This, however, is to set aside peculiar tenets of eccentric sects, which ordinary Protestants themselves would not consider germane to the issue.

[5] In any event the Scotch-Irish were largely inarticulate. The only signer of the Declaration of Independence the Presbyterians supplied was Dr. Witherspoon, the President of Princeton, who was also, incidentally, the only clergyman who signed that document.

members. Usually the community was inclined to appoint
liberals in theology and, despite the furious protests of the
orthodox, its right to do so was upheld by the courts. The
consequence was an endowed Unitarianism. The dissenting
Congregationalists of the Calvinist school were perforce
obliged to set up their own churches and support them out
of their own pockets. Even they had now an excellent reason
for approving the separation of State and Church.

Already the Anglican establishment had not only ceased to
exist as such but had lost much of its former political and
social prestige. Two-thirds of the Signers of the Declaration
of Independence had belonged to that communion—which
may be credited with having helped to civilize them by its
polite tone and its stately ritual; but so many of its ministers
had taken the wrong side in the Revolution as to destroy their
influence and to bring about a virtual collapse of their church.
As Thomas Cuming Hall remarks, "All the States where
episcopacy had been recognised passed easily over to complete
secularism."[6] Or again to quote Hall, "The eighteenth-century
conception of Greco-Roman Paganism has completely sup-
planted Puritanic Judaism."[7] The truth is that Anglicanism
had often been accepted in Virginia and elsewhere as a "gentleman's religion" that demanded very little of a man beyond
respectability—which its adherents had almost to excess—and
practically nothing in the way of dogmatic subscription. Before the Revolution it was honeycombed with Deism. Now
the Deists gave hardly so much as a perfunctory attention to
the forms of their nominal faith.

Yet I think it should be candidly admitted that it was upon
the whole fortunate that the making of the Constitution was
primarily in the charge of such men—by nature indifferent to
dogma and determined to see that no dogmatic adhesions
should be used as a test for political office. It was the professed Deist, Thomas Jefferson, who was the author of the
Virginia Statute of Religious Liberty of 1785, a fact of which
he was so proud that he directed it to be engraved on his
tomb. (That he had been President of the United States he
did not think worth recording, or perhaps merely thought
there was no need to record it.) His Statute reads: "Be it en-
acted . . . that no man shall be compelled to frequent or
support any religious worship, place or ministry whatsoever,

[6] *The Religious Background of American Culture*, p. 172.
[7] *Ibid.*, p. 185.

nor shall be enforced, restrained, molested or burthened in
his goods, nor shall otherwise suffer on account of his religious
opinions or beliefs; but that all men be free to profess, and
by argument to maintain their opinion in matters of religion,
and that the same shall in no wise diminish, enlarge, or affect
their civil capacities." Having so legislated, that session of the
Virginia Assembly acknowledged its impotence to control subsequent assemblies, and that "therefore to declare this act ir-
revocable would be of no effect in law." Nevertheless, it
affirmed its conviction that the rights asserted in the statute
"are the natural rights of mankind," and that any infringement of them would therefore be an infringement of natural
law. It is this last expression of opinion—though confessedly
of no legal force—which is perhaps the most important thing
in the famous statute. For if religious liberty, of the most absolute sort, was really part of the natural law, as Jefferson so
confidently asserted, it logically followed that it ought to be
embodied, not merely in a revocable law, but in the basic
constitutions of all states.

I trust nobody will wilfully misinterpret me or imagine that
I have any sympathy with Deism if I confess my gratitude to
Deists in this matter. If it comes to that, I have a much closer
theological affinity to even the most rigid Calvinist than
I can have to any Deist.[8] All I wish to convey is that the
religious liberalism (or the doctrinal indifference) of the
Deists as a body—gaining control of the more influential political positions at the moment of the collapse of Anglicanism
and the schism in Congregationalism—powerfully tended, despite its insecure theoretical foundations, to bring about

---

[8] Deists of course were of various sorts. Tom Paine, so unjustly
described by Theodore Roosevelt in a rash moment as a "dirty little
atheist" wore his Deism with a tinge of the Quakerism in which he
had been brought up. Jefferson (a more typical Deist) was hardly
distinguishable, except for his hardheadedness, from what the Vic-
torians were to call a reverent agnostic. And Franklin gave a quaint
twist to the doctrine (such as it was) and may be described as a kind
of polytheistic Deist. His attitude was that men should pay divine
regard to SOMETHING—the capitals are his—and he conceived that
this SOMETHING had "created many beings or gods, vastly superior
to men," and that "each has made for himself one glorious sun,
attended with a beautiful and admirable system of planets." He
concluded, "It is that particular wise and good God, who is the
author and owner of our system, that I propose for the object of
my praise and adoration."

liberty of conscience. Each sect was free to consider itself, if it chose, as the sole depository of truth; but no sect was free to interfere with any other. Any man might continue to hold that dogmatic correctness was of overwhelming importance in this life and in the life to come—and that *he* possessed that correctness; but he only had the right to propagate what he believed by means of preaching and discussion. Constitutional law placed itself entirely aloof from offering even a hint as to what religious truth might be.

In all this the Catholic Church was the main, if not the sole beneficiary. Quakers and Baptists had formerly been persecuted to the death in New England, but had long enjoyed freedom from molestation. It was only Catholicism that was under civil disabilities at the time of the Revolution. And though we may suppose that the proscription against Catholics was removed largely because their numbers were insignificant and (as Orestes Brownson was afterwards to say) their dogmas were considered moribund, it must also be granted that nobler and more luminous minds unhesitatingly accepted religious liberty as a philosophical principle. American liberty was recognized as containing that as an inevitable corollary.

Years later (in 1827) Charles Carroll of Carrollton was to write to a Protestant minister: "To obtain religious as well as civil liberty I entered zealously into the Revolution and, observing the Christian religion divided into sects, I founded the hope that no one would be so predominant as to become the religion of the state." Dr. Guilday seems inclined to discount the statement as an old man's reflections long after the event. But I can see no reason for this scepticism about Carroll's motives. It was not in his nature, or in that of his almost excessively cautious coreligionists, to "gamble desperately" on the bare possibility that somehow the Revolution would bring religious freedom. The leaders among them were in personal contact with those who had risen against British rule and so must have known their minds. I think we might credit Carroll and the other prominent Catholics with grasping the true character of the struggle.

Even apart from the legal enactments in favor of freedom, there was now a much better feeling in the country towards Catholics. This comes out in the reply George Washington addressed in 1790 to the congratulatory letter they sent him. Similar letters arrived from other religious denominations, and he made suitable replies to all. But as Dr. Guilday points out, there is generally a somewhat formal tone in the President's replies; whereas "he sounds another note to the Catholics." No doubt he intended to speak over their heads to the nation at large when he wrote: "I presume that your fellow-citizens will not forget the patriotic part, which you took in the accomplishment of the Revolution, and the establishment of their Government—or the important assistance, which they received from a Nation, in which the Roman Catholic Faith is professed." Something of the sort needed to be said—as it still needs to be remembered—because the complete establishment of religious liberty in some of the states was then only in process. As an instance of the rumblings of bigotry that had not yet died down, the *Independent Chronicle* of Boston, in its issue for September 4, 1788, violently protested against the return from abroad of John Thayer, formerly a Congregationalist minister but now a priest, or (as the *Chronicle* put it) "in the character of a Popish bishop." The fulmination flashed, "Americans are much too enlightened to be easily imposed on by the dogmas of Rome—and we are too well acquainted with the history of 'the whore' not to detect every idea, that involves in it martyrdom-inquisition and pontifical tyranny." But such rumblings were as ineffectual as they were absurd. Nobody could pretend to be more American than the Founding Fathers themselves. The Constitution of the United States maintained the complete religious equality which the states one by one confirmed.

The immediate progress of Catholicism could not, in the nature of things, be very striking. There were still only a handful of priests ministering to a handful of scattered people. The timorous attitude that had been engrained in them by persecution did not disappear at once. But hope had revived. Even before the formal religious guarantees under the law, liberty was being exercised. It appears in the fact that in 1784 an edition of Reeve's *History of the Old and New Testament* was openly published in Philadelphia, to be followed the next year by Challoner's *Catholic Christian Instructed*. Previously Catholic books had to be smuggled in from abroad or privately printed for the clergy, who circumspectly disposed of them by subscription. From the very beginning of the Revolution a decided change in the intellectual atmosphere of America had occurred. Thus, as early as February 28, 1779, John Carroll had written to his English friend, Father Charles Plowden: "You enquire how congress intend to treat the catholics

in this country. To which I must answer that congress have
no authority or jurisdiction relative to the internal government, or concerns of the particular states of the Union. . . .
I am glad, however, to inform you that the fullest and largest
system of toleration is adopted in almost all the American
states." Then with prophetic exultation Carroll exclaims, "I
am heartily glad to see the same policy beginning to be
adopted in England and Ireland; and I cannot help thinking
that you are indebted to America for this piece of service."
Catholic emancipation was obliged, as it turned out, to wait
a good many years. But Carroll was right: it was already on
its way; the American example was proving infectious. What
had been accomplished in the United States was destined to
have an effect on the whole English-speaking world.

A final word should be added. Throughout the Revolution
the Catholics in America remained nominally under the jurisdiction of the Bishop of the London district. But even during
the colonial period the successive English bishops had accepted the charge reluctantly and were too far away to exercise
any real control. During the war, when the jurisdiction was in
the hands of Bishop James Talbot, the brother of the Earl of
Shrewsbury and coadjutor to Challoner, he refused to have
any communication with those who were still technically his
ecclesiastical subjects. This was because neither he nor Challoner had any sympathy with the American rebels. They did
not realize that American Catholics (though rebels) were ren-
dering, as John Carroll said, a service to their English brethren.
But they, for their part, rendered an unwitting service to the
American Church by refraining from touching its affairs. If
that was not conducive to good discipline, at least it removed
all possibility of the accusation that American Catholics were
subject to an Englishman. At the close of the war Bishop Talbot went so far as to refuse to give faculties to two Maryland
priests who proposed to return home. There may have been
some pique in his attitude, but it was based on the argument
that American independence had removed from his shoulders
a responsibility he had never wanted. The ground was therefore cleared for Rome to make entirely new arrangements for
the government of American Catholics. It was now possible to
put them under one of their own countrymen, and with that
there opened—coinciding with their civil and religious liberty
—a vast opportunity for the American Church.

CHAPTER TEN

THE NEW START

We should fasten clearly in our minds that the Catholic body in America shared the universal sentiment of their fellow-citizens that something strange and of vast import had happened. To this, Catholics added a conviction—it may have been only a hope in the beginning but it had now become an assurance—that in this they would share as Catholics as well as Americans. When Cornwallis surrendered at Yorktown, the band came out playing "The World Turned Upside Down." If it seemed so to the astounded British, it must have seemed still more so to the colonists who had in fair fight defeated them. They had set out merely to insist upon their rights as Englishmen—and then had discovered to their surprise that they were Americans, the people of a new nation. It is important to remember this feeling because it explains much of the turbulence of the early years of the country, when the wine of independence went to many unstable heads and liberty was so often wildly misunderstood. A good deal of the same feeling was to manifest itself during the period when an ecclesiastical organization was being built up in the face not only of stiff material difficulties but of an unruliness among both priests and people. It is true that most of the insubordination was shown by newcomers; but that they showed it at all was due to a notion they found already prevalent that in every respect the American slate had been wiped clean. Therefore in the new start there was in some quarters little inclination to submit to the authority which must always be the living center of Catholic life.

Those in command, however, were very conscious of Catholic continuity. They kept their heads and their hands firmly (if with some difficulty) on the reins. What eased their problem was that they had as a nucleus the most homogeneous group in the United States. American Catholics would have been swamped had Canada thrown in its lot with the rebelling Colonies. For then there would have been a French predominance, and they might even have been put for a time under the jurisdiction of the French bishop already at Quebec. This danger was providentially averted. In due course the distinctively American Church was able to absorb the various racial strains that were soon to flow into the United States. It would have been at a loss to deal with them had they arrived, in any considerable numbers, earlier than they did. In the existing situation it was possible to forget that there had been a French missionary effort in northern New York and elsewhere, and the Spanish missions of California and the South-west did not impinge as yet upon the American consciousness. They were, in any case, thought of as foreign and faraway. All that Carroll and his associates had to address themselves to at the moment was building up an ecclesiastical organization for the Atlantic seaboard. And though they did what they could for the scattered settlements of the newly acquired territory beyond the Appalachians, Carroll certainly never imagined that he would also be obliged to act for the last seven years of his life as Administrator-Apostolic of Louisiana.

The first problem confronting the Church was simplified by the fact that, if the Catholic people were homogeneous—being mostly of English descent, with a sprinkling of Irish and a German group in Pennsylvania—the clergy were still more homogeneous, for they were all ex-Jesuits. Their Order was suppressed, it is true, but they retained the Ignatian spirit and were hoping for a restoration. They could therefore act as a body, though they had no canonical standing as such, and their Superior at the time of the suppression in 1773 functioned as Vicar-general for the Bishop of the London District. Added to this was the fortunate lack of complications which some of the other denominations had to meet—the presence among them of Loyalist factions. A few Catholic Tories were indeed to be found among the laity, but there were none at all among the clergy. Untorn by political dissensions, they were as American as they were Catholic.

This does not mean that the Church encountered no difficulties. It encountered many—only of a different sort. The physical ones are described in a letter written by Father James Moseley to his brother, a priest in England, concerning conditions in the sixties, but applying equally well to the years following the Revolution. "Our journeys," says Moseley, "are very long, and our rides constant and extensive. I often ride about three hundred miles a week, and never a week but I ride one hundred and fifty to two hundred. In our way of living we ride as much by night as by day; in all weathers,

in heats, colds, rain, frost, and snow. You must not imagine
that our chapels lie as yours do. . . . They are in great forests,
some miles away from any house of hospitality. Swamps, runs,
miry holes, lost in the night, etc.—this, as yet, and ever will
in this country, attend us. Between three and four hundred
miles was my last Christmas fare on one horse." The country
roads, however, were at least free from highwaymen, in contrast to England; the reason being that travellers were few and
there was always an honest living to be earned.

Life was simple and primitive. The inns were extremely
bad, eight or even ten people being often put up in one
room. The sprightly Madame Knight was to record, without
any special surprise, that when she was on her way from Boston to New York, two men shared her apartment. As for the
roads, they had such deep ruts that passengers had to crowd
from side to side of the coach to keep it from toppling over.
There were frequent upsets and broken axles, and the crossing of rivers often resulted in drownings, the drunkenness
prevalent at the time adding to the perils. Farmers habitually
left their heavy hauling until the winter, when they could use
sleighs.

The priests had managed to hold on to the property their
predecessors had obtained as private gentlemen, but were far
from being well off and, after the suppression of the Society,
lived in constant fear of the confiscation of what little they
had. Father Theodore Schneider—who had once been Rector
Magnificus of Heidelberg—had been obliged to make two
manuscript missals, printed ones being hardly procurable until after the Revolution, so as to have one at each of the stations he visited and not be obliged to carry more than was
absolutely necessary on his journeys. And in 1766 Father Moseley had written exultantly, "I've now a sort of house, a table,
a desk, some chairs, paper and ink, candles etc., which in great
part, I wanted all last year. . . . I have now my cows, my
sheep, hogs, turkeys, geese and other dunghill fowl, and I've
my own grain and make my own bread." He thought himself
in clover. Such being their circumstances, we must not wonder
that the ex-Jesuits, exhibited what might seem, if we did not
bear conditions in mind, an excessive concern over their property. It was pitifully small, and they had scant time to spare
for attending to the farms without which they could not have
existed at all. For there was no financial support to be expected from a poverty-stricken flock. Their cares must there-

fore be understood as springing from a fear that they would be reduced from poverty to complete destitution.

Obviously this state of affairs did not promote active missionary work. But worse than the lack of material means was the sense of isolation that descended upon the Fathers after the suppression. The penal laws had instilled a natural timorousness, evidenced by the fact that some among them were still obliged (or believed they were obliged) to use an alias. After 1773 they were more discouraged than ever. Many of them were growing old, and as they had lost their novitiate, they could expect no generation of young priests to take their places. It is no wonder that they developed a tendency to perform their duties in a spiritless and half-hearted routine fashion. There was no future for them in America—not unless God performed a miracle and their Order were restored. And though the Revolution had brought freedom,[1]—even while it was still in progress—there was still no sign as to how or where they might recruit their dwindling numbers.

Such was the situation when John Carroll came into control in 1784. He had held rather aloof from his brethren, of whom his ability and energy and prudence came by degrees to mark him as the future leader. It was John Lewis, the Superior before the suppression, who had been acting as vicar-general during the war, and it was his name that was first sent to Rome by his fellow-priests when the question came up as to which of them was to take charge after the peace. This was probably done only in deference to his age and former position; in any event Rome decided against him and in favor of a younger man.

Carroll was, however, by no means eager to accept the government of the American Church. He did so only out of fear that Rome might appoint a foreigner as bishop to America. And Rome, for its part—or rather Cardinal Antonelli, the head of the Congregation de Propaganda Fide—accepted Carroll mainly out of fear that the American clergy would elect their own bishop and that the Holy See might ratify their

[1] That Ferdinand Steinmeyer—better known under his alias of Farmer—was made a trustee of the University of Pennsylvania in 1779 suggests an improved position for the Catholic clergy. But too much must not be made of this: the arrangement was that the senior pastors of all six of the denominations in Philadelphia were to be given places on the board. He could therefore hardly be excluded. His appointment indicates no special influence or prestige.

choice. His policy was to keep the American Church under his own control. This could be done by making Carroll a Prefect-Apostolic, in which office he would be removable at the discretion of Propaganda. A bishop would be a different story.

Antonelli's fears were, had he only known it, quite unfounded. There was nothing the American Catholic body desired less than a bishop. The mere mention of the possibility was enough to scare them out of their wits. As there was some talk of a Frenchman being sent over, they jumped at Carroll, while they had the chance.

About this a word or two of explanation should be supplied. Up to the time of the Revolution the hatred of episcopacy was so strong that the Anglicans in Virginia had decided it was inadvisable to admit a bishop. And if this was true of them, it was still more true in the case of a papist bishop. When it was suggested that Briand of Quebec visit Maryland and Pennsylvania to administer Confirmation—for which Clement XIV had given him special faculties—his coming was opposed, lest his presence on American soil cause trouble. The Catholics preferred to forego the sacrament of Confirmation rather than run the risk of having revoked even such slight toleration as they then enjoyed.

The matter, however, was still more complicated. Antonelli was known to be an enemy of the Jesuits. Anybody he appointed would be certain, it was supposed, to be a man sharing his prejudices. As Dr. Guilday puts it, "Episcopal authority could mean only one thing to the beaten remnants of the Jesuit Society—confiscation of all they possessed, and with the confiscation the fall of the missions and the end of their own maintenance." Carroll did not altogether share these apprehensions. He could not believe that a bishop—however anti-Jesuit—would do anything to ruin his own diocese. Nor did he delude himself, as many of the ex-Jesuits did, that there was an immediate likelihood of the Society being restored. But he did think, like the rest of American Catholics, that it was upon the whole probably inopportune to have a bishop for the United States. Accordingly he moved circumspectly and without the least motive of personal ambition. Indeed, when he was at last selected for the see of Baltimore, he expressed his dread that, by showing inadequacy in so responsible a position, he should lose his soul.

The attitude of the American priests was a curious one.

They thought that, if America *had* to accept a bishop, it had better be Carroll than a Frenchman. At the same time, in order to keep any bishop away, a delegation of them met at Whitemarsh in October, 1784, and passed resolutions to the effect that "a bishop is at present unnecessary" and that "if one be sent . . . he shall not be entitled to any support of the present estates of the clergy." Not content with this, they sent a memorial to the Pope the following month protesting that "we are convinced that [the appointment of a bishop] will be much more detrimental than otherwise to the interests of religion." They wrote, however, to Carroll to assure him that, if a bishop had to be appointed, "we have not any objection to your person and qualities." It was only that they objected to having any bishop whatsoever, things being as they were.

It seems that a foreigner—though nobody in particular was mentioned—came very near to being chosen. Beginning with Shea, nearly all the historians of the Church in America have believed that there existed a French intrigue to effect this. Charles Plowden wrote to Carroll on September 2, 1784, to warn him of what he had heard was afoot: "The policy of the French ministry . . . who, by bringing forward a Frenchman, or perhaps an Irish-Frenchman, would use religion as an instrument to increase their own influence in America." It is upon this letter that the allegation of French interference mainly rests.

What would seem to be true enough is that such a project was broached by Antonelli and the Nuncio at Paris, Prince Doria Pamphili. It is not true that the atheist Bishop of Autun, the famous Talleyrand, had a finger in the pie.[2] And the Sulpician Father, Jules Baisnée, has disputed—to my mind successfully—the contention that the scheme, which included the establishment at Bordeaux of a seminary for the training of priests for the American missions, originated with the French authorities. If he is correct, "The initiative in the negotiations was taken by the Holy See and . . . the French government was counted upon to lend its good offices and give its material support to the undertaking." This was only because the Prefect of Propaganda did not know of any American priest qualified for the episcopate, not because of special tenderness for France or animosity towards men who had once

[2] This was universally believed until Baisnée's article in the *Catholic Historical Review*, Vol. XXIV (1938), p. 177. Talleyrand did not become Bishop of Autun until 1788.

been Jesuits. Yet allowing for all this it is likely enough that the French government was not altogether disinterested in backing the project.

Benjamin Franklin, who was as a matter of course consulted about American affairs by the French government, also approved. He may have thought it a cheap and inoffensive method of compensating France for her help in the war. But he did not commit his own government in a matter which, as he pointed out, was beyond its province, so merely expressed an opinion on general principles. He understood nothing of American Catholic sentiment. Probably he considered (like the French government itself) that France was being generous in offering to come forward to help the struggling Church in the United States, and that there would be a happy combination of profit and good-will all round. Therefore Dr. Guilday's judgment is perhaps a trifle severe when he writes, "It is hard to enter upon the story of the effort made in France at this time (1783–1784) to give an organized hierarchy to the Church in the new Republic without considerable suspicion of all concerned." We may at least give credit to the good intentions of Franklin who, as soon as the name of Carroll was mentioned, instantly perceived that he was the right man for the office and threw what influence he had to his support.

I think we may scout the notion that there was a dark conspiracy to bring the nascent American Church under the domination of a foreign power: the whole affair has been too often discussed in terms of melodrama. What is true is that the Catholics were terrified—unnecessarily terrified, as it turned out—that if they got a bishop, they would antagonize their Protestant compatriots. But if a bishop had to come, they realized that there might be less of an outcry if he were nominated by their ally, France, than if he were nominated by the Pope direct. They knew that many Americans had the strange idea that spiritual allegiance to the Holy See must involve at least some degree of allegiance to the Papacy as a temporal power. Nevertheless they were perfectly clear—and perfectly right—in not wanting a Frenchman for bishop. They were, on the other hand, in error in believing that a bishop, as such, would be an offence to Americans. They did not yet understand how vastly the American temper had changed.

Soon the problem was solved for them. It was solved—or its solution was pointed to, as it happened—by the Episcopalians. They, like the Catholics, had formerly been careful to avoid having a bishop. Now Samuel Seabury—a doughty Tory during the Revolution—proceeded to Scotland and had himself consecrated by three non-juring bishops. This happened in 1784, but as the consecration was not approved by Canterbury (though its validity was not questioned), Seabury's audacious action did no more than provide a precedent. It served its purpose, however: in 1787 the Archbishop of Canterbury himself consecrated bishops for Pennsylvania and New York. As these happenings, instead of provoking the expected storm, gave the Episcopalian body in the United States a new prestige (of which it was sorely in need), Catholics perceived that the time had come when they might safely accept a bishop too. Dr. Arthur L. Cross, the Episcopalian historian, has written, "Undoubtedly, there is something to be said in favour of the argument that the attempt to introduce bishops and the opposition thereby excited, formed one of the causes of the Revolution. There can be no doubt that the opposition to bishops was based on political grounds: this fact is indicated by the absence of any resistance to the establishment of an episcopate after the Revolution."[3] That the Episcopalians managed to "get away with it" became an encouragement to the Catholics. When John Carroll at last crossed the Atlantic to be consecrated, he had as his fellow-traveller, both going and returning, Dr. Madison, who had been chosen Bishop of Virginia.

As early as February 27, 1785, Carroll, while still Prefect-Apostolic, had written frankly at length to Antonelli to inform him that American independence had changed the situation; that there was now perfect religious freedom; that there could hardly be any opposition to a Catholic bishop "as the Protestants are thinking of appointing one for themselves;" and to suggest that a bishop would be less likely to arouse "Protestant jealousy of foreign jurisdiction" than a mere ecclesiastical superior removable at will by Propaganda. But he delicately, though sufficiently definitely, hinted that it would be as well for the Holy See to give the American clergy the right—for this first occasion—to elect a bishop themselves, as by doing so it would further dissipate the idea of foreign control. This was the solution agreed upon by the band of priests working in the United States, and it was accepted by Antonelli. The very fact that the Prefect of Propaganda did accept

[3] *The Anglican Episcopate and the American Colonies*, p. 264.

it so readily would seem to prove that the prevalent distrust of Propaganda, as a pro-French and anti-Jesuit department, was not securely based.

I have, however, gone somewhat too far ahead in my story: much had to happen before it was generally agreed between Rome and the American clergy that a bishop was really necessary. The guidance of the Church was in the beginning—from 1784 to 1789—committed to Carroll as a Prefect-Apostolic.[4] Only when it became patent that he lacked adequate powers to deal with the situation did the idea of the episcopate find acceptance.

A Prefect-Apostolic, it should be explained, is in some instances a missionary bishop without a see, though the usual procedure is to confer the title of Vicar-Apostolic in such cases. Carroll, however, remained a simple priest on whom had been conferred some part of a bishop's authority and special faculties for administering Confirmation. But the very fact that he was not a bishop in his case weakened even the authority with which he had been invested. The system of "Archpriests," which had begun in the reign of Elizabeth and had continued (except for a brief interlude) until that of James II, had proved anything but conducive to good order in England. Nor did it work satisfactorily in America. To make matters worse, John Carroll had his powers limited by what he described as "cramping clauses" in the brief of appointment dated June 6, 1784. In particular, he was instructed not to give the ordinary faculties to priests except with the permission of the Sacred Congregation at Rome. However, when he protested against the imposed limitations, Cardinal Antonelli removed them with the explanation that a mistake had been made: the brief had followed the usual form for new missionary fields, but the restrictions had never been intended to apply to the United States. They were accordingly struck out.

So far, so good. But Carroll's authority as a mere Prefect-Apostolic was of a kind that could be, and was, questioned and even resisted by some of the clerics who now began to flock into the country. He was obliged to receive them, so desperately was he in need of priests, although among them were men of undesirable character who were not very ready to submit to any sort of rule. The havoc caused by the lack of

---

[4] Until 1785 Carroll was no more than the superior of the missions. The title of Prefect-Apostolic gave him but little more authority, though it indicated that the episcopate was likely to follow.

priests is indicated by Bishop Shaughnessy's moderate estimate that the country already contained about a quarter of a
million Catholics who had lapsed—or were descended from
those who had lapsed—simply because there had been no way
for them to practice their religion. As a large proportion of
these were among the most bigoted opponents of the Church,
they had to be regarded as permanently lost. If he were to
retain the remnant still in the fold and to minister to the newcomers Carroll saw that he would first have to augment the
number of his clergy.

What the state of affairs was in 1785 we know from his
letter to Antonelli dated March 1st. There were, he says, about
15,800 Catholics in Maryland, of whom about 9,000 were
freemen above the age of twelve, with about 3,000 children
and an equal number of negro slaves. In Pennsylvania there
were a rough 7,000, with about 200 in Virginia who were
visited only four or five times a year by a priest and, as he had
been told, about 1,500 in New York who, at the time of writing, had lacked a minister of religion, except for a Franciscan
Father who had just arrived. The Marylanders, he went on to
say, were mostly planters; and the Pennsylvanians, except for
some merchants and mechanics in Philadelphia, were all farmers. Rather ominously he adds, "While there are few of our
native Catholics who do not approach the sacraments of Pen-
ance and the Holy Eucharist, at least once a year . . . you can
scarcely find any among the new comers who discharge this
duty to religion, and there is reason to fear that the example
will be very pernicious, especially in commercial towns."

There was another way in which the newcomers soon became a problem. The native Americans, for the most part,
took their independence calmly. But many immigrants—both
priests and people—arrived with the most exaggerated notions
of liberty, which only too often they confused with license.
On all sides their truculence caused trouble. The hitherto
peaceable Germans in Philadelphia started to complain that
they were being discriminated against in favor of the Irish in
the matter of the allotment of the pews. Before long they
were demanding in that city, and even in Baltimore, that they
have their own churches and their own priests and even—so
old is Cahenslyism—that they be put under the charge of a
German bishop.

The racial problem, however, was, for the moment, a minor
one. Far more serious; a kind of Presbyterian government had

come into being in the Catholic Church in America. This had been all very well in the old days, but now some of the people got it into their heads that they had a prescriptive right to "hire and fire" their pastors and that the Prefect-Apostolic had no right to interfere. Similarly some of the clerics arriving from abroad brought with them, or rapidly acquired, a fantastic notion of their own importance, imagining American independence to include independence of all ecclesiastical control.

If the story is sad, it has also some comic aspects. There is, for example, the case of the French secular, rejoicing in the name of Claude Florent Bouchard de la Poterie, who had been a chaplain with Rochambeau and who settled in Boston in 1788. One of the first acts of this eccentric gentleman was to issue a "Pastoral Letter—given at Boston, in North America, under our hand and the seal of our arms." It assured "all faithful Christians entrusted to our care and . . . our spiritual jurisdiction" that "My Lord Carol [*sic*], the ecclesiastical superior of the Roman Hierarchy in the United States of America, did on the 24th of December last, communicate to me very ample powers." He informed his flock that he had posted with the French Consul his "credentials," which included a "patent of Count Palatine, which His Holiness grants as Sovereign in his Dominions, to those he thinks worthy of that dignity," another patent showing him to be a Knight of the Holy Sepulchre of Jerusalem, and a diploma "of his admission to the number of Protonotaries of His Holiness." And probably Poterie really did have these gauds and decorations: after all, a stuffed shirt is rather a suitable place to hang medals. "My Lord Carol," however, so far from being overwhelmed by his honorifics, decided that the man was "a sad rascal" and therefore suspended him, after having sent William O'Brien, a Dominican from New York, to enquire into the state of affairs. The best that can be said of Poterie is that he attempted no schism. The worst is that he issued a mendacious pamphlet charging Carroll with attempting a surreptitious revival of the Jesuits and putting upon O'Brien the name of "Friar-Inquisitor."

Poterie was succeeded by another Frenchman, Louis Rousselet. He, too, had to be suspended on account of misconduct, after which he went to Guadeloupe in June, 1791, where he died as a victim of the French Revolution. He made a pious end, preparing those for death who were awaiting the guillotine and regretting that he himself had to die "without having the efficacious graces of the Sacraments applied to my poor soul."

Both these men were manifestly unbalanced, and it transpired that they had had rather dubious careers in Europe. Nevertheless they arrived in America with what appeared to be excellent credentials from their bishops, who, it is to be suspected, regarded America as a convenient dumping-ground for rubbish. It is a story that was to be frequently repeated during these early years.

Boston was not very fortunate in its first pastors. The next priest, John Thayer, was a convert Congregationalist who had served in the war as chaplain to Governor Hancock. He was a man of some ability, and no complaint could be brought about his morals. But he was "difficult," retaining much of the stern inflexibility of the Puritan minister. It was not until Matignon and Cheverus arrived that any real headway could be made in New England.

Boston, however, was at all events free from positive insubordination. That was not true of New York. There there came an Irish Franciscan named Whelan (the one alluded to in Carroll's letter to Antonelli), who was soon joined by another Irish Franciscan named Nugent. Before the year was out each man had his faction, with that of Nugent in the ascendency. Carroll wrote to the men, trying to get them to make peace, and when that failed, he went himself to New York at the end of 1787.

The root of the dissension here, as in nearly all the cases of which we shall hear, was that the trustees of the church considered that they possessed the right to appoint to the pastoral office. Carroll gently explained to the trustees that they were under a misapprehension but failed to convince them. While the Prefect-Apostolic was vesting for Mass, Nugent went into the pulpit and commenced to denounce him violently. And though Carroll then and there suspended Nugent, the man said Mass in defiance of his authority.

On this occasion the trustees sided with Carroll and locked the door of St. Peter's to keep the Nugent faction out. It was no use. They broke the door down and filled the church, accompanied by a gaping crowd of Protestants. The case had to be taken to court, where the trustees were sustained. With Nugent ousted, William O'Brien, also an Irishman but a Dominican—La Poterie's "Friar-Inquisitor"—was put in charge of the church. The one good thing to come out of all this was that the American clergy laid aside their former trepidations and asked Rome to give them a bishop.

Rome wisely allowed them to elect the bishop themselves, and unanimously they chose Carroll. It might have gone against him that there had been rebellion against his rule had not all the assembled priests recognized that he had shown himself gentle but firm in the way he had met his difficulties. The tribute is all the greater because of the fact that the ex-Jesuits had begun by looking upon him as an interloper. Now they could not fail to see that he was the obvious choice. It is hard to imagine what would have happened to the Church in America without him.

Yet at the last moment something happened that might have made Rome refuse ratification. An unattached Irish priest, one Patrick Smyth, had landed in America in 1787 and had been sent to work in Frederick, Maryland—which in those days was known as Fredericktown. After a year he had had enough of a country in which he imagined that, as an Irishman, he had been slighted—especially by the wealthy Henry Darnell, a relative of Carroll's. The Prefect-Apostolic assured him that he had taken offence over nothing, but Smyth was not to be placated and sailed for home.

Before doing so he published a pamphlet entitled *The Present State of the Catholic Missions Conducted by the ex-Jesuits in North America*, in which he charged that all the best parishes were reserved for former Jesuits, who left all the hard work to seculars while they themselves lived in magnificent mansions and were waited on by cruelly treated slaves. It was an accusation all the more calculated to be damaging because it coincided with Poterie's charges that Carroll was seeking to effect a secret restoration of the Society of Jesus in America.[5]

Carroll was very much alarmed. It was not that he feared personal calumny—and he had no wish for the prospective bishopric—but charges of this sort, circulating in Ireland, might have the effect of deterring priests from coming to work in the American missions. Therefore he wrote at length to Archbishop Troy of Dublin refuting Smyth and proposing to publish a reply. Troy advised against this and undertook to see that the truth was made known.

[5] The title of Poterie's work was *The Resurrection of Laurent Ricci*. Ricci was the Jesuit General at the time of the suppression. Carroll of course was the new Ricci.

One passage in Carroll's manuscript is of special interest. Of priests and their slaves he says that "The few to whom this management is committed, treat their negroes with great mildness and are attentive to guard them from the evils of hunger and nakedness; that they work less and are much better fed, lodged and clothed, than labouring men in almost any part of Europe; that the instances are rare indeed, and almost unknown, of corporal punishment being inflicted on any of them who are come to the age of manhood; and that a priest's negro is almost proverbial for one, who is allowed to act without control." As for Smyth, Carroll hints that his troubles were due to intemperance. And for Troy's information in the matter of sending other priests he quietly adds, "Sobriety is expected from a clergyman to a great degree. That which in many parts of Europe would be esteemed no more than a cheerful and allowable enjoyment of friendly company, would be regarded here in our clergy as an unbecoming excess." Here too is a story that was often to be repeated.

Archbishop Troy was sympathetic, and probably knew Smyth's true character. But neither his sympathy nor that of any of the Irish bishops, reached such a height of enthusiasm as to make sacrifices for America. It was for a long time hard for Carroll or his successors to obtain a desirable type of priest for the missions. Most of those who consented to go out were men whom, for one reason or another, their bishops were not sorry to lose. In the years immediately to follow, France was to supply nearly all the laborers who are now remembered for their devotion in the Lord's vineyard.

If Smyth's preposterous accusations had any effect on the Irish clergy, they had none upon the Holy See. On November 6, 1789, John Carroll was appointed Bishop of Baltimore, with his see coterminous with the entire territory of the United States. Baltimore was chosen as the see only because of its central location: it was then a small shabby insignificant town. Until 1787 Carroll had continued to live with his mother at Rock Creek, near the present Washington.

Carroll decided to go to England rather than to Canada for his consecration. This was partly because he had already promised his friend Charles Plowden that he would do so if made a bishop. But it was also because he hoped to raise money in England for his projected College of Georgetown, and perhaps even persuade Plowden to become its President. He did, in fact, obtain some handsome gifts, enough to warrant his making a beginning with the college, but Plowden refused his offer. And if Carroll failed in this, he failed too in his efforts to obtain English recruits. By now he had grown somewhat weary of eccentric Frenchmen and quarrelsome and bibulous Gaels. But all the priests in England were in demand for work in their own country. Not one of them felt drawn to the idea of America.

At Carroll's consecration, which was by the aged Benedictine, Bishop Walmesley, in the private chapel of Lulworth Castle, the country seat of Thomas Weld, his host's son, a youth of seventeen fresh from his marriage, held the missal for him. Thirty years later the acolyte, after the death of his wife, was ordained. He died a cardinal in 1837.

It is interesting to notice that both Carroll and Washington came into office—the one in the Church, the other in the State —at about the same time. An attempt has been made to show that they were close friends. All that one can say, however, is that they had a considerable respect for one another; there are few records of their meeting. But they were in many respects alike. Neither was an obviously brilliant man; each rose by force of character.[6] The difference between them was that Carroll achieved his results by calm and steady pressure, whereas under Washington's icy exterior lava boiled. We hear of huge laughter, of amazing bursts of profanity, of an earth-quaking rage. These ebullitions were rare—he was more commonly slow, patient, persistent, and always selfless—but they did occur. Carroll lacked his violent, if well-controlled, temper. He was invariably imperturbable and good-humored. Nobody was ever able to say of him, as General Knox said of Washington after Charles Lee's treachery at the battle of Monmouth, "He swore that day till the leaves shook on the trees. He swore like an angel from heaven." If Carroll was an angel, he was one of a more placid variety; he never swore at all. Yet many have noticed the similarities of the two men. Each was, in his own field, the captain demanded by the dangerous and difficult times. Clever men might have ruined everything. These had prudence and courage as their most characteristic virtues.

[6] The essential nobility of Washington's character remains untarnished even by the recent extremely critical study, Bernard Knollenberg's *Washington and the Revolution*. This reëxamination of the evidence does not so much lower Washington's reputation as raise that of some of his subordinate generals.

CHAPTER ELEVEN

THE CHURCH TURBULENT

It might be rather unjust to call the period between the suppression of the Jesuits and John Carroll's appointment as Prefect-Apostolic that of the Church Somnolent—for the priests of that harassed and disorganized and disheartening time did what they could under difficulties—but it would not be inappropriate to call the next period that of the Church Turbulent. Yet, even in doing so, I must make certain qualifications. The turbulence was by no means limited to the Church. There were several local disturbances, such as Shays' Rebellion and what is known as the Whiskey Rebellion and the dangerous sectional furore caused by the visit of Citizen Genêt. It was inevitable that the Catholic body should also tend to get out of hand.

These incidents—whether in Church or State—were not altogether deplorable: at least they were a sign of vitality. The young colt had to be broken in, but it was good that it showed spirit. And though one hears more about the disturbances than about the orderly (and sometimes even idyllic) life which was more general—on the principle that crime is news and that virtue is not—in all sections of the nation strong foundations were being laid down. They were all the more solid because the accomplishment had to be brought about in face of serious difficulties. The reader therefore need not be alarmed: he will soon learn of the striking development of the Church in the United States under the administration of Carroll, even if he will have to be told in subsequent chapters of other upheavals. They may all be regarded as growing pains, as marks of a healthy adolescence. America in due course did grow up, and the American Church grew up too. What we have for the moment before us is a gangling, rowdy, obstreperous youth. But be comforted: the "problem child" will reach sedate maturity. Just as Jefferson, the wild Jacobin radical, showed during his presidency great wisdom and moderation—for responsibilities tame even a revolutionary—so even the most unruly Catholics came in the end to settle down.

The defection of the few malcontents who did not, proved a blessing to the Church, if not to themselves.

What was more alarming than the turbulence was the great defection of numbers who fell away, not out of malice, but simply because there were no priests to reach them. Even as late as 1820 Father William Vincent Harold—who himself caused not a little disturbance—wrote a long letter for the information of Propaganda. He says, "On their first arrival from Ireland they feel a horror at the idea of entering a Sectarian Conventicle, but persons who have been longer in the country, and who have fallen into this external apostasy, tell newcomers that their interests will be affected and their characters suspected if they do not go to some church, and to this counsel they fatally, though reluctantly yield." More explicitly he adds of these immigrants who are "almost exclusively Catholics" that "from the moment they enter the interior of the State of New York they never see a priest nor a Catholic church; in the State of Pennsylvania they are nearly in the same deplorable condition. The inference is as evident as it is painful, that these poor wretches who are now filling the vast frame of the country must in a few years cease to be Catholics, that their children will not have even an idea of the true Faith, that, as apostates they will be even more hostile to the Catholic religion than those who have had the misfortune to be educated in heresy from their childhood."[1] Reading that, one feels that Father Harold's insubordination was, at least in part, due to his zeal and to his impatience with slower-moving men.

Harold, however, was speaking of slightly later conditions, of a time when the flood of immigration was beginning. The earlier troubles were caused not so much by the lay Catholics who were coming from abroad as by the priests who descended on America. They were of various nationalities and tongues and they intruded into a Catholic population which was as yet largely homogeneous. Their coming precipitated strife. Until then the German Catholics of Pennsylvania had contrived to get along with their English and Irish neighbors. It was the German and Irish clerics who set the people at loggerheads.

Further difficulties were created by the influx of French priests that occurred as a consequence of the French Revolution. If Poterie and Rousselet had not been quite the kind of clerical material America needed, nobody could ask for better

[1] Guilday, *John England*, Vol. I, pp. 19, 21.

men than were most of their successors. They were, in fact, almost too good; men so learned, so able, so pious as Cheverus and DuBourg and Dubois and Flaget and Bruté and Maréchal simply *had* to be made bishops. And the Irish bitterly resented being passed over in favor of so many "frogs."

One serious deficiency these French bishops and priests must be admitted to have had: few of them ever learned English very well. And in those days American Catholics set great store on preaching ability. This is hardly comprehensible now, when practically any amount of ineptitude in the pulpit is easily condoned in the clergy; then a priest was judged mainly by his "gift of the gab." Such being the standard of judgment, it was the simplest thing in the world for an Irish ecclesiastical adventurer, who happened to have a glib and humorous eloquence, to acquire a personal following. So also was he likely, because of the vanity which is the besetting sin of the orator, to fall foul of the bishop's authority when reproved, to kick over the traces and, backed by his admirers, to enter into open schism. Carroll soon encountered people of this sort, in whom, as he put it, "much ignorance was joined to consummate impudence."

One can nevertheless have a sneaking sympathy with their views about the importance of preaching. A good preacher, after all, did make Catholics proud of their religion. And sometimes these priests had zeal even if they also had conceit. As for the people they misled, it is hardly to be wondered at that they had a curious concept of their rights and duties. American Catholics had lived for generations without effective ecclesiastical control, and when at last it was imposed upon them they did not like it. In a democratic country they considered that they should be allowed to appoint their own pastors, to pay them their salaries, and even withhold their salaries when they saw fit. Here and there a man among them had read in a book something about the *jus patronatus*, and they imagined that they possessed it, not knowing that as yet there was, in the view of canon law, no such person as a parish priest in the whole United States. It was this misunderstanding that lay at the root of everything: the people (always associated with some turbulent priest) honestly believed they had the right of presentation, and when the bishop denied that they possessed it, they set him down as a high-handed autocrat who had no place in a land dedicated to liberty.

Those who caused the trouble were, as I have said, for the

most part, newcomers. Invariably there were such among the clergy. The Irish—clerical or lay—not unnaturally had the idea that their being English-speaking made them at least half-American upon landing. At all events, Germans and Frenchmen were foreigners in a sense that they were not. When after a year or two in the country they felt themselves to be more American than the Americans themselves, they displayed what may perhaps be described as a kind of "nativism" that anticipated the nativism of the movement from which they were afterwards destined to suffer. Who, they demanded to know, were these French bishops and priests that were lording it over them? If they were told that they were extremely devoted and devout pastors, the answer was, "But they can't preach. We want Irish priests."

I am not suggesting that all, or even a majority, of the new arrivals were of this stamp. They were not. Most of them were admirably obedient sons of the Church. But there was certainly a large Irish element which was ready to fight the Bishop and the Germans and the French, as, for that matter, a good many Germans were also stirred into revolt. If Carroll had found it hard to maintain discipline while invested merely with the authority of a Prefect-Apostolic, things did not become much easier for him after he was invested with the full panoply of a bishop. It is a marvel of tact and prudence that he and his confrères and successors managed to keep control at all. For there were moments when, in some quarters, rebellion against the bishops almost passed into a rebellion against the Pope himself. We may of course discount many of the things said by the hot-heads, for angry men—especially when they happen to be endowed with eloquence—are liable to vent opinions they do not really hold but which are immediately useful as debating points. But if we are to take these utterances at their face value, there undoubtedly arose a disposition to question the authority of the Holy See as being "foreign," as well as the authority of the see of Baltimore as being arbitrary.

It would be a dreary business, except for those who revel in ecclesiastical scandal, to trace the origin and outcome of the various disturbances that occurred. There are too many even to list in a short chapter, and they have a dreadful sameness. In almost every instance an uninvited cleric—often a free-lance member of a religious order—lands in America with apparently excellent references from his bishop or superior; he is accepted by Carroll, partly because he is in dire need of priests but also, in part, because he retains, in spite of repeated disillusionment, a sanguine trust in human nature; the new priest seems at first to be an acquisition; but finally, having gathered a party, he sets himself up against his bishop. This leads to a suspension, though usually only after patient attempts to make the unruly gentleman see the error of his ways; and only too often the suspension precipitates a schism. Several times we hear the threat to set up an "Independent Catholic Church of America"—something which the schismatics deem to be in accordance with American independence. And though all these schisms are eventually healed—by the submission of the excommunicated cleric and his recalcitrant trustees—occasionally they result in the permanent apostasy of individuals and always in grave damage to souls.

I have already noted the rebellion of Nugent in New York. The fact that on this occasion Carroll was supported by the trustees perhaps led him to repose a little too much confidence in trustees ever afterwards. But there was another reason for his leniency; his just and good-humored mind—and his very Americanism—obliged him to admit that there was good in the trustee system, or that it might conceivably be put to a good use. As Archbishop Hughes, who even in his day had to contend with the same system, long afterwards said, "The venerable Archbishop Carroll, who himself took part in the revolution by which American independence was won, wished to assimilate, as far as possible, the outward administration of Catholic Church property in a way that would harmonize with the democratic principles on which the new government was founded. With this in view he authorized and instituted[2] the system of lay trustees in Catholic congregations. Regarded *a priori*, no system would appear to be less objectionable." Hughes proceeds to list those apparent advantages—the freeing of the priest from the necessity of making appeals for money or appearing to be a money-seeker, the legal security of the property, and the forging of another bond between priest and people.

We should also remember that the Episcopate had no choice but to accept trusteeism—for the state laws concerning church property had been drawn up by men who were ac-

---

[2] Hughes was not quite correct. Carroll did not institute the system, nor even approve of it. He accepted it because there was nothing else to do. (See Guilday's *Carroll*, Vol. II, p. 830.)

quainted only with the Protestant system under which such property was incorporated under the names of the vestrymen or the deacons or the elders. The legislators had no wish, broadly speaking, to subject the Catholic Church to any injustice; it was merely that in their ignorance of canon law they could not begin to understand why Catholics were unable to operate upon the same basis as the other denominations. In these circumstances, Catholics had to accommodate themselves to the law.

There was, however, this great difference: in the case of Protestant churches the lay officers in whose name the property was held were always men in good standing who could be depended on to serve the best interests of their communion. But the Catholic Church was able as a rule to draw no line between "good"—that is, practicing—and "bad," or merely nominal Catholics. If a man had been baptized, he was a Catholic, and his interior disposition was something of which only God could judge. This is still true: even the excommunicated, or men who have never in all their lives practiced their religion, are often able to claim under canon law their privileges as Catholics, although their Catholicism may go no further than their baptism. Thus marriage annulments are demanded by, and cannot be refused to, such men and women on purely technical grounds. Therefore when they find it convenient to appear as Catholics, their rights have to be admitted, however irreligious or immoral their lives may be.

There was accordingly no way of keeping lax Catholics out from trusteeship, if they were duly elected to it by the other pewholders. In many instances it was the laxest variety of Catholics—parish politicians avid for power—who contrived to insinuate themselves upon the board of trustees. They were not necessarily bad men—on the contrary, most of them, if we except their spirit of insubordination, were respectable enough—but they had commonly had a feeble Catholic life and among them were ignorant men whose ignorance was made all the more dangerous when they picked up a phrase or two of canon law they did not properly comprehend. When some clerical adventurer, whose ignorance of canon law was almost as vast as their own, told them about the right of presentation which prevailed in settled Catholic societies, they considered themselves defrauded if the bishop informed them that this right did not exist in a missionary country. If nothing else served, they fell back upon the state law regarding the incorporation of ecclesiastical property.

There is another factor which should be borne in mind. The American clergy had made strong representations to Rome that they be permitted to elect their own bishops, and this privilege was granted, however reluctantly, in the election of the first three members of the American hierarchy—Carroll, Graessl[3] and Neale. The clergy did not, it is true, demand this as a right, and Rome retained its freedom to reject any bishop so elected. But the laity must be pardoned if they did not fully grasp the significance of all this. They could not see why, if the clergy might elect their own bishops, they might not elect their own pastors. It appeared an extension of the same principle—and a very American one. Nothing else was consonant with democracy, as they understood it.

One must allow for their point of view. They had built the church; therefore they considered that they owned it, and in this they were upheld by the law. The point escaped them that, their gift being made to God, it was the Catholic Church itself which became the real owner of the property. Even so, the bishops would have had no objection to trusteeism had it been treated as a partnership between priest and people in the administration of temporalities. The evil of the system, as it existed, was that what should have gone no further than a responsibility for the upkeep of the edifice was turned into an assertion of a right to interfere in spiritualities. The parish— if we may use the term when there was, according to canon law, no parish in America—thought it was for the people (through the trustees) to engage any pastor they pleased, to sustain him in office as long as they pleased, and to dismiss him when they pleased. If he did not give satisfaction, the trustees, as holders of the money-bags, could withhold his salary. On the other hand, if they were satisfied with him, the bishop had better mind his own business. The result was that plausible clerical scamps who had the support of the trustees thought they were immune from episcopal control. They might go into the pulpit, flushed with the previous night's hard drinking, and rant to their heart's content: it was called

[3] Lawrence Graessl, a very lovable Bavarian, was elected but did not live to be consecrated. He wrote to his parents telling them, with dismay, of what had happened to their "poor Lawrence." The confirmation of his election was made by Rome, though after his death, of which no news had then reached the Holy See.

eloquence. Why should a strait-laced bishop interfere with a little harmless conviviality? The kind of men he approved of were solemn fellows, dull dogs, kill-joys: and more often than not they were not effective preachers.

The issue was complicated by the racial one. The Germans and the Irish could not get along together, though the Germans had been quiet inoffensive people before the arrival of mischief-makers from abroad. For example, a German Franciscan named Caesarius Reuter had come to Baltimore, where he was at first stationed at St. Peter's, where Bishop Carroll was himself living. When he said that he wished to work among his fellow-countrymen in that city, Carroll encouraged the worthy project, until Reuter announced his intention of founding a separate parish for the Germans. This the Bishop disapproved of, though merely on the ground that the new church—St. John's—was unable to support a pastor. Reuter, however, attributed Carroll's opposition to racial prejudice, so went to Rome where he gave out that the Bishop threatened to excommunicate any priest who preached in German. The remedy he took it upon himself to propose was that a German bishop be appointed for America. His charges were investigated, whereupon he was politely informed that he was a liar, because there were no less than twelve churches under Carroll's jurisdiction in which sermons were regularly preached in German. The demand for a German bishop was dismissed with contempt. Nevertheless upon Reuter's return, when Carroll refused to give him faculties, he and his congregation went into schism and assembled for Mass, as Archbishop Hughes was to relate, "with muskets in their hands" in order to keep Carroll out.[4] The case had to be carried to court, where in May, 1805, the jurisdiction of the Bishop over Catholics of all nationalities was upheld.

An earlier instance of Teutonic truculence was what happened in the first German church of America, that of Holy Trinity, Philadelphia, which had been established at the end of 1789. Charles Helbron was elected by the trustees as pastor and his election was confirmed by Carroll, though with some hesitation. When the priest left for a visit to Europe in 1791, leaving his brother Peter as *locum tenens*, Carroll devoutly hoped he would not return; nor did he, for he perished in the French Revolution. Things went fairly well under Father

[4] *Works*, Vol. II, p. 551.

Peter until the arrival, in 1796, of John Goetz, who intrigued against the incumbent and induced the trustees to depose Helbron and appoint him in his place.[5] He was joined by a William Elling, and after the two men were excommunicated, they took up the position that Carroll's authority extended only to English-speaking Catholics and (as that did not suffice) went on to maintain that the authority of the Pope was a "foreign jurisdiction." When Carroll visited Philadelphia, having vainly tried to bring priests and trustees to reason by means of letters, they brought legal action against him. It was not until 1802 that submission was obtained.

The dissensions, however, were by no means caused solely by Germans. They were indeed the instigators of the first schisms, but the worst troubles had Irishmen at the bottom of them. In so far as the clashes were between incompatible races they were those between a later generation of French clerics and an alliance of Irish priests and people. But as these belong to a somewhat later period, they must be deferred for the moment. All that is necessary now is to touch upon the preparatory part played by the gifted but rather refractory Harolds. A couple of paragraphs will suffice.

William Vincent Harold, an extremely brilliant Irish Dominican, arrived in Philadelphia in 1808 to be joined three years later by his uncle James, a secular priest. The elder man had "done time" in Botany Bay, from which he had escaped. As one persecuted by the British government, he was of course received with enthusiastic sympathy by his compatriots. Meanwhile his nephew cast a spell on all who listened to his magnificent oratory.

Both these priests were worthy men, except for vanity and ambition. What the younger Harold was after was a bishopric, to which he considered his parts entitled him and in which he probably sincerely believed he could do a great deal of good. Zeal both of them must be admitted to have had, though

[5] On October 15, 1796, they wrote him a letter: "Rev. Sir: We hereby inform you that in consequence of your refusal to sign the twenty-six resolutions you are hereby dismissed and deposed from your office in this church. Furthermore your salary is withdrawn. . . . In case you refuse to give up the property of the church we will prosecute you with the law." The terse clarity is admirable. But that any Catholics should hold such views is astounding and something never heard of before. The views, however, were those commonly held by trustees.

Christian humility was not much in their line. Therefore when all the strenuous and artful pulling of wires failed to obtain the desired promotion, William Vincent grew disgruntled. He was periodically suspended and reinstated, and lived to put his finger in the pie of the Hogan schism, though he did not proceed to Hogan's lengths. His chief complaint came to be that only Frenchmen were getting all the plums of ecclesiastical preferment.[6] But nearly everything done by the authorities was wrong in his eyes. His milder uncle, who was actuated rather by the hope of seeing his nephew advanced than by a wish for his own advancement, eventually returned to Ireland. But William Vincent Harold lived on in America, alternately edifying and scandalizing the Church.

The rebelliousness of these early years was not confined to the Irish and Germans. On the contrary, it seems to have been common to all races, and was probably fostered by the American soil and atmosphere. John Carroll's burden was, at all events, increased when, as an outcome of the Louisiana Purchase, he had to assume the administration of the new territory, there being as yet no other bishop in the United States. His difficulties there were at once like, and unlike, those he had to meet in New York and Baltimore and Boston and Philadelphia. Louisiana, under the Spanish regime, had enjoyed (or suffered from) the special privileges granted by the Holy See to the Spanish Crown. No ecclesiastical office could be made without the King's personal consent. Previously under the period of French occupation, when it was governed by vicars-general under the nominal jurisdiction of the Bishop of Quebec, things had got into a very bad state, with Jesuits and Capuchins perpetually wrangling. Therefore church government was in disorder and Catholic practice at a low ebb by the time the United States acquired Louisiana.

The position taken up by some of its recalcitrant priests—who were not well pleased to come under the jurisdiction of Carroll—was that, though the province had passed to new political hands, the privileges given the Spanish Crown remained in force—but had been transferred to the various congregations. In other words, they would not recognize Carroll. Their leader was a friar named Antonio Sedella—a man of

[6] See the letter from one of his supporters in Guilday's *Carroll*, Vol. II, p. 680. The Doctor remarks that it has hitherto escaped the notice of research students and is one of the few documents in English in the Propaganda archives.

loose morals and a Freemason. He defied the vicar-general, Sibourd, as he afterwards defied DuBourg, when he arrived as Bishop, so that Carroll in his perplexity wrote to Madison, then Secretary of State, for advice and support. Madison in his official reply, dated November 20, 1806, pointed out that under the Constitution he could not intervene. At the same time he sent a private enclosure assuring Carroll that the government would raise no difficulties with regard to any action he decided to take and that "of the Spanish friar Antonio di Sedella the accounts received here agree with the character you have formed of him." What we see is not a well-meaning but misguided cleric who is more the victim of circumstances than a deliberate contriver of ill. Sedella's is an altogether different case. He was a reverend rascal cynically taking advantage of the existing confusion to perpetuate his power and to protect his scandalous life. He did not even possess the virtue of rash courage. For when things got too hot for him he made a pretended submission, in order to be left alone. When he died in 1829 he received a masonic funeral.

The amazing thing about this man is that when DuBourg was looking for a coadjutor who would live in New Orleans, so that he himself could be free to devote his attention to the St. Louis area, he actually went so far as to propose Sedella's name to Propaganda.[7] It is true that he intended to give him only delegated authority and he added that, on account of Sedella's age his deficiency in learning and "the sad memories of the past," as he charitably expresses it, another coadjutor should also be supplied, one who should have the right of succession. All of which was "appeasement" with a vengeance. Before long, however, DuBourg realized that he had blundered and so wrote to the Cardinal Prefect of Propaganda, "The only means I can think of to settle matters is to have Your Eminence oppose in the Sacred Congregation this appointment on account of the age of the person, and have an official letter sent to me with the remark that, no matter how great the merit of this religious might be, his advanced age would preclude the hope of his surviving me . . . ; that therefore it would be against the spirit of the Church to appoint him as my coadjutor."[8] DuBourg, through his very kindness of heart, had got himself into a mess and had to fall back

[7] See Rothensteiner, *History of the Archdiocese of St. Louis*, Vol. I, pp. 386, 387, 388.
[8] *Ibid.*, pp. 388–389.

upon naïve duplicity to extricate himself! Rome, it need hardly be said, did not appoint the disreputable old friar.

DuBourg of course was a man of books[9] rather than of affairs, though he conceived many fine schemes and even carried some of them out. But he was a poor judge of men. This came out not only in the case of Sedella but in that of Angelo Inglesi. This young man was also thought of by DuBourg as his coadjutor, and was sent to Europe, where his handsome presence and ingratiating manners were valuable in extracting large sums of money from exalted personages, including the Kings of France and Holland and the Emperors of Austria and Russia. But in the end he had to be run out of Rome because of highly unclerical conduct. On returning to the United States, he was mixed up in the Hogan schism, and we hear of him as a strolling actor and then as a saloon-keeper. He had of course married since his excommunication. His end, it is consoling to record, made amends for his career: he died at Port au Prince in the West Indies on June 13, 1825, while ministering to the dying during a cholera epidemic. He had no faculties for this, but in such cases of extremity, faculties may be presumed. Inglesi, by exercising them, was showing that he wished to return to the Church.[10]

These incidents serve to show how easily a thoroughly good man like DuBourg could be imposed on and that something more than the best of intentions was necessary to steer the Church through the heavy seas of the time. It was, however, all too much for him. Though able and notably energetic, he was disheartened by the opposition of the trustees of the cathedral at St. Louis, so in 1825 resigned, returning to France where he was appointed to Montauban and died as Archbishop of Besançon in 1833.

DuBourg was not the only bishop who failed to control his diocese. There was Patrick Kelly, who did not last two years at Richmond. And most abject of all, there was Henry Con-

[9] His library in the wilderness consisted of 8,000 volumes, a huge library for those days.

[10] The best account of his career is in Rothensteiner (*op. cit.*). Dr. Guilday mentions him in his *Carroll* but cautiously leaves out his name from the index. Archbishop Spalding in his *Flaget* (p. 255) points out that it was Inglesi who proposed in 1822 the formation of what came to be the Association for the Propagation of the Faith. Here we have a case of some kink that ruined what might have been an edifying life.

well of Philadelphia, whose story must be deferred to a later chapter. Yet the main fact that emerges from the turmoil is that, in spite of a few prelates who proved unequal to their task, the hierarchy, taken as a whole, succeeded in mastering the situation. Charlatans, cranks, mischief-makers and schismatics did their worst; in the end the American Church came to a happy haven.

CHAPTER TWELVE

UNDER CONSTRUCTION

It is a relief to turn from the story of insubordination and schism to the steady constructive work going on during these years of conflict. This work was, after all, of far greater significance than the upheavals. The turmoil cannot be ignored: it was a real danger to the American Church, and was to remain a danger for more than a generation. But what was of much greater importance was the quiet progress being made, for the turbulence was only in spots, whereas an orderly Catholic life was the general rule. If the explosions manifested an energy of a kind, that energy was of its nature wasteful and sterile. The true energy went into patient organization and into a heroism which was not less heroic because it tried to conceal itself.

If I had to single out the most important happening under Carroll's administration, it would not be the restoration of the Jesuits or the founding of the colleges of Georgetown, and St. Mary's at Baltimore, and Mount St. Mary's at Emmitsburg, or the introduction of various religious orders of men and women, or even the division of the diocese in 1808, with the vast expansion that followed, but the founding of the Sulpician seminary. It was this that provided a place where priests might be trained for the missions; it was this that sent out priests to the frontier; it was this that supplied most of the early bishops. Without the Sulpicians it is hard to see how Carroll could have coped with his problems. Yet their seminary looked, for a time, so complete a failure that it came near to being abandoned; indeed it would have been abandoned had it not been for the personal intervention of Pius VII.

When Carroll went to England in 1790 for his consecration, he hoped to be able to secure English recruits for the American missionary field. In this he did not succeed. Instead, out of a clear sky, an astounding offer was made him. It came from Jacques-André Emery, the Superior General of the Sulpicians, who invited the new Bishop to Paris that he might explain in detail what he had in mind. So faintly was Carroll interested that he declined to go, though it must be remembered that he was pressed for time and that the French Revolution had broken out. It had not reached, however, such a pitch of fury as to make a visit to France dangerous, and Emery himself was to survive the storm, however close he was to execution during his imprisonment in the Conciergerie.[1] Nor can we suppose that merely because Carroll had recently had unfortunate experiences with Poterie and Rousselet he imagined all French priests to be of the same stamp. He knew better than that, for he had been educated in France and had lived there and in Belgium for twenty-five years. His lack of interest in Emery's proposal is therefore somewhat strange. The most likely explanation is that he feared it would call for a considerable outlay on his part, or would clash with his project for Georgetown College, which he thought of as a nursery for a native American clergy.

Emery was not to be put off: as the mountain would not go to Mahomet, Mahomet went to the mountain; Father Nagot was sent to London to see Carroll. He assured the Bishop that this was something that would cost him nothing. The Sulpicians would themselves finance the entire undertaking, for which they had 130,000 livres available; and they would not only supply the professors but the first students. As for Georgetown, they would help to man its teaching staff.

Such an offer could hardly be refused. Georgetown had not as yet actually begun its work, though the year 1789 is the "official" date of its founding.[2] And two American students for whom the often-maligned Antonelli had provided scholarships at Rome had not persevered in their vocation. As Carroll wanted priests and wanted them at once, he agreed that the Sulpicians should open a seminary at Baltimore.

Four priests, accompanied by five English-speaking students, crossed the Atlantic—having the young Chateaubriand[3]

[1] An interesting account of Emery and the period is in Helen C. White's recent novel, *World Without End*. That will be more accessible to most readers than Gosselin's *Life*.

[2] There is a letter from William Gaston, Georgetown's first student, to his mother, which is now in the University archives. It begins: "At length, I am safe; arrived here after a journey of three days. . . . The college will be opened immediately." That letter is dated November 5, 1791. It is printed in full in the Rev. W. C. Nevils' *Miniatures of Georgetown*, pp. 52–53.

[3] Chateaubriand, who was twenty at this time, interested himself while he was in Philadelphia in the religious condition of the West

as a fellow-passenger—and started work in September, 1791. Their story has been told by Dr. Herbermann and more recently by Father Ruane. The first students left or proved unsatisfactory, and it seemed impossible to attract native-born Americans to the clerical state. Two men, however, were ordained in 1793, one of whom—Badin—was to prove a zealous if troublesome missionary in Kentucky; and in 1795 the Russian convert, Prince Gallitzin, was also priested. We shall hear more of him, and of Badin, later. Yet the enrollment in the seminary declined to such an extent that we find only one student registered for the years 1799, 1801, and 1802. There is no wonder that the Sulpicians thought of giving up in despair.

Soon they were confronted with dire poverty, for they had used up all their money. And having little to do in an almost empty seminary, they were obliged to undertake missionary work. Thus DuBourg started the first parish for colored people in Baltimore, and thus Flaget was sent in 1792 to the West, where eighteen years later he was to return as the first Bishop of Bardstown. But all this involved, for the Sulpicians, something worse than material hardship—the danger of losing their distinctive vocation. Now that the upheaval in France had subsided, Emery was for recalling them.

We have some light on the Sulpicians' lack of success in a letter Carroll wrote to Plowden in 1800. He attributes it to "errors committed at the outset, and, above all, national prejudices, in my opinion very ill-founded, against the worthy priests of St. Sulpice and the system of education pursued in the seminary," and concludes, "If those of St. Sulpice, the most edifying and inoffensive clergymen I ever knew, have failed to give satisfaction amongst us, I think none of their countrymen ever will."

Carroll here of course is only expressing the common American judgment about French priests, one that was later to be expressed by others with more bitterness. His unfairness in this matter is indicated by his attributing—as he does in his letter to Plowden—Georgetown's languishing condition to the fact that it was the seminary that supplied most of the

---

Indian negroes there, and wrote a French hymn for their use, which is still sung in English translation as "Hail, happy Queen!" (See *American Catholic Historical Researches*, Vol. XVI (1899), p. 151.) Unfortunately the future author of *The Genius of Christianity* never had a very clear idea that its genius contains a moral principle.

teachers there. A more accurate explanation of Georgetown's state is the one supplied by Father Ruane: "There was no large middle class of Catholics as exists today. Those few boys of the old English stock, endowed with the world's goods, were not attracted to the life of heroic labor and sacrifice which was the lot of the missionary priest."[4] But no doubt there was some basis for what Carroll wrote to DuBourg, that it was desirable "that Americans be educated by Americans." However, as neither American teachers nor American students for the priesthood were available, it was hardly generous of Carroll to make his complaint. St. Sulpice might well have flourished better than it did had it not been obliged to deplete itself in order to lend Georgetown teachers.

That Carroll knew the value of the Sulpicians to his diocese is amply manifest in his dismay upon hearing that the seminary was to be given up. Then he wrote off to Emery begging him "by the bowels of Christ" not to abandon the work, but slipped in a tactless remark that, if he did so, the only monument "which the Society of St. Sulpice would have in the United States was a college." Emery replied with some warmth: "There has been nothing like that which we did for you and your diocese. A small Society like ours, in fact the smallest of all societies, makes you the offer of establishing a seminary in your new diocese." He went on to remind Carroll that they had done everything at their own expense and had sacrificed nearly the whole of their savings, only to find themselves no further advanced at the end of ten years than at the beginning. The promised students had not been forthcoming, and though he did not impute blame to the Bishop for not having been master of matters beyond his control, he felt obliged to add, "I hoped that you would hold as something, all the services which its members have rendered you during the space of ten years. If there were any complaints to be made, it seems to me that I have the right to make them." Emery therefore turned a deaf ear to Carroll's pleadings that the Sulpicians should not be withdrawn. It was only Pope Pius VII who saved the situation. He was in Paris for the coronation of Napoleon, and he said to Emery, "My son, let this seminary subsist. To recall the directors in order to employ them in France would be stripping St. Paul to clothe

4 *The Beginnings of the Society of St. Sulpice in the United States,* pp. 158–159.

St. Peter." Had it not been for this conjuration the Sulpicians would have left America.

From the Baltimore seminary other works eventually flowed. A school at Pigeon Hill, Pennsylvania, was started and after a short period transferred to Emmitsburg. And from the enterprise of Dubois and Bruté there came not only a secular college but a seminary, which are still in existence, though not under Sulpician direction. The founders both became bishops. So did McCloskey, the first of the American cardinals. So did that remarkable man, John Hughes, who started as a gardener at the college—where he directed the slaves working among the cabbages and tomatoes while mumbling his conjugations and declensions. One so earnest to be admitted as a student, simply had to be admitted—and he inevitably rose to the top of the ecclesiastical tree. He, like Dubois and Bruté, and their associates, Flaget and DuBourg, will appear again later in these pages.[5]

But DuBourg must be mentioned at once. He had joined the Sulpicians after their arrival in the United States and immediately proved his worth. Carroll appointed him President of Georgetown in 1796, and as Father Ruane puts it, he "gave Georgetown a brilliant reputation, for in those days the prestige of a college depended upon the personal ability and merit of its president."[6] But Georgetown, despite DuBourg's brilliance, did not prosper until it was taken in charge by the Jesuits after their restoration. So we find DuBourg establishing St. Mary's College in Baltimore in 1799, somewhat to the chagrin of Carroll, who naturally disapproved of a rival to his pet project, especially as in the beginning it showed signs of outstripping Georgetown.[7] In the end, however, it was suppressed as a secular college, not being in accord with the true Sulpician objects, upon which the university charter that had

[5] Among the secular students of distinction at Mount St. Mary's are Chief Justice White (who also attended Georgetown), John La Farge and sons of the Emperor of Mexico, Iturbide, and Jerome Bonaparte, as well as a nephew of George Washington.

[6] *Op. cit.*, p. 99.

[7] St. Mary's College was, for a time, the fashionable college of the South, and was attended by both Catholics and Protestants. Dolly Madison sent her son there, but the bills he ran up for finery—especially for a prodigious number of dancing pumps—indicate a youth more intent on his pleasures than his studies. These bills are in the seminary archives.

been conferred by the state of Maryland was transferred to the seminary. DuBourg, it should be added, left it rather heavily in debt, and seems to have been somewhat deficient as an accountant. But he was a man of vision, as he showed again when he became Bishop of Louisiana and transferred his center of operation from New Orleans to St. Louis, to which city he brought the Vincentian Fathers and the Religious of the Sacred Heart. And he threw his personal fortune into his enterprises. So that, though he came to regard himself as a failure and resigned his see, looking back we cannot but observe that few men have left a deeper mark upon the Catholic Church in America. Whatever faults he had were those of a generous man.

Georgetown, as we have seen, opened its doors to students in November, 1791. Carroll's hope was that it would supply priests for the missions, and in later years it supplied many, along with those distinguished in other fields of activity. But at the start it conspicuously failed in fulfilling Carroll's designs. Moreover, it dissipated the energies of the seminary, which was expected to give it teachers. Many of these, because of being taken away from their theological studies, lost their vocation to the priesthood. The outlook, in fact, grew so disheartening that the Jesuits, after their partial restoration, were for moving to New York, as they considered themselves buried in Maryland and the District of Columbia. But Carroll was firm. Times changed. Georgetown developed into one of the great educational institutions of the American Church.

A word might be said about its location, as a good deal may be explained by this. Carroll had picked out a magnificent site overlooking the "Potowmack." But except for its scenery, the college had, in those days, few advantages. As Washington had not been able to get along with Major l'Enfant, whom he had employed to lay out the "city of magnificent distances," the District of Columbia long remained an insalubrious swamp. Pennsylvania Avenue was a dirt road in which pigs rooted. The representatives and senators lived in ramshackle and sometimes not very respectable boarding-houses, in which few of them had a room to themselves. That the national capital was built in such a place was due merely to a political deal. As the marvellous artificial improvements that have since been effected were then scarcely imagined, it is quite possible that Georgetown's early lack of success was due to the tatterdemalion aspect and the unhealthy climate of the District, as its subsequent success was in part due to the city's growing prosperity and prestige. Never would Carroll hear of abandoning Georgetown, and he has been justified by events. He, like DuBourg, had vision.

But this was only a detail in a situation which was generally discouraging. There were still very few Catholic churches. In many of the towns and villages visited by the missionaries the common procedure was for the priest to ask for the loan of the meeting-house from the local minister. There, if he found any Catholics, he might say Mass; otherwise he could do no more than preach a sermon explaining Catholic doctrine. Carroll did not have much faith in these itinerant efforts. It was far better, he held, to confine the work to the settled centers Catholics already had, where, if fewer people could be reached, more could be done for them. This haphazard preaching, however, was the method which John England and even Cardinal Gibbons, in the days when he was a young bishop in North Carolina, were obliged to use.

That they were able to use it at all suggests a fairly widespread good will among Protestants. The good will comes out in other ways. Thus we find both Washington and John Adams giving subscriptions for the erection of Catholic churches. It was shown again—along with plain justice—in the famous confessional case in which Anthony Kohlmann, the Administrator of the diocese of New York, was upheld by the courts. Kohlmann had handed back some stolen property and, upon the arrest of the suspected thieves, was summoned to tell what he knew. He took the position that, as a priest, he was not free to reveal what he had been told *sub sigillo*. "If I did," he said, "I should render myself liable to eternal damnation." De Witt Clinton, who presided at the trial, ruled that the secrets of the confessional were inviolate, and so laid down a principle that the law has never again challenged.

Perhaps a good indication of the prevalent fair-mindedness of Americans at this time was a little incident that happened early in June, 1792. Miers Fisher, a Pennsylvania assemblyman, attacked a lottery, saying it was "like the Papal indulgences, forgiving and permitting sins to raise money." Matthew Carey—though he soon afterwards became a leader of trusteeism and was not at this stage in his life particularly devout—quickly took him to task. Upon being challenged, Fisher handsomely apologized, explaining that he had meant no offence, but had gathered "from his reading" that the Pope claimed and exercised this power. He asked to be given a book on the subject, for he admitted "a prejudice which may have arisen from his being more conversant in the writings of [the opponents of Catholics] than their own." If all Americans had shown Assemblyman Fisher's intellectual honesty, the story of the Church in the United States would be very different.

A final instance of American good will may be seen in the reception on arrival accorded Jean Dubois, the founder of Mount St. Mary's and the future Bishop of New York. He had been educated at the Collège Louis-le-Grand, where Robespierre and Desmoulins were his fellow-students, but had to flee France at the Revolution. He came to America bearing letters of introduction from Lafayette to James Monroe, Patrick Henry, the Randolphs, the Lees and the Beverleys. They were charmed with him, and he remained giving his new friends French lessons (receiving from them English lessons in return) and saying Mass on Sundays at the capitol at Richmond. A little later the attitude of Protestants was not nearly so friendly. But friendliness must be gratefully admitted to have existed during these years among those who had worked and fought side by side with Catholics for the winning of American independence. Men were still sufficiently entranced by their newly gained liberty to set no limits to its application.

Conditions were, in this respect, so favorable that religious orders of men and women now began to be introduced. The Augustinians settled in Philadelphia; the Franciscans projected an American province, but got no further than sending out a few isolated friars;[8] the Dominicans, under Edward Fenwick, established themselves in Kentucky; and even the Trappists wandered about in the western backwoods unable as yet to find a permanent home and nearly killing themselves practicing austerities unsuited to the American climate. It is instructive to note how early the contemplative life was found in a country where even the vast majority of the Catholics of that period thought it decidedly out of place.

The most important event of this sort, however, was the re-establishment of the Society of Jesus. Since their suppression in 1773 they had been very downcast; but in the vague hope of a restoration they had clung to their property, though

---

[8] It was not so much that they were *sent* as that they wandered out, like some of the free-lance Dominicans, without authorization. Many of these unattached religious, being out of their proper element, caused trouble.

always in fear that a bishop would come who would confiscate it. There was, however, some reason for their not despairing. The rump of the Society managed to exist in White Russia, where they were protected by—of all people in the world!—Catherine the Great. And elsewhere in Europe some former Jesuits organized themselves into congregations known as the Society of the Sacred Heart of Jesus, and the Company of the Faith of Jesus—both of which sought to preserve the Ignatian spirit until such time as Rome relented. In 1801 Rome did relent, to the extent of publicly recognizing the canonical existence of the Order in Russia. By 1805 American Jesuits received permission to affiliate with the Russian province, and it was evident that it was only a matter of time before full restoration would come. By the time this happened only Carroll and his coadjutor, Leonard Neale—who, being bishops, were cut off from the Society—and one or two other men survived.[9] But in the interval other Jesuits had come to America and two of these—Grassi and Kohlmann, especially Kohlmann—were exceedingly able men. Under their vigorous direction, with Georgetown as headquarters and novitiate, a new beginning was made, one destined to have an enormous effect upon American Catholicism.

Yet some have often wondered how it happened that the religious order which came to be by all odds the most numerous and powerful in the United States has managed to produce relatively so few outstanding men. No group of religious is so intensively and extensively trained; no group has ever maintained so high a general level, intellectually, morally and spiritually; but with all this it is hard to find among the hundreds who have shown marked ability many who have shown anything still higher. I have of course no qualifications to explain why this should be, but I surmise that American Jesuits have decided upon a policy of teamwork rather than of "giving the ball" to exceptionally brilliant players, or—to put it in other words—their genius has been to discourage genius in favor of working as a disciplined phalanx. If this is the case, it has certainly achieved results. As the plateau has been so high

---

[9] Molyneux, a fat, old, infirm and therefore not very energetic man, was appointed American superior, but he was not the Provincial. There was no American Province, in the canonical sense, until 1833. Carroll and Neale both seriously thought of resigning to rejoin the Jesuits, but eventually decided that duty demanded that they retain their episcopal office.

it would be beside the point to complain that towering peaks have been few and far between. It is contrary to the constitutions to allow members of the Society, unless under special circumstances, to accept bishoprics. Yet sixteen of them—exclusive of Carroll and Neale—have been raised to the episcopate, though usually they accepted with reluctance and in several cases—among which that of the lovable and saintly Miége may be cited—they resigned at the earliest possible moment to return with a sigh of relief to the cloister. American Catholicism must be said to have been, in its inception, wholly a Jesuit affair, and to have largely remained so.

The first orders of women in America should be noted. Of all the convents in the present territory of the United States, the earliest was that founded in 1727 by Mother Tranchepain and her Ursulines at New Orleans. Their school was a success from the start and received colored children as well as white. It is still in existence and flourishing. During Kohlmann's administration of the diocese of New York a group of nuns established themselves there for a while, and about the same time the Ursulines went to Boston. But all these were teaching orders, and that at New Orleans was as yet in foreign territory. The first American convent was that of the Carmelites whom Carroll brought back with him from Europe in 1790 after his consecration and settled at Port Tobacco in Maryland.

The Carmelites, though dedicated to a strictly contemplative life, were nevertheless asked to open an academy for girls. They pleaded that their vocation disqualified them for any sort of active work, but later, under the pressure of poverty, agreed to establish a school. As might be expected, it was not a success, and was soon given up. Much the same story has to be told of the Poor Clares—also contemplatives—who came to Frederick, Maryland, before the eighteenth century was ended. By 1801 we find them conducting an academy at Georgetown. A year or two later they, too, had reached the conclusion that it was impossible for them to teach and at the same time observe their rule. Accordingly they packed up in 1805 and returned to Europe.

They had employed, however, as lay teachers a Miss Alice Lalor and two other young women. These took over the Poor Clares' school and, affiliating themselves with the order of the Visitation, founded what has become one of the most famous of Catholic academies.[10] They at last solved the problem as to how to combine the contemplative life with teaching.

But what was destined to be a still more important event in the history of Catholic education occurred in 1805 when Elizabeth Seton became a Catholic. She was born in 1774, a Bayley, and therefore a connection of the Roosevelts, and when twenty married William Seton, a well-to-do New York merchant. He died of consumption in Italy in 1803, having lost most of his fortune and leaving his widow with five children to support. Her reception into the Church, which occurred soon afterwards, cut her off from aid from her relatives, so for the sake of a livelihood she started a school in New York City. In 1808, however, prompted by Carroll and DuBourg, she went to Baltimore, where she opened an academy in a house adjoining St. Mary's College on Paca Street. Her conversion had been largely effected by correspondence with Cheverus, who was to be the first Bishop of Boston, though she was never to meet him but once, and then some years later. But the initial Catholic influence was that of the Felicchi brothers of Leghorn, business friends of her husband's.

In 1809, encouraged by DuBourg and financed by Samuel Cooper, a Virginian merchant who was then studying for the priesthood,[11] she transferred her activities to Emmitsburg. We have her own account of the two-days' journey under the August sun: "Heat, dust, bad roads, streams unbridged, jolting, crowding, fatigue, and fear of freshets; partly on foot and partly in one of those huge canvas-covered, creaking wagons ('Prairie Schooners') in use among the country people of Maryland. The expense was $50. We were obliged to walk the horses all the way and walked ourselves nearly half the time (all except Cecilia); this morning four and one half miles before breakfast. The dear patient was much amused at the procession and all the natives astonished as we went before the carriage."[12] Emmitsburg had the advantage of a Catholic college in Mount St. Mary's and friends capable of appreciating what a treasure they had in Mrs. Seton. They took charge

[10] It is now also a junior college.

[11] He served as a priest at Emmitsburg later, and in the South; then went to Bordeaux with Cheverus, where he attended the Cardinal on his death-bed, himself dying in 1843.

[12] Quoted in Meline and McSweeny's *Story of the Mountain*, Vol. I, p. 26.

of her boys, while she kept her daughters with herself. But two of her three daughters died in youth, as did the young sisters-in-law who had entered the Church and had joined her; and in 1821 the rigors of Emmitsburg proved too much for Elizabeth Seton herself.

She was a natural writer, though she never set up as an author, and—what is more important—a soul at once valiant, wise and humorous. "Had I been a man the whole world would not be enough for me," she was to say. "I would tread in the footsteps of St. Francis Xavier." But her friends Flaget, DuBourg, David and Bruté went to the *ultima thule* of the American frontier as bishops; all were inspired by her. "I shall be wild Betty to the last breath," she wrote, and to do her justice, she was. Perhaps that is why she is now one of the American candidates for canonization.

Though Mother Seton never wore the habit of the Sisters of Charity, she was their American foundress. From her, therefore, spring a large number of corporal and spiritual works of mercy, of which I must for the moment confine myself to her educational projects. And here her great glory is not even that she established St. Joseph's Academy (now also a college) but that she began the parochial school system in America.

Before her, there had been Catholic schools as St. Mary's, Philadelphia, and elsewhere, but these were conducted by lay teachers and charged fees. It was Mother Seton who set up the first completely *free* parochial school and staffed it with her Daughters, so providing a model which was afterwards everywhere adopted. Brief as her life was—with only sixteen years of it spent within the Church—she, quite unconsciously, left an unforgettable impression, and this was due rather to what she was than to what she did. Katherine Burton, her most recent biographer, has well said that she offset "the malady of the period: the decorating of all landscapes with funeral urns and weeping willows." No, weeping willows were not at all in Elizabeth Seton's line. Rather it was brilliant gayety and passionate fervor and good sense that were the manifestations of her strong piety. America has never produced a greater woman, and few as great. And no other country but America could have produced anybody just like her.

But of course the founding of religious orders was only auxiliary to the main work of the Church, which was diocesan and in charge of the secular clergy. That was why the founding of the seminary at Baltimore was of paramount importance: it provided a place where secular priests could be trained. The proof of the expansion already reached, and the expectation of further expansion to come, was indicated in 1808 when John Carroll's vast diocese was divided.

He had long been asking that this be done, but at first the only result of his pleading was that Leonard Neale was given him as coadjutor in 1799. Nine years later, however, the Holy See lessened his burdens, which were increasing every year with a rapidly growing Catholic population. Then the diocese of New York was entrusted to Concanen, that of Boston to Cheverus, and that of Philadelphia to Egan. But Concanen, an Irish Dominican, never managed to leave Italy and died at Naples in 1810 while waiting for a boat; therefore the Jesuit, Kohlmann (who would have been appointed had he not been a Jesuit) was obliged to administer the diocese in his absence. As for the Franciscan, poor Michael Egan, he struggled against unruly priests in Philadelphia until it was too much for him and he died in 1814, most piously ordering that he be laid on the floor to take his last breath.

The most notable—or at all events, the most charming—of these suffragans to Carroll, who was made Archbishop in 1808, was Jean-Louis Lefebvre de Cheverus, who, when Matignon refused the see, was appointed to Boston. Already as a priest he had endeared himself to everybody, so that when John Adams visited the city as President, it was Cheverus who was given the place of honor by his side. Now as Bishop he lived in a two-room shack, chopping his own firewood, and with his own hands carrying corporal and spiritual charity to the needy. Carroll would have liked to have had him as his coadjutor, or to have secured him for Philadelphia (then the largest Catholic center); and had either of these things happened the history of the American Church would perhaps have taken a somewhat different course. But it was not to be: the health of Cheverus was not robust enough to permit him to assume too heavy burdens. In 1823, when he was offered the see of Montauban in France, he accepted it, though he had become an American citizen. In 1836 he died, Archbishop of Bordeaux, a Cardinal, and a Peer of France. Channing, the celebrated Unitarian minister of Boston, wrote his epitaph: "Who among our religious teachers would solicit a comparison between himself and the devoted Cheverus? . . . How can we shut our hearts against this proof of the Catholic religion to form great and good men?" When Channing himself died in 1842, Bishop Fenwick ordered that the Catholic church bells in Boston be tolled. Though by then the period of violence had begun, large and luminous minds on either side were still able to recognize one another's merits. It would be a bad man indeed who failed to see in Cheverus one of the most beautiful spirits of the American Church.

If Cheverus was, of all the new bishops, the only one given new soil to break, he was at the same time the continuer of one part of the old tradition. It was he who took the Indians of Maine under his care. It was on foot that he made his way through their forests, and there he mastered their language—a Black Robe in their midst again! On the other hand, Benedict Joseph Flaget, though he went to a western territory which had once known Jesuit and Recollect, found a wilderness from which nearly every evidence of Catholic life had disappeared. He did not have, like Cheverus, so much as the basis of a settled civilization to build upon; hardly anything was there but the wild lawlessness of the Frontier. If the story of the dioceses of the East is largely one of internal conflict, the problems of the West were even more difficult, for there there was nothing (except for the Marylanders settled in Kentucky) but small scattered communities of French Catholics who, because of their long neglect, were often Catholics merely in name. The vast diocese of Bardstown was created to bring succor to these lost sheep. And though I must defer the Frontier for fuller treatment to a later chapter, I pause now to remark the keenness of vision of those in America who advised the appointment of its bishop. In their bones they felt that what we now call the Middle West was destined to be the heart of America, and they set out to capture it before there seemed to be anything to capture at all. They guessed wrong in selecting Bardstown as the see, for that place, as time was to show, had no future, and has long since been absorbed into the diocese of Louisville. But they were right in choosing a spot in Kentucky. In 1792 it had been admitted to the Union as the fifteenth state, the first of those in the West. For the moment no other center served for the radiation of western Catholic effort.

As for the eastern dioceses, a word should be said at this point about the accusation that bishops in Ireland, and in particular Troy of Dublin, pulled wires to see that Irishmen obtained bishoprics in America. Shea has been rather caustic on this subject, but his contentions have recently been shown by Peter Guilday to be without foundation. It is true enough that Richard Luke Concanen, the first Bishop of New York, was an Irish Dominican, as was the second, John Connolly. And it is natural to infer that the Dominican Troy had something to do with their selection. But Shea, it would seem, was displaying touchiness in this matter, as he did in bringing the charge that France intrigued to get a Frenchman appointed at the time the American Church was being organized. It was an instance of that suspicion of foreigners destined to do so much harm to American Catholicism—and to Americans generally. What must be conceded, however, is that Connolly's nomination was singularly tactless, as he was a British subject, and at the time he was made a bishop England and the United States were at war. But if in that respect a blunder, it is at least proof that Rome was anxious to supply the new Republic with English-speaking prelates in the belief that these would be more acceptable than any others. The line of French bishops that was so soon to begin—that in fact had already begun with the appointment of Cheverus and Flaget—was not due to Roman machinations, or to the intrigues of France, but to the simple fact that these were the men American ecclesiastical authorities rightly considered most suitable for the episcopal office. Among the American born, as they themselves recognized, there was a dearth of men of the right timber. Hence Rome's appointment of Irish friars; hence too Carroll's selection of Frenchmen. Though he had taken as his coadjutor Leonard Neale, the descendant of one of Lord Baltimore's settlers, he knew perfectly well that Neale was a man of no great ability, as Neale himself on several occasions disarmingly admitted. Carroll would have preferred Cheverus.

The Archbishop of Baltimore was now an old man, and though his health was good, he felt his weakness increasing. Much had happened to drain his powers, much to sadden him. The second war with England was a grief additional to those caused by his rebellious subjects. Like most of the people in the East he did not approve of the war, although I cannot recall his having said anything about its real—as distinguished from its ostensible—cause. We know that the true object of the "War Hawks" was the seizure of Canada, the extension of territory, even if the object given out was the British claim to the right of searching American ships for deserters. It is now admitted that there were many such deserters, however much the British must be blamed for taking off rather indiscriminately any sailor who spoke with an English accent. Yet it was precisely the commercial East, especially New England—the very part of the country that suffered most from the high-handed British refusal of the liberty of the seas—that was most strongly against a declaration of war.

The whole affair was as inglorious as it was inconclusive. After several brilliant American naval forays, the British blockade of the Atlantic coast became absolute. The city of Washington was burned, following the rout of the American forces on the Bladensburg road, and British officers at the White House ate Mr. and Mrs. Madison's dinner. The most striking American success, and almost the only one on land, was that of Andrew Jackson at New Orleans over the foolhardy Pakenham. It was obtained after peace had already been signed at Ghent.

This battle has a certain interest to Catholics. The Ursuline nuns at New Orleans had spent the night in prayer for an American victory. And it was while DuBourg was still saying Mass that news of Jackson's triumph arrived. The services concluded with the *Te Deum*. The next day General Jackson, though far from a pious man, called with his staff to thank the good Sisters. Commodore Macdonough's exploit on Lake Champlain, however, really did have something to do with the termination of the war. The unique naval battle of Plattsburg was won by a Catholic.[13]

It gives one a curious sensation to read the letters Carroll addressed to his old and intimate English friend, Charles Plowden, during this period; they might have been written today. He points out, indeed, the "impolite actions of your government," which he sees to be all the more unfortunate because of their effect upon "the busy intriguing French and headstrong Irish amongst us." But he concludes, "Heaven knows that [England] is the bulwark of public welfare—*spes ultima mundi*." Another letter might have had Hitler and the Battle of Britain in mind: "To have stood alone against an overwhelming power, which compelled submission from every power in Europe, until it was met by British arms, and to have at length reanimated the trembling nations to shake off

[13] Another little matter of Catholic interest is that James Ord, reputed to be the son of George IV by his morganatic Catholic wife, Mrs. Fitzherbert, served in the American Navy. He had been a Georgetown student, and rose to be a judge.

their yoke, is the exclusive merit of Englishmen." He could hardly be other than unhappy about a war in which the issues were so confused and which, in the end, accomplished precisely nothing.

The last years of John Carroll were clouded with a sense of failure. But, as is so often the case, such a feeling is the measure of a man's greatness. Thus Virgil, when dying, asked that the *Aeneid* be burned; thus St. Thomas dismissed the *Summa* as a lot of straw. In the same way his achievements seemed to Carroll so little when compared to the unachieved design. We can estimate the value of his work more accurately now. His monument is not merely his cathedral—which he never thought of as such; it is rather the whole history of the Catholic Church in the United States.

But as for the cathedral in Baltimore, it might be remarked that, to obtain funds to build it, he initiated the system of a voluntary tax, and also used the less original device of a lottery. When he won the first prize in the drawing, he handed it back to the building fund. He even approached Napoleon, then First Consul, for a subscription, so hard pressed was he for means to gather money. In its day the cathedral was the most imposing ecclesiastical building in the United States, and Latrobe's noble and simple design may still be admired. The building is all the more touching because of the confession it openly makes of the economy that was necessary to put it up at all. Its slightly quaint dignity—which would be like that of a child in brocade, if it had any sort of gorgeousness— is vastly greater than that of some edifices whose pretentiousness has cost ten times as much.

Yet if Carroll had done a great deal—more than he ever suspected—a great deal remained to be done. In the whole country east of the Mississippi there were only ninety-two priests. Maine, Virginia, South Carolina, and the various "territories" had each but one priest apiece. Except for Massachusetts, which had three, there was no resident priest in any of the New England states, nor in New Jersey, Delaware, North Carolina and Tennessee. Nearly half the clergy were stationed in Maryland. So meagre a growth after the strenuous work of thirty years may account for Carroll's feeling of failure. But there can be no doubt that the shadow upon his mind was also due to the constant calumnies which, like Washington, he had suffered from those who should have been most grateful to him. As Dr. Guilday writes: "To the Germans [he] was Irish; to the Irish, he was English, or at least pro-French; to the secular clergy, he was an ex-Jesuit; and to the partially restored Society of Jesus, he was looked upon as an uncertainty in the efforts they were making for full canonical revival." He never, it must be confessed, inspired much love, for he was reserved and, though kindly, aloof. Except for Plowden, far away in England and not seen since 1790, he had no close friend. He had given himself too completely to his work to permit much flowing of the warm human juices that we catch sight of now and then in his nature.

It might be added that, like many priests of the time, he was slightly puritanical. His letters often contain warnings about dances and the harmful effects of novel reading—and one wonders what were the delirious romances he had in mind. The novels of the time strike us as intolerably insipid. However, we must remember that he was fearful lest any of his priests or people—all of whom were keenly watched by their Protestant neighbors for any defect—should fail to give good example. The conduct of some of the convivial Gaels gave him no inducement to unbend in society.

His main mistake was that he had permitted the trustee system to take root. However, in the circumstances in which he found himself, he cannot be justly blamed on this account. For the rest, he had done his duty to God and man, though as he himself sadly admitted, his judgment of men had sometimes been poor. His temperament was too sanguine to allow him to think anything except the best of his fellows; it was a generous failing. There was nothing of the mystic about him; his piety was sober and steady rather than fervent. Courage, persistence, prudence, honesty—these were always his. He had never flagged in service. He had fought the good fight. His end came quietly in Baltimore on December 3, 1815: he was eighty years old.

Shea records[14] that a man named John Engle died in 1881 at the age of ninety-five. He had been confirmed by Carroll in 1796 and had lived to see the original diocese divided and subdivided "till the hierarchy numbered fourteen archbishops and fifty-six bishops and holy mass was said throughout the land in more than six thousand churches and chapels by as

[14] *History of the Catholic Church in the United States*, Vol. II, pp. 494–495.

many priests." During the same time the American Church had passed through raging tempests to peace. It was providential that during the first critical years the hand upon the rudder was that of John Carroll.

CHAPTER THIRTEEN

ENTER JOHN ENGLAND

John Carroll had been accused freely enough of pro-French leanings, for all that his Americanism was of the sturdiest sort. Now it really did grow evident that the control of the Church was about to pass into French hands. Leonard Neale, the new Archbishop, secured the appointment of Ambrose Maréchal as his coadjutor with right of succession. Already Flaget was at Bardstown, DuBourg in Louisiana, and Cheverus at Boston. And Dubois was appointed to New York in 1826. There was a moment, just before Irish bishops arrived from abroad to man the new sees of Richmond and Charleston, when there was only one bishop in the United States not of French blood and birth—and he was the incompetent Conwell. If it is now hard to imagine what would have become of the Church without these learned, virtuous and devoted guides, at the time it had all the look of a Gallic plot to capture America.

This fact must be sympathetically allowed for. The Irish have received so many injustices that they are quick to take offence when none is intended. And the question of bishops was no trifling matter. It would only have infuriated them to have pointed out that such Irishmen as did get sent to American sees were of no great capacity. Egan of Philadelphia and Connolly of New York did not show themselves able to cope with their problems. As for Henry Conwell, who at the age of seventy-five was appointed to Philadelphia, he proved to be so abject a failure that he had to be forbidden by Rome to exercise his functions. Nor was Patrick Kelly who was sent—through an intrigue—to Richmond in 1820 anything but a pious nonentity. He soon gave up. It was John England alone of all these first Irish prelates who proved himself capable of dealing with the situation. England was the exceptional, the incalculable: England was a genius.

Some of the distinguishing marks of the period have already been indicated. The old struggle between trustees and bishops went on throughout it all—aggravated now by the new factor of resentment against what was considered French domination. Yet obviously it was not French domination that led

Conwell of Philadelphia to make a virtual surrender to his trustees, for he was an Irishman and as such should have been acceptable to his Irish subjects. All the same the Irishman, William Vincent Harold, gave him trouble, and the Irishman, Hogan, led what was to be the gravest schism of the American Church. The thing that really comes as a dividing line between the administrations of Carroll and Maréchal was that a new claim was made by the laity. Not content with attempting to assert, as before, their right to choose their own pastors, they began—in Virginia and South Carolina—to assert their right to choose their own bishops as well. The first phase had resulted, at worst, in parochial schisms that were all eventually healed. The second phase very nearly resulted in the setting up of an Independent Catholic Church of America, with its own bishops free of the jurisdiction of the Metropolitan of Baltimore or, for that matter, of Rome itself.

It may be said in passing, however, that though this movement was, in its extreme form, confined to the southern states, there was to be found elsewhere a disposition on the part of the lay trustees to force the bishops to do their bidding by withholding their salaries. This was attempted in the case of Conwell; it was attempted also in the case of Dubois. The bishops in these instances did not have their authority formally rejected; it was merely that they were to be starved into submission. The trustees held the money-bags and so had no need to rebel: for those who paid the piper could call the tune. That was so much simpler and could be just as effective.

The southern states went a good deal further. They sought to establish by appeals to Rome and the civil authorities their right to have only bishops that were to their liking. And they decidedly did not like the Frenchman, Maréchal, any more than he pretended to like Irishmen. He might possibly have handled matters more tactfully than he did; he could (and perhaps he should) have refrained from sending to Norfolk and Charleston French priests who were obnoxious to congregations largely Irish. He might also have recognized his mistake and tried to rectify it. On the other hand, he did not have so many priests at his disposal as to be able to pick and choose among them. And he was dealing with stubborn and hot-headed men who made such extravagant demands that it was difficult to appease them without seeming to surrender the cardinal principle of episcopal authority. It was his plain duty to apply that principle, as it was the plain duty of priests and people to accept it. The thing therefore developed into a knock-down-drag-out fight.

I must remind my readers that when Carroll's diocese was divided in 1808, Virginia, the Carolinas and Georgia—because there were very few Catholics in those states—remained within the jurisdiction of Baltimore. This meant that they came directly under Maréchal. And if it be said that the disturbances began before Maréchal was Archbishop—that is, while Neale was still Metropolitan—the answer is that everybody saw what would happen. Frenchmen were already in the American sees; they were in charge of the seminary; Neale was old, and died eighteen months after Carroll; and Maréchal's appointment as coadjutor with the right of succession was being sought. It was not held in the Sulpician's favor that he had already refused two American bishoprics and did his best to avoid appointment the third time. The one fact that glared out was that he was to be Archbishop and therefore would be in a position to advise Rome as to future ecclesiastical appointments. The Irish thought of themselves as being bound hand and foot and delivered to perpetual servitude to their enemies.

They were of course as mistaken in their estimate of the situation as they were at fault in the action they took. But an effort at least must be made to see things from their point of view. They had a high—a legitimately high—opinion of their own capacity. Every preacher of note in the country was Irish, and we have seen how in those days an excessive importance was attached to preaching. It may be that Father John Power was slightly exaggerating when he said in 1829 of Dubois: "[He] is thirty-six years in America, and when he attempts to give common instructions, thirty-six out of three thousand [*sic*] cannot understand a word of what he says. Hundreds leave the Church and go into the Rum Shops while he is speaking";[1] but undoubtedly he voiced the Irish disgust, not only with Dubois but with many of the foreigners. The eloquent Irish could not see why they should be passed over and all the appointments given to Frenchmen.

Historical truth demands the admission that it was the Irish who were the great trouble-makers at this time. We should, however, also gratefully admit that, taking the history of the American Church as a whole, it is the Irish who have

[1] Guilday, *England*, Vol. I, p. 447. Yet Dubois had received lessons in English from Patrick Henry!

done by far the most to build it up. In the end the American episcopate became almost an Irish preserve, and though this, too, was to cause some dissatisfaction, it can hardly be denied that the Irish showed themselves to be the men best qualified to captain the Church. I say this because I may be accused, as an Englishman, of an anti-Irish prejudice. Actually, if I have any prejudices, they are in the opposite direction. As we proceed in our story we shall see, I think, how not the least of the contributions of the Irish was their work in Americanizing Catholics of other nationalities. But having given the credit where it belongs, I repeat that it was a certain turbulent element among the Irish that came very close indeed to wrecking the Church by creating a schism that would have had Irish bishops. And if that had happened, a doorway would inevitably have been opened to heresy, and a large part of the Catholic population would have been forever lost, not only to the Roman obedience but to theological orthodoxy.

The hot-heads went so far, after their preposterous representations had been rejected by the Holy See, as to concoct a plot for getting an Irish priest to proceed to Holland and receive consecration at the hands of a Jansenist bishop; after which he was to come to America and preside over the projected Independent Catholic Church. It is an astounding instance of how racial passions and prejudices can override judgment. It is even more astounding that at least one American priest in good standing—the Dominican Carbry of New York —lent himself to the scheme. And though in this I suspect his motive was the hope that Rome would be sufficiently scared by the mere threat as to appoint him bishop, there is little doubt that the congregations of Norfolk and Charleston were prepared to do more than threaten to gain their ends—freedom from the detested Maréchal.

Dr. Guilday in his *Church in Virginia* and *The Life and Times of John England* relates the sad story and gives the documents in full. I can attempt no more than a summary. In 1817 the "Vestrymen of the Roman Catholic Apostolic Christian Congregation" of Norfolk sent a petition to Propaganda protesting their unwavering loyalty to the Holy See but asserting their right of patronage, as they had erected the church edifice. They complained about their French pastors and the "strangeness and extravagance" of the character of Maréchal, writing, "We have fixed our wishes on and beg leave to present to His Holiness the Reverend Thomas Carbry

. . . and we do not cease to offer to the Almighty Bestower of all gifts, our most ardent prayers that he may vouchsafe to inspire our Holy Father, to confirm him our Bishop and Spiritual Head." At the same time they issued, for the instruction of their delegates to Rome, a series of resolutions. One reads, "In consequence of our inalienable right of patronage our first Bishop will be elected by us." The implication is plain: they understood their right of patronage (which they did not possess) to extend not only to the choice of priests for their churches but to the choice of the bishop too.

In this we have, it need hardly be said, the claim as a right to something which the Holy See had never accorded even as a privilege. It is true that Rome had made special concessions to the American clergy as to the election of the first bishops. It is also true that sometimes under a concordat the Holy See has granted the civil power the privilege of nominating bishops—but only to the civil power, not to individual congregations. Under the Civil Constitution of the Clergy during the French Revolution such powers were made legal, but so far from their being recognized by Rome, those of the clergy who accepted the arrangement were excommunicated. It is also true that the Spanish Crown had enjoyed, since the days of Queen Isabella, the privilege of appointing to all ecclesiastical offices in its dominions in the New World. But that obviously did not apply here. Finally it is true that the British Crown was given, for the sake of peace, the so-called right of vetoing episcopal appointments contemplated by the Holy See. But again the two cases are not on a par. What the Norfolk congregation had in mind was the state of affairs that had existed during the French Revolution. As America had had its Revolution, it too was entitled to a similar system. They ignored, or failed to understand, that it involved schism.

It is difficult to imagine upon what theory of canon law Norfolk reposed its claim. For even before the congregation had sent their petition to Rome, they met in January, 1817—after a visit from Maréchal had failed to pacify them—and resolved that their French pastor, "the Rev. James Lucas, having abandoned the Church, violating the duties of a Pastor, a conduct in opposition to the Spirit of the Gospel, Maxims of the Holy Fathers, and the Canons of the said Councils of the Church, treating with disrespect the Board of Trustees lawfully elected, depositories of the power and views of this Congregation, and moreover, by not having complied with the

Laws of our State, in consequence of which he is amenable to law: he is hereby declared no Pastor of this Roman Catholic Congregation of Norfolk." It would almost seem that they believed they were endued with the power of excommunication! The preposterous language of their rigmarole would convey as much. In any event, it is clear that they claimed the right to dismiss him.

It is not necessary to defend Father Lucas. Even if he was not "an incendiary French clergyman," even if he was not as grasping and as high-handed as his people charged, it may be that he was a rather disagreeable man and he had certainly made himself unpopular. But if Norfolk wanted him withdrawn, the proper procedure would have been for the congregation to have laid representations before the Archbishop and abided his decision. The course of action followed was utterly indefensible in his case, and led on to the monstrous proposal that the South set up its own Church independent of Maréchal and therefore also of the Pope.

Rome was seriously alarmed. The authorities there had a very vague idea of the topography of America for, as Maréchal wrote on July 8, 1820, when it was proposed to erect Virginia into a diocese, they intended to have the Bishop reside at Hartford! But at least they now saw that it was advisable to create two new sees and to put them under prelates of the same race as the majority of the people. Later in that same month they appointed Patrick Kelly and John England.

We need not concern ourselves with Bishop Kelly, except to remark that his subjects at once divided themselves into a "bishop's party" and a "trustees' party." As John Gilmary Shea says, "The very men who had clamoured for an Irish priest now turned against an Irish bishop." The culmination was a riot to secure possession of the church and the arrest of twenty-one men. But the malcontents did succeed in getting rid of Lucas, who went to Washington where (as in Norfolk) he was unpopular. He entered the Jesuit Order in 1825. As for Kelly, he struggled with his difficulties for about a year; then this physical giant resigned, regarding the situation as hopeless, upon which Virginia came once more under the jurisdiction of Maréchal as administrator of the vacant diocese.

The more important scene was that of South Carolina, for there the problem was solved by the one man capable of solving it—John England.

But before we come to England's career, it is necessary to

look at the condition of Charleston before his arrival. It was much the same as that of Norfolk, down to the detail of coincidence that in both places the leader of the rebellious trustees was a physician. But in the case of Charleston there was this difference: the Archbishop had wished to get rid of the Irish priest already in charge and to put a Frenchman in his place. Which of course was adding insult to injury.

The priest in question was Dr. Simon Felix Gallagher about whom two things are not open to doubt—that he was a brilliant orator, and that he was a drunkard. Neale, and afterwards Maréchal, had written to him several times very frankly concerning his failing, and they had warned him that he would have to be suspended unless he turned over a new leaf. This Gallagher promised to do, but soon relapsed to the bottle. And his parishioners—many of whom we may suspect to have been addicted to the same widely prevalent vice, for the documents they issued are unmistakably redolent of whiskey—would not hear of the removal of one whose sermons they so greatly relished. He was supported in contumacy by Robert Browne, an Augustinian canon, who in any event had no business to be in Charleston, to which place he had wandered without permission from his station at Augusta, Georgia. Browne, as the less able man, played only the rôle of second to Gallagher, but as a priest was of course a great support.

The man to whom they—and their Irish congregation—objected was Joseph Picot Clorivière. He was a Breton who had had an adventurous history. Born at Nantes in 1768, he had been a fellow-student with Chateaubriand, and is mentioned in the *Mémoires d'Outre-Tombe*. An officer in the King's Guard when the French Revolution broke out, he had fought in the counterrevolution of the Chouans as a general. Later he was implicated in a plot to assassinate Napoleon but escaped, making his way to America in 1803 disguised as a sailor under the name of Guitry. Three years later he entered the Baltimore seminary and after ordination was appointed as assistant to Dr. Gallagher. He ended his days as chaplain to the Visitation convent at Washington.

Up to 1815 there does not appear to have been any special friction between the two priests, so that one surmises that it was Carroll's death, and the French influence that followed it, that brought matters to a head. But one can see that Clorivière had never been really liked—simply because he was a Frenchman. It may be, however, that he took no pains to conceal his Bourbon sentiments and that these grated upon the violently republican sentiments we know the trustees to have had. As the trustees make no mention of his part in the attempt to assassinate Napoleon, we must conclude that the congregation knew nothing of that dark episode in his life: otherwise they would have been sure to have used it against him. His pronounced Gallicism was enough.

When Gallagher was, together with Browne, suspended by Archbishop Neale in 1816, their response was to drive Clorivière out. The French priest, so Gallagher told Neale in a letter, had expostulated with him for defying the Ordinary but had removed to another place, leaving him in possession of St. Mary's. This, however, was not enough to bring peace. Gallagher sent his assistant a document—formally written in Latin for further weight—forbidding him to open another chapel in the city. Whereupon Neale sent Gallagher a long letter begging him to submit. "Probably my never having entertained an idea of possessing supereminent abilities," he wrote, "I feel less sensibly at hearing of your entertaining the public with your strictures on me. . . . But, Sir, is it not surprising that you of renowned abilities, splendid qualifications and highly boasted knowledge, especially of the canon law,[2] should have committed such a blunder as to plead your appeal to Rome as a sufficient authorization for the exercise of those spiritual powers, which I have revoked."

It was his appeal that caused further confusion. Browne went to Rome to explain the matter and put such a construction upon it that Propaganda upheld him and Gallagher, ordering Neale to reinstate them. It was at this stage that both sides quibbled. Neale took up the attitude that, as Propaganda had been misinformed, he was free to disobey the Sacred Congregation. I am no canon lawyer, but it appears to me—speaking under correction—that what Neale should have done was to have obeyed and then made his own representations to the Holy See. These representations, indeed, he did afterwards make, and the result was that Rome reversed itself and wrote to Neale giving him full authority to deal at his discretion with the rebels. But as Neale died before these instructions were drawn, Gallagher now quibbled in his turn. He wrote at once to Maréchal, the new Metropolitan, hinting broadly that the document was forged but arguing that "if it

[2] This was perhaps a piece of gentle sarcasm.

were genuine, it only granted the power to proceed to Archbishop Neale on whom alone that power was conferred. But no such person, name, or character was then in existence. It was therefore null according to all laws." The argument was clever, but Gallagher must have known that, at best, it would merely gain him a little more time, for the evident intention of Propaganda was to support the Archbishop's authority, not a particular person. The Charleston congregation followed this up by addressing a petition on May 13, 1818, to the Holy See similar to the one sent by Norfolk the previous year. That it was relatively void of the Norfolk absurdities, we may credit to Gallagher's having supervised the composition, if he did not compose the petition himself. The trustees asked that Clorivière be removed and Maréchal rebuked and that "our revered civil and political institutions, the spirit of which he attempts to violate and frenchify" be upheld by Rome.

But that was not quite all. Less truculently than Norfolk, and without demanding it as a right, Charleston asked that Carbry be sent there as bishop. The document advances the reason, "He has . . . with us, we must confess, the peculiar merit of being obnoxious to the Baltimore Junta." It was at this point that Gallagher (if he was the author of the petition) overshot the mark. There we can smell the whiskey. For the sake of scoring a small debating point he writes what, in his sober judgment, he must have known would destroy all chance of his obtaining what he wanted. This attack on the "Baltimore Junta" gave him away completely in Rome.

It was now that the most extraordinary thing of all happened. On January 4, 1819, a letter was forwarded through Father Carbry to a Franciscan named Hayes in Dublin. Carbry sent it on without comment except that Hayes was to use his discretion, and that he himself was acting disinterestedly, for the Catholics in South Carolina had asked Rome to appoint him their bishop. The instructions were as follows: "On receipt of this letter to proceed to Utrecht in the most secret manner, carrying testimonials of good conduct from some of the clergy, and to have yourself consecrated Bishop of South Carolina in North America, and to set out for that state as soon as possible. On your arrival in America your expenses shall be made good to you, but you must agree to consecrate other Bishops, when settled in this country, otherwise your salary may be doubtful." Hayes, thoroughly alarmed by the letter, turned it over to the Roman authorities and they, in their turn alarmed, decided—against Maréchal's known wishes —to send Irishmen as bishops to Virginia and South Carolina. To that extent the machinations of the malcontents had a good result. Had Propaganda not acted at once the Independent Catholic Church of America would in all probability have been set up.

Some doubt has been expressed as to whether the Charleston group (who were of course in collusion with Norfolk) were really sincere. It is possible that they intended nothing more than to frighten Rome and so get what they wanted— new dioceses with Irish bishops. But we must remember that practically every heresy and schism has been carried much further than its initiators ever intended it to go. In the same way Charleston, having made this move, could hardly have drawn back had it met inflexible opposition. But there are some suspicious features about the whole business: no money was sent to Hayes for his expenses, and conditions were laid down—enforceable by the withholding of his salary—which no prospective bishop would be likely to accept in advance. It may be that Charleston expected Hayes to refuse and was merely trying to force the hand of the Holy See.

Maréchal brought the accusation that Hayes was selected because he had attained some notoriety by an excessive boldness that had been drastically reproved by Rome: he was therefore looked upon as a potential schismatic. But evidently Charleston did not know much about the man they had picked. He had been associated with John England in opposition to the Royal Veto, and was "Papal" almost to excess. I am left with the feeling that it was Carbry who suggested his name, in the expectation that Hayes could be counted upon to act as he did. It is quite possible that Carbry hoped the outcome of the scare would be that he himself would be given the bishopric for which the congregations of both Norfolk and Charleston had previously taken it upon themselves to nominate him. If this be so, the Dominican was playing an extremely Machiavellian game. But it would at least exculpate him of any guilt of countenancing schism. In any event Rome passed him over and he disappears from history. Patrick Kelly was chosen for Richmond and John England for Charleston.

If it is instructive to note how England, from the moment of his appointment (and probably before) went to the very heart of the troubles of the Church in the South, so also is it instructive to note that, however reprehensible the rebels were in their methods, however unsound in their general theories, they too had got hold of some valuable ideas. For example, there exists a paper addressed in 1819 by Browne to Propaganda in which he urges, among other things, the sending of an Apostolic Delegate to Washington and the erection of a national Catholic university in that city. These projects had to wait a long time, the country not being ripe for them; yet they came to be recognized as of vital importance to the American Church. Therefore we may assume that the exasperation of the Southern congregations was due, in part, to misplaced zeal.

England soon came to share the views of his people about the French. It was not, however, in his case an unreasoning prejudice. He saw very clearly that, whatever the high personal merits of the French priests and bishops might be, and however excellent their intentions, they were not the men most fitted for work in America. At any rate, they were not the most fitted, American racial feeling being what it was. On this subject he expressed himself freely—and not always tactfully. As he wrote in 1825, "If Rome wishes to have our religion establish itself here, the reasonable wishes of our people must be taken into account." Still more downright is a letter written ten years later: "I am daily more convinced that the genius of this nation and the administration of the French are not easily reconciled. Besides this, one of the strongest topics of prejudice against our religion is that it is a foreign Religion, and it is not American, that it is the religion of strangers, of aliens. . . . The French can never become Americans. Their language, manners, love of *la belle France*, their dress, air, carriage, notions, and mode of speaking of their religion, all, all are foreign. An American then says, 'It might be very good, but 'tis a foreign aristocracy.' . . . The French clergy are generally good men and love Religion, but they make the Catholic religion thus appear to be exotic, and cannot understand why it should be made to appear assimilated to American principles." It is evident that he is speaking of intangibles —in which bearing and cast of thought and gesticulation should be included. But intangibles are never to be ignored in human relationships. John England was from the outset an American in a sense that Ambrose Maréchal and some of his colleagues could never hope to be, or perhaps wanted to be.

The result of this view of the French was far-reaching. England would no doubt have subscribed to Father Harold's opinion, contained in a long letter addressed to Propaganda in 1820: "Subjects [for the priesthood] alone are wanted. They are not to be found in the United States, and a French clergy will never look for them in Ireland where they abound." Though there was another side to the story—for many of the Irish priests who did come over were those of whom their bishops wished to be rid, so that England himself eventually came to the conclusion that he had better set up his own seminary in Charleston rather than invite unknown Gaels to his diocese— the main objection was sound. And it was not merely that the French bishops did not greatly hanker for Irish priests: no Irishman of ability was particularly anxious to go to a country where, under a Gallic episcopate, he believed he would have no chance to get on. Some of the Frenchmen talked about *la canaille Irlandaise,* and the Irish—rabble or not—fiercely resented their attitude.

In this respect England was at one with his people and with the majority of Catholics throughout the country. But of course it brought him under the grave suspicion of Maréchal and others, while his method of solving the trustee problem did not raise him in the esteem of some of the prelates who were not French—Conwell of Philadelphia, for example. Most of them came to agree that he was a dangerously democratic man.

It must be admitted that he *was* democratic, very much so. His justification is that Conwell, after struggling against refractory priests and lay trustees, surrendered to them, with the result that he was summoned to Rome in 1829, deposed and ordered not to return to his diocese. Nevertheless he did return, though for this his brother bishops obtained his pardon. He was, however, obliged to give up all exercise of his episcopal functions and saw the administration of his diocese pass into the hands of Francis Patrick Kenrick[3] who, because he was only thirty-four as against Conwell's eighty-five was always referred to by the old man as "the boy." Kirlin[4] tells how once, when Kenrick was away, Conwell even had the young Bishop's furniture moved out of his room so that he

[3] It is interesting to note in passing that Kenrick had, as a youth, worked in the same office with the ill-starred poet James Clarence Mangan. He left Dublin to study at Rome when he was eighteen. Though he was not one of the greatest of administrators among the American hierarchy, he was by far the greatest of their theologians.

[4] *Catholicity in Philadelphia,* p. 266.

could take possession of it. On his return Kenrick good humoredly did not disturb the intruder but moved to another house nearby. Poor Conwell lived to be ninety-seven and was blind for the last nine years of his life. Kirlin, the historian of the Archdiocese of Philadelphia, has a charitable explanation of his conduct with regard to the trustees: it is that the Bishop deliberately made a martyr of himself, knowing that Rome would condemn him but believing also that it would be forced to clean up the mess. "By what seems to be an inspiration," he says, "Bishop Conwell had acted in the one way calculated to settle once and for all the disputed position of the clergy and the laity in temporalities."[5] That his action had this effect is perfectly true. Nevertheless it is a little difficult to believe Conwell had the cleverness to perceive what would be the outcome.

John England's solution of the trustee problem that had vexed nearly all the American bishops was the introduction of a formal constitution for the government of his diocese. Upon the framing of this, as he wrote in a long statement to Propaganda dated January, 1833,[6] he had spent three entire years of intense study, and to get it accepted everywhere by his diocese took another six years. In its main lines the Charleston Constitution was based upon that of the Church of England. To admit this, however, is not to deny its usefulness; the system prevailing elsewhere—in so far as a muddle can be called a system—was Presbyterian, each congregation asserting the right of running its own affairs under the "Moderatorship" of the bishop. England probably did not consider his device as more than something which would meet immediate needs. He did not think of it as a new code of canon law but as a temporary *modus agendi*. As such it must be judged. If it is so judged, there can be no question but that it achieved its object of bringing peace to a diocese which a short time before had been on the point of becoming an Independent Catholic Church.

England started off by saying, "I do not know of any system more favorable to the security of religious rights and of church property than that of the American law. . . . I prefer it to the law of almost every Catholic country with which I

[5] *Ibid.*, p. 251.
[6] See Guilday's *England*, where the statement is quoted at length. Vol. I, pp. 524, 525.

am acquainted."[7] But having made this frank—and probably too sweeping—acknowledgment, he set his face against all interference on the part of the lay trustees with spiritualities. His achievement was that he did not rest upon generalities but proceeded to definite rules, to the positive as well as the negative. As pew-rents gave the trustees an opportunity to interfere, he began by abolishing pews—which are in any case a Protestant innovation. They might remain for the time being, he said, in churches that already had them installed. But no new church was to have them; and any pastor who permitted their introduction would be suspended. At the same time, he recognized that the laity should be given something to do in the management of affairs. Therefore he organized his diocese so that, under the Bishop, whose authority was not to be challenged, there should be a Convocation of Clergy and a House of Representatives for the Laity. Both bodies were to be advisory rather than legislative.

Dr. Guilday has written: "The trustee system was an obvious response to an apparent need. Some one must hold the property for legal purposes, and the simplest system was for the congregation to elect a number of its members to represent it before the courts."[8] Had the system gone no further than this it would have been unobjectionable. Unfortunately, as we have seen, the trustees were only too often intoxicated with a sense of their own importance and claimed the right of engaging and dismissing their pastors and even—as in the case of Charleston and Norfolk—of nominating their own bishops. England cut to the root of the problem. As Orestes Brownson afterwards explained, "The representative system [of Charleston] was adopted in a way to satisfy the cravings of a few for distinction, and yet to make them weary of the trouble and formality." Or as England put it himself, "Under the Charleston Constitution, I can truly say that the clergy, and especially the Bishops, are entirely free; and on the other hand the laity are empowered to cooperate but not to dominate."

All this was accomplished in what probably was, as England

[7] The question of the legal incorporation of Catholic church property in America still awaits adequate treatment. Father Dignan's doctoral dissertation on the subject is the best so far, but though full of valuable information, it too often turns into a discussion of trusteeism. An earlier and somewhat wider discussion, is that in Father Charles Augustine's book.

[8] *England*, Vol. I, p. 353.

often said, the poorest Catholic diocese in the whole world. Though the Bishop introduced a system of taxation under his Constitution—fifty cents a quarter from each adult Catholic, a tax which served to emphasize their unity and responsibility —he could hardly have managed except for the contributions sent him from the missionary societies of Vienna, Munich and Lyons. Even these he obtained only after 1833 when at last he decided to put his squeamishness aside and ask for outside assistance.[9] And as it was, he was always in debt.

It is a marvel that, so hampered, he effected so many projects. One of these was for a seminary. He did not want men trained by the French Sulpicians at Baltimore: these were likely to have French ideas. Nor, after some sad experiences, did he want clergy direct from Ireland. Students from Ireland were another matter: he would mould their spiritual lives himself, at the same time indoctrinating them in the American spirit. But the Bishop had to conduct many of the classes, including that in Algebra, which he confessed he had largely forgotten. In view of his other countless activities, we must describe him as:

> At once a cook, and a captain bold,
> And the mate of the *Nancy*, brig,
> And a bo'sun tight, and a midshipmite,
> And the crew of the captain's gig.

Greatly daring, considering the prejudices of the South, he also set up a school for colored children, for which he formed an order of nuns. In this, too, he often taught. He established a book-society and library—following the lead of Carroll: it is a branch of work still shamefully neglected in the United States. He preached incessantly. Up and down his vast diocese he wandered, borrowing a court-house or a church from a friendly parson, and in this way did much to dissipate the fantastic notions prevalent about Catholicism. He was also in frequent demand as a preacher outside his own territory, and on one occasion—January 8, 1826—was invited to address Congress; many senators and representatives, and President John Quincy Adams himself, being present to listen to the celebrated orator. Everywhere he won people by his personal charm and kindness. Perhaps the only ones he did not win

[9] *Ibid.*, p. 526. He first applied to the Holy See, but was told there were no funds at the moment available. Rome, however, helped him with the missionary societies.

were a group of his fellow-bishops, who looked at all these proceedings askance.

They did not even regard with enthusiasm his magazine, the *United States Catholic Miscellany*, which was a little too outspoken for their liking. Yet the need for such a magazine was obvious, and England's natural talents as a journalist are now universally granted.

The *Miscellany* was the first Catholic paper in the United States. The honor has sometimes been claimed for the little sheet Father Gabriel Richard got out in Detroit. But that— the *Michigan Essay and Impartial Observer*—was hardly more than a substitute for the town-crier and did not last long. Richard has some title to be remembered as the only Catholic priest ever to be elected to Congress and for his share in founding in 1817 what was to become the University of Michigan. This was the "Catholepistemiad," of which he was Vice-president and occupant of six chairs, a Protestant minister being President and occupant of the remaining seven! But without derogation to Father Richard, I think we must consider Bishop England as the father of American Catholic journalism.[10]

In this he had as sub-editor his sister Joanna, who sank her little fortune in the enterprise. It was with difficulty that she was dissuaded from going off to join Mother Seton at Emmitsburg. Her early death was a great loss, for she toned down the too vigorous passages in her brother's compositions and, one suspects, gave them polish. England, though lucid and forceful and with an immense amount of varied information at his command, was inclined to be somewhat "spread-eagle" in style. But that of course was the mode demanded by the period: when men could not listen to oratory, they liked to read it. England was not what can be called a literary artist; the orator rarely is. "Did the speech read well?" asked Pitt, and when told that it did, answered that it must have been a bad speech. In the same way, we must believe that the overwhelm-

[10] Matthew Carey's *Columbian Magazine*, founded in 1786, and his *American Museum*, founded the following year, were not Catholic publications, though published by a Catholic. Robert Walsh, a Catholic, a Georgetown man, was the editor of the first American quarterly, *The American Review of History and Politics*, established in 1811. But this was in no sense Catholic. Walsh afterwards edited other journals and became American Consul in Paris, where he died in 1859.

ing presence of England and his glorious voice and his beguiling manner gave what he uttered an effectiveness that is not quite so apparent in what he wrote. However, this is a judgment long after the event. At the time, people relished his rolling periods. As they were completely satisfied, we have no right to complain.

In spite of all these activities—and largely because of them —England was not regarded with much favor by Maréchal and his party. As Kenrick wrote in 1834 to the future Cardinal Cullen in Ireland: "The talents, learning, fame, eloquence of Bp. England rendered him not an object of envy, for I believe the good Prelates superior to this narrow passion, but fear, for they dreaded lest his active mind and liberal views might lead them into the adoption of measures that might weaken their authority and disturb the repose of the Church."[11] Or as England himself wrote of the Bishops to the same correspondent the same year, "They are well disposed but their minds and mine are cast in different moulds, and cooperation is out of the question; for I cannot approve of their methods of administration, and at the last Council, they plainly manifested the most distinct want of confidence in me."[12]

Perhaps there is little cause for wonder that this should have been so. England had kept begging Archbishop Maréchal to summon a Provincial Council to introduce uniform legislation for the Church. This Maréchal would never consent to do; so the First Provincial Council was not called until 1829, when James Whitfield had succeeded as Metropolitan.[13] And when Whitfield was pressed to summon the Second Provincial Council he had promised should meet four years later, he kept putting the matter off, until England approached Rome direct, with the result that the Council was ordered.[14] All this

11 Guilday, *England*, Vol. I, p. 532.

12 *Ibid.*, Vol. I, p. 537.

13 Whitfield was born in England in 1770, but was not ordained until 1809. Coming to Baltimore in 1817, he specially interested himself in work for the negroes, and was made coadjutor to Maréchal in 1828, succeeding to the see the following year. Whitfield was a man of considerable private means. But he had no great ability and, though without Maréchal's French leanings, was not at all pro-Irish. He did, according to his lights, what had to be done, but was never very closely in touch with the true needs of his adopted country.

14 It is worth remarking that these Councils of Baltimore, through their inclusion in the collection published at Maria Laach, have had

did not exactly endear England to the Archbishop. As Kenrick was to put it in the letter to Paul Cullen[15] already cited, "The greatest evils with which this country has been afflicted, are attributable to good men." The remark was directed against the French bishops; it has some application to Whitfield too.

It is a sad but humanly understandable story. One wishes that the opposition had not degenerated, as it sometimes did, into mere petty spite. Thus when Whitfield was consecrated, the Bishops of Cincinnati and Boston—the two Fenwicks, cousins and members of an old Maryland family—and John England were not invited. This was because they were not members of Maréchal's faction.

But Conwell of Philadelphia was also offended with England. He disapproved of the Charleston Constitution. Still more did he disapprove of what he considered England's intrusion into the affairs of Philadelphia. "With respect to the Schism [that of Hogan]," he wrote to Maréchal in 1824, "I think nothing can support it any longer if Dr. England would have the goodness to desist from interfering." We can sympathize with the harassed Bishop's irritation over the contumacy itself and the war of pamphlets it provoked. England's were convenient shoulders on which to throw the blame. Conwell would not acknowledge his own incapacity. Nor did he see, what Dr. Guilday points out, that "the appointment of incompetent prelates had lessened the respect the clergy ordinarily had for Rome."[16]

As a matter of fact England had been most careful not to see any of those implicated in the schism while he was passing through Philadelphia. It was instead Hogan who followed England to New York where, on neutral ground, there was no impropriety in their meeting. England may be accused with some justice of lack of judgment, of being too easily taken in by the specious rascality of Hogan, but at least he observed

---

a remarkable influence on conciliar legislation and Catholic life throughout the world.

[15] England tried to persuade Cullen to become his coadjutor, but he remained in Ireland where he died as Cardinal-Archbishop of Dublin.

[16] *England*, Vol. II, p. 103. As for the pamphlets, Finotti has 36 pages of his bibliography devoted to them, though his list is probably incomplete. Some of them were written by Matthew Carey, though he afterwards abandoned Hogan in disgust.

the episcopal courtesies towards Conwell. If he did harm in this matter, it was because he had so beautiful a trust in the inherent goodness of human nature. It was he, after all, who had subdued Gallagher and Browne and made them tolerably respectable members of his clergy. He hoped he could do the same with Hogan.

Hogan appealed to him because he believed the framer of the Charleston Constitution would be sympathetic. Conwell, however, distrusted the young Bishop as one who had justified trusteeism, failing to see that what England had really done was to leave it alive—with all its fangs drawn. But he suspected, with some reason, that Hogan might be brought to submit except for being encouraged by what was going on in the South and by the personal contact he had established with England. It was a tangle of cross-purposes in which nobody —perhaps not even Hogan himself—should be altogether blamed.

L'affaire Hogan need not long detain us: I would not deal with it at all were it not for the fact that it has a feature distinguishing it from similar fantastic episodes, so many of which were associated with Philadelphia.[17] The difference is

---

[17] Though it is of no great historical importance, I cannot refrain from giving the account of "Crazy Norah" which is contained in Finotti's *Bibliographia Catholica Americana* (pp. 172–173) and is quoted from a local Catholic paper for 1865, the date of her death: "She sported an immense *stove-pipe* [hat] . . . which, together with a long woollen cloak, and the inevitable accompaniment of a couple of huge carpet-bags stowed full of novels and bills for collection, set off her gaunt, raw-boned figure rather conspicuously. . . . She was the daughter of Mr. Gower, a respectable farmer, Co. Limerick, Ireland. After his death she came to this country. . . . She espoused Mr. Hogan's cause, but when she saw the officers of the law, who had been called upon to quell the riot, trampling on the sanctuary, her reason gave way, and from that time she wandered in the streets . . . an especial favorite with children. . . . Her ostensible business was that of collector. . . . She would present her bill, and, on payment being refused, would take up her station, opposite the debtor's house, surrounded by a crowd of children. . . . Shame would soon bring the debtor to terms, and Norah would hand over to the principal the amount, *minus her commission*. . . . The Litany of the Saints was her favorite prayer. She frequently repeated it over insolvent debtors . . . enumerated among the celestial inhabitants her *grandmother*. Up to a few days of her death, . . . a regular attendant at St. John's. . . . She was buried from her sister's house: a hearse and a solitary carriage composing the funeral cortege." It is not only inter-

this: the first schisms were instigated by newly arrived clerics who, having secured a following, persuaded lay trustees to oust their pastors to insinuate themselves; these were succeeded by the plot for setting up an Independent Catholic Church— a plot which was fundamentally a clerical scheme, though ostensibly emanating from laymen; but in Hogan's case the priest would have yielded to the Bishop except for trustees who would not permit him to do so. It therefore marks a new stage in trusteeism.

William Hogan was a stage-Irishman, one of those weird creatures who do exist, though they need a foreign scene for their setting. He had come to this country in 1819 under a cloud, but all that people noticed about him was his glib tongue and his winning way—especially with women. A contemporary description quoted by Monsignor Kirlin[18] says that in his complexion were blended the lily and the rose—and this wonderful complexion was not impaired it would seem even by the liberal use of the bottle. His beautiful head of hair was also remarked, and the ladies thought (perhaps because of this) that he had a "spiritual effulgence" about him. Hard-boiled men were disposed to set him down as a dandy and a fop, and even the kindly England described him as "deficient in the most common branches of an English education." He made up for this by blarney, visiting the ladies in their pews and patting their children on the head. And even men had to acknowledge that he was a good talker. That counted for more than anything else in a priest in those days—with some people.

When he first got at odds with Bishop Conwell, he proposed to his cousin that they offer themselves to the Protestant Bishop Hobart of New York, Mother Seton's rector in the days before her conversion. In the end he married in 1824 a widow of twenty who had some means and, after her death, married another well-to-do widow. He became a lawyer; he was mixed

esting in itself but reveals something as to the atmosphere of Philadelphia at the time. That Crazy Norah is still not quite forgotten appears in a poem about her in a recent privately printed book of poems by William Bacon Evans, of which this is one stanza:

> "To young and old,
>   Abroad she wails,
> 'Keep tight your hold
>   On God's coat-tails!' "

[18] *Op. cit.*, p. 215.

up in the malodorous Maria Monk matter; he was United States Consul in Cuba in 1843; and he died in apostasy at Nashua, New Hampshire, in 1848.[19]

John England was at first taken in by Hogan, thinking he perceived good in the fellow. Out of pure kindheartedness he thought to re-establish him by receiving him into his own diocese. But this was on condition—one accepted by Hogan with tears and on bended knees—that so long as he was in Philadelphia he refrain from saying Mass. Within forty-eight hours that promise was broken—whereupon England added his suspension to that of Conwell.

Hogan was unfortunately by no means the first clerical apostate in America. While Carroll was still Vicar-Apostolic a relative of his, an ex-Jesuit named Wharton, had left the Church and married. But he committed his crime in a fairly gentlemanly sort of a way and showed no special bitterness towards the Church. And in Augusta, Georgia, the local priest, John Egan, had married in 1819 and had then proceeded to make public attacks on the doctrine of the Real Presence. But these defections were of no great historical importance: Hogan's was; if it was important for nothing else it throws a good deal of light on conditions that led to the drawing up of the Charleston Constitution. As England wrote to Maréchal in 1822, when defending the innovation he was about to introduce: "Hogan was my adviser to this; the unfortunate young man told me when he was, I believe, disposed to follow my advise, that he never intended to oppose the Bishop, but that the Trustees had prevailed upon him to do so. . . . With tears in his eyes he besought me, if I valued the religion of Jesus Christ, never to suffer a lay trustee in my diocese, be his piety what it may, or the restrictions under which he is placed ever so great. He told me that if he left Philadelphia, as he was determined, the Bishop would have no peace; for though he may obtain good trustees one year, they would be either supplemented or worried out or be made bad before the next year." In the same letter England expresses the opinion that "Hogan is not the author of this evil, though he should leave Philadelphia, the evil would not be removed. It is the natural consequence of the system upon which Catholicity has been established in Philadelphia. The same evil is in New York, the same is here, and I suspect you

[19] Finotti (*op. cit.*, p. 138), however, says it was at Peterborough, and in a tavern.

are not free from it in Baltimore, guarded as your by-laws appear to be."

There is nevertheless another side to the story. Hogan cannot be held to have been merely the victim of his trustees. These were in turn stirred up by clerics. For example, Shea tells us[20] of two strange priests who constituted themselves advisers in canon law to the trustees of St. Mary's. One was an unattached Franciscan named Rico who gave out that he had been "Vicar-general to the Armies of Spain." In Philadelphia he was not exercising any sacred office but kept a cigar store. The other learned authority on canon law was a priest named Mier who had barely escaped the Inquisition in Mexico, from which country he had fled to England to fall in with Blanco White, the apostate Spanish priest who is still remembered as the author of a sonnet Coleridge vastly admired. As Mier was known to have used pulque instead of wine at Mass, his notions of ecclesiastical propriety could not have been of the strictest. He argued that as Hogan had arrived in America with faculties from his bishop in Ireland, he had a perfect right to exercise his priesthood in what was a missionary country, regardless of what the Bishop in Philadelphia thought.

The remedy for trusteeism, as England saw it, lay in a Provincial Council and uniform regulations for all the dioceses. As his advice was not taken, we must regretfully conclude that Maréchal as well as Conwell cannot escape all condemnation. They failed to act. This does not mean that the only possible remedy was the one England had applied to Charleston. When at last the Council met in 1829 it did not accept England's solution, though it explicitly exempted Charleston from the legislation it adopted. What can, however, hardly be denied is that Maréchal's refusal to call a Council helped to prolong the wretched state of affairs.

It is a great pity that England did not live to be translated to one of the great dioceses of the North. He was lost in Charleston, although his achievements there stand as a perpetual inspiration to the American Church. Kenrick, whose task it was to straighten out the muddle into which Conwell had brought Philadelphia, wrote with extraordinary generosity to Cullen in 1834: "I would at any moment resign my mitre to make place for him. This I authorize you to make known to the Sacred Congn."[21] It was not to be. Most of the Ameri-

[20] *Op. cit.*, Vol. III, pp. 236–237.
[21] Guilday, *England*, Vol. I, p. 534.

can bishops felt quite differently. The last place they would have liked to see England was in Philadelphia. They were all good men, but many of them were out of touch with American needs. That is why I set down here an estimate of England's work written by his friend William George Read, the famous lawyer of Baltimore. "When I style him 'the great apostle of the western world,' I mean only to say that he was the first to make the Catholic religion respectable in the eyes of the American *public*." In this he anticipated Cardinal Gibbons who, like himself, was sent at the age of thirty-four to the South as a bishop and who came to be regarded, by the nation at large, as the very embodiment of American Catholicism.

But though England understood the genius of America, his one excursion into American politics was not altogether happy. Before I relate it, it should be remembered that, just as the ending of the second war with Great Britain introduced a new era, when the attention of the country was given to domestic rather than to foreign problems—a political event which, happening to coincide with the death of Carroll, was also the beginning of a new era in ecclesiastical history—so the "Jacksonian Revolution" of 1829 was, among other things, the defeat of a man who represented the old Puritan tradition. The Irish had their reasons for rejoicing in the downfall of the Federalists, who had attempted discriminatory naturalization laws, and Catholics could not be expected to grieve overmuch at the elimination of John Quincy Adams.[22] Naturally therefore, John England, who entered so fully into the sentiments of the Southern states, was inclined to support Van Buren, the Democrat, against the Whig, Harrison. Unluckily he discovered, or imagined he had discovered, that Van Buren had supported the attempt to exclude a Catholic member from the New York state legislature in 1806. When it was shown that England was mistaken, he withdrew his charge. In spite of this an effort was made to exhibit England as a Harrison backer. As "Tippecanoe" was being supported by the Native-Americans, and was therefore likely to lose Catholic votes, England, it was hoped by his managers, would serve to hold at least some of the Catholic voters in line. The whole election was ridiculous and has been called the "apotheosis of tom-

[22] An attempt was made, however, to placate Catholics by putting some of them on local tickets in Maryland. (See Shea, *op. cit.*, Vol. III, p. 104.)

foolery," with accusations on the one side, that Van Buren used scent and wore stays and silken underwear and lived a life sybaritic to the point of "sissiness" and, on the other side, that Harrison was an uneducated backwoodsman who inhabited a log-cabin and drank nothing but hard cider. The "he-man" argument prevailed. "Van, Van is a used up man" destroyed him. Miniature log-cabins and cider-barrels became Harrison's most effective emblems, and insured his election. In all this nonsense what Bishop England had to say counted for very little. Though he switched to Van Buren he refused to take any active part in the political contest except to denounce the bigotry of the Native-Americans. "Tippecanoe" got in, promptly died, and "Tyler too" succeeded to the presidency.

The Native-American Movement did not reach its height for another decade. By then John England, whose voice and pen would have been of such inestimable service to the Catholic cause, had passed to his reward. Here was at least one Irishman whom all men honored both as a great Catholic and a great American. In 1842 he died and was buried beside his sister Joanna in Charleston cathedral.

CHAPTER FOURTEEN

THE FRONTIER

Inspired in a way Macaulay could never have intended when he wrote his review of von Ranke's *History of the Papacy*, I have often meditated an apologue matching Boccaccio's fable of the Jew who was converted by visiting Rome and becoming convinced that an institution that could survive such flagrant corruptions must be divine. Macaulay's thesis, as everybody knows, is that the Catholic Church has survived —escaping even that period at the opening of the nineteenth century when nearly everybody expected it to collapse—because of its marvellous organization. Catholics of course smile at this, not only because they know the life of the Church to be supernaturally guaranteed, but because (if they have seen much of the working of the machine) they are somewhat sceptical about the suppositious Catholic efficiency. The triumphs of the Church have often been achieved in the face of almost unbelievable muddle and dilatoriness on the part both of Rome and the local ecclesiastical authorities. The hierarchic structure of the Church does indeed give it strength and cohesion. But the details of organization, on their human side, have only too frequently been mismanaged, and Catholics have often shown a disposition to rely so confidently upon God's promises as to have no need to use ordinary intelligence. Almost any Protestant church, in short, is better managed than the average Catholic parish. And much the same thing is commonly true as we work upwards to the Ordinary and the Vatican itself. It might almost be said that it is Catholic *inefficiency* that proves the Church divine.

What must be granted, however, by everybody is that, though the Church has made many errors of general policy, as well as errors of detail, its catholicity induces a certain wideness of vision. It knows its mission to be to the whole world, even at such times as it fails to carry out this mission. Whatever golden opportunities the American Church has, for its part, missed—that of evangelizing the negro, for instance —we can see how clearly it recognized, when Carroll's original diocese was divided into smaller sections, that despite the fewness of priests, it must at all costs push on to the Frontier. Right in the backwoods at Bardstown, Kentucky, a diocese was created in 1808.

Even before the war which ended in the wresting of Canada from France, groups of settlers had crossed the Alleghenies. And they continued to go when, after the peace of 1763, the British government attempted to prohibit the occupation of the lands to which various colonies had set up claims. Though the prohibition was not intended to be more than a temporary measure to maintain order—for sometimes several colonies claimed the same territory—and to protect the Indians and the fur trade, it was resented and had much to do with bringing on the Revolution. So, for that matter, did the land question have much to do with the war of 1812. The "War Hawks" had their eyes on Canada, and though it was officially given out that the American invasion of the country was merely part of the military strategy, Canada would assuredly have been annexed had the United States decisively won the war. It was the true, but unacknowledged, *casus belli*.

After the Revolution there remained great irritants to the young Republic. England did not withdraw its troops from the West until 1796, on the pretext that the United States had not fulfilled some of the treaty obligations. But, after all, the withdrawal was eventually made. The significant fact is that, almost immediately afterwards, in 1803, the country doubled its extent by the bargain-counter purchase of Louisiana. However much Jefferson doubted the constitutionality of the transaction, the times—and the basic notions of Jeffersonianism itself—demanded unbounded room for the founding of what was thought of as an agrarian civilization.

America was then, and expected to remain, a nation of villages. There were only six towns of any size, of which Philadelphia, the largest, had about thirty thousand inhabitants. If one added the people living in New York, Boston, Charleston, Baltimore and Salem, one would still have no more than three percent of the population of the United States. The rest was wholly rural.

It was to extend this rural domain that the first settlers crossed the mountains. Yet in 1790 the West, which twenty-five years later was to have more than a million and a half inhabitants, had hardly a hundred thousand. The immigration that came after the Revolution of course increased the population of the cities too—Charleston alone remaining stationary—but the rate of increase in the West was far greater. There it was 400,000 by the end of the century and two and a half millions—or a quarter of the population of the whole United States—by 1820. Through the Cumberland Gap from south-western Virginia and thence to the Ohio River (Daniel Boone's trail), from the Potomac to the Monongahela, and by the route from Philadelphia and Baltimore to Pittsburgh they poured in, as they did also along the Genesee road from Albany to Buffalo. The West appealed at once to the romantic and those who hoped to better their fortunes.

All this confronted the Church with a challenge. Most of the original settlers of the West had been French, though small groups had gone from Maryland to Kentucky in 1785, and even earlier, in search of a greater religious freedom. Now these Catholic settlements were in danger of being swamped and swept away by the sudden Protestant inundation. Already their religious practice had become feeble, for after the war with France the religious orders had withdrawn until now there were only two secular priests in the entire region whose chief villages—they could not be called towns—were Cahokia, Vincennes and Kaskaskia. When Flaget, who was afterwards to be the first Bishop of Bardstown, arrived at Vincennes in 1792, he found the church falling to pieces from neglect and recorded that out of nearly seven hundred souls "only twelve could be induced to approach holy communion during the Christmas festivities." Furthermore, many of the French, feeling themselves to have been tricked by the American authorities, were migrating to Spanish territory on the other side of the Mississippi. It was to save these remnants and to recall them to Catholic practice that Carroll laid his western plans. The work had to be done all over again by men sent from the East, for it is evident, from the correspondence that passed between Bishop Plessis of Quebec and Carroll, that Gibault, however great his services in winning the West for the United States, was not a particularly edifying pastor. In any case he and the other French priest now left could not cope with the situation.

As part of the great trek went priests, travelling like the rest of the migrants much of the way on foot, riding horse-back when they could, floating down the Ohio on flat-boats, and sharing the dangers and hardships of the people. Kentucky, Tennessee, the Ohio valley and the Illinois country were filling like so many cups.

Relatively few of those who went out were newly arrived immigrants. These did not make good backwoodsmen, even if their sons often did. One had to be thoroughly American to enjoy playing the rôle of Daniel Boone. All Americans, in fact, dreamed of themselves in that rôle, as many of them still do. If the life was rough, log-cabins could be made fairly comfortable. Nobody was looking for elegance: the westerners professed to prefer their deer-skin trousers and moccasins to the habiliments of the effete East. Their isolation brought about wild sprees and fights when they met together; and yet among them were many women of some education who taught —as did Andrew Johnson's wife at a later date—their husbands to read. Never was the West quite so wild as romance has often made it. But one thing at least is certain: nowhere were the "self-evident" truths of the Declaration of Independence so evident as upon the Frontier. Its hard-drinking, hard-fighting communities were notable schools of practical democracy.

The Frontier colored the American imagination and did much to develop the American character. Some would even make it the most important factor in that development. Frederick Jackson Turner's theory, first advanced as part of "scientific" history in 1893, caught the country in the most propitious mood for its acceptance. Stated in its most radical form it was that "an American is a born enemy of all European peoples"; and this illiberal doctrine became instantly popular in academic circles because it permitted highbrows to wallow without shame in the self-righteous self-sufficiency whose other name is isolationism. Fifty—forty—thirty—perhaps even ten years ago it flattered Americans to hear that they had attained their uniquely stalwart and virtuous character by taming the wilderness. There was nothing—or hardly anything—that could be learned from decadent Europe.

Since that time the Frontier Theory has steadily lost ground. Daniel Boone was no doubt a stout fellow, but he is not the most representative—and still less the best—American. We may reasonably admire the resource of the frontiersman without decorating his rather limited good qualities. He served his time and passed. He was only one, and not the most important of the factors that have gone to the building up of America. All our mythology need not center around Paul Bunyan. There were to be found among the pioneers—as is testified by the preservation of classical works of English literature by descendants often unable to read them—men of wide cultivation. Whatever rudeness there was is scarcely to be thought of as admirable. In any event it was modified by European and Eastern American contacts. Let us rather remember how extremely well-read a body of men were the Founding Fathers—who were, after all, the first and most adequate exponents of the American idea. And though it came to be the American fashion to regard cultivation as somehow effeminate, the rail-splitter Abraham Lincoln (whatever his appeal to the electorate in that capacity) had not only a first-class mind but a first-class literary style.

Turner's theory is therefore now somewhat flyblown. It leaves so much out of account—including what France and Spain had already done to tame the wilderness and the civilizing work the missionaries were to continue. If we look through Turner's eyes we see a backwoodsman happily reverting to semi-savagery, whereas the truth is that—although there was a certain amount of such reversion—the cultural progress of European civilization, only slightly modified by frontier conditions, persisted. The primitive life soon passed and was never primitive from choice. In any event various factors operated to prevent the degeneration into the mere rough boorishness that was always possible. One of the most important factors was that the settlers came so soon into touch with Catholic priests, many of them *émigrés* from the French Revolution, and nearly all of them men of considerable learning. One might cite Loras as an instance. He became the first Bishop of Dubuque in 1837. His fine manners remained as fine as ever in the backwoods. When he visited Ireland in 1849 the Abbot of Mount Melleray said that they surpassed even those of Archbishop Murray, and Queen Victoria said that Murray was the most elegant courtier she had ever met.[1] Hardly a typical backwoodsman, of course; but there were others like him.

What really arose on the Frontier was a life not radically different from that of the villages of the Atlantic seaboard (or even of Europe) but a life simplified out of necessity and which disappeared as soon as conditions made this possible. Nor did American democracy originate in the West, however much it may have been affected by the western temper; it originated in the stately homes of Virginian aristocrats and

[1] See Hoffman, *The Church Founders of the North West*, p. 264.

the less stately but still dignified homes of New England lawyers and merchants. Turner's theory is little more than a fanciful notion that appeals to the immature imagination. It is the small boy peeping out of the pedant. This glorification of the Frontier may be all very well for Tom Sawyers. But how dreary, in sober fact, was the life of Hannibal, Missouri! Only a genius could gild it; only a dull man can now think it beautiful.

Fortunately the Frontier was not nearly so uncouth as it has been painted. It is, however, true enough that the rigors of the life there and the war of 1812 combined to give America —not only in the West but to some extent in the East as well— an aggressive truculence which was perhaps a useful sort of article to have just then but which can scarcely be described as admirable *per se*. The Revolution had left in the country a large element—perhaps a third—strongly Anglophil, and an equally large element (that of the radicals) strongly Francophil. This was one of the main causes of the feud between Hamilton and Jefferson. It explained, though it does not excuse, the moody and embittered career of that shady grandson of Jonathan Edwards, Aaron Burr. But after the war of 1812 Americans thought of themselves as simply Americans. Franklin, when he heard somebody refer to the war of independence, commented, "Say, rather, the war of the Revolution: the war of Independence has yet to be fought." The second war, inglorious as it was, proved to be just that, because it engendered so much bad feeling against England as to set Americans free from any sentimental attachment. Some such catalysis was needed. Though neither side won the war, the firm conviction of the majority of Americans in their "victory" had the moral effect of raising the national morale. This feeling was greatly accentuated by the conquest of the Frontier.

But if it gave America a further thirst for personal as well as political liberty, I think I shall not be unjust in saying that it brought into existence a type of American who was not a very pleasant person. Dickens, who made his first visit to the United States in 1841, full of a vast vague enthusiasm for the young Republic, was so thoroughly disgusted by the exploitation of immigrants by the Mississippi land companies as to be so indiscreet as to set down his impressions. Yet allowing for the exaggeration and caricature habitual in Dickens, we must believe that he encountered many Jefferson Bricks who declared that the libation of human liberty has often to be quaffed in human blood. Chateaubriand, writing in 1832 after the revolutions in France, Belgium and Poland, said, "We fall asleep to the sound of kingdoms crashing in the night, and every morning they are swept up before our doors." The American who witnessed these happenings complacently assured himself that the decadent old world was now learning something from the new. It heightened his mood of supreme confidence, and also his contempt for Europe. The crassness, the brassiness with which Europe, for its part, came to credit America dates from this time, and that false idea persisted long after the American of the aggressive species was about as extinct as the bison.

In all this, however, we must remember, what Turner himself pointed out, that there were several frontiers—the missionary had one, the trapper another, the soldier another again, and the farmer his. Or as Father Fintan Walker has put it in one of the many excellent monographs now appearing that reveal something of the hitherto obscured work accomplished by the missions of the West, "The frontier movement in American history may be looked upon as a line, a region, and a process."[2] It is with the process that I am principally concerned.

It was fortunate that the evangelization of the Frontier was so largely in the hands of French priests, with whom, for our purposes, we may group Belgians like Nerinckx of the impossible and unforgettable name. For though the presence of foreigners did no doubt accentuate, in the minds of non-Catholics, the notion that Catholicism was an exotic imported product, they could afford to be tolerant, as the missionaries were primarily there for the benefit of the scattered French communities. As yet, there were few Irish in the West to make the racial protests already being heard in the Eastern cities. Nor did the "wandering friars" who so troubled the peace in Philadelphia and elsewhere consider that the backwoods provided an adequate outlet for their distinguished talents. The field was accordingly left to extremely zealous Frenchmen who were willing to renounce all hope of promotion, or of an easy life, or of scholarly seclusion, in order to save neglected souls. Nobody envied them the lot they had chosen. An advertisement for recruits for the American missions circulated at this time in France read. "We offer you: No salary; No

[2] *The Catholic Church in the Meeting of Two Frontiers: the Southern Illinois Country*, p. 4.

Recompense; No Holidays; No Pension. But: Much Hard Work; a Poor Dwelling; Few Consolations; Many Disappointments; Frequent Sickness; a Violent or Lonely Death; an Unknown Grave."[3] If this deliberately painted the picture in darker colors than was necessary, it was because only heroes were wanted, and heroes are summoned by an appeal to heroism.

French priests and bishops were, as we have already noticed, frequently criticized at this time. Smarting under it, De Courcy came to the defence of his fellow-countrymen. "Surely," he says, "the ecclesiastical spirit that animated them, their knowledge of the governmental traditions of the Church, were in a Flaget, a Cheverus, a Maréchal, qualities far more essential than a greater or less elegance in speaking the language of Milton." Without fully accepting that point—for the language of Milton was more important than De Courcy is disposed to admit, and the "governmental traditions of the Church" were sometimes understood in a sense too narrow to apply to a new country—it may be gratefully granted that in the West, at all events, the French priests were the best men that could have been supplied, as they were almost the only men who would consent to go. Carroll's first biographer, Brent, has written, "If in many instances the French Revolution has been fatal to religion, this country promises to derive advantage from it." That is an understatement: without the French *émigré* priests Catholicism could hardly have survived in some parts of America. While we must always bear in mind the work done by the Sulpicians in their seminary and at Mount St. Mary's, and the spell Cheverus laid on Boston, it was in the West that Frenchmen found their most fruitful field of labor.

It would of course be easy to make too much of the French-Irish antagonism. Against it the authors of *The Story of the Mountain* quote an unidentified writer who points out that at the Council of 1829, "Bp. England has chosen for his theologian Simon Bruté, of Emmitsburg; Bp. Flaget, Francis Patrick Kenrick—an Irishman chooses a Frenchman, a Frenchman an Irishman."[4] But this was among great men who, despite their general policy, were above petty racial jealousies; antagonism was, after all, very widespread in the East. In the West there was no room for it. There the French missionaries

[3] Hoffman, *op. cit.*, p. 23.
[4] Vol. I, p. 218.

had a free hand and were, at first, working mainly among their own people. So that John Gilmary Shea, though his leanings are never very pro-French, quotes with approval from a pastoral Archbishop Eccleston addressed to his flock in 1841: "Why is the solemn chant of the ancient liturgy heard far beyond the Alleghenies? Why are the prairies of the distant West dotted with Catholic temples, while in Virginia the very name is scarcely known, or known but to be abused?" The answer is that in the West the efforts of the devoted missionaries were not as a rule hampered by internecine war. Such non-Gallic groups of Catholics as there were in those regions—and even before the Revolution some Marylanders had migrated to Kentucky to escape persecution—were relatively free of racial prejudice.

There were, however, difficulties of another sort. Immediately after the Revolutionary War, as Shea remarks, "Military expeditions treated Catholic settlers in the West as though they were hostile Indians. This was especially the case in the wanton destruction of the village of Ouiatenon by the forces under General Scott in 1791."[5] But these happenings were political rather than religious. Their friendly association with the Indians was now proving a disadvantage to the French, who were despised for the very reason they should have been admired. The policy was to drive the red man beyond the Missouri to those plains where it was then supposed the white man could not support himself.[6] As friends of the Indians the French were, for a time, under suspicion. It was in vain that Carroll appealed to the Federal authorities to adopt a policy of religious protection: this was smugly ruled out as involving Federal interference in religious matters. Consequently any white group that sided with the Indians had to pay the penalty.

The United States did not emerge with luster either on this occasion or on most of the others in which it came into contact with the aborigines. The warmest friends of the Indians saw clearly that they were doomed before the irresistible onrush of the American settlers, and that nobody could do anything about it. The Indians were thought of as vermin to be exterminated.

At this period, however, there was something to be said in favor of the whites. Because the English had not yet completely withdrawn from the Western outposts the American

[5] *Op. cit.*, Vol. II, pp. 464, 465.
[6] See Paxson, *History of the American Frontier*, p. 277.

settlers not unnaturally supposed that any opposition raised by the Indians was inspired by the British.[7] There was probably some foundation for this suspicion. The confederation formed by Tecumseh in 1809 did at any rate receive encouragement from Canada. But the ideas of this chief and his brother "The Prophet" were noble. In order to preserve their lands from the rapacious whites they organized and—marvellous to relate—even managed to persuade their people to stop drinking so that their morale might be strengthened. Their intention, however, was not to eject the settlers but to protect their own interests. It would have been possible for the government to have reached a *modus vivendi* with them, and this in simple justice and humanity should have been done.

The cause of Tecumseh was hopeless from the start. He could muster only 4,000 braves against the 200,000 settlers in the Ohio valley. The result we know: General Harrison took advantage of the absence of Tecumseh to force hostilities and won the victory of Tippecanoe which was to become his rallying cry when he was elected to the presidency nearly thirty years later. The policy of Indian eradication was popular. As Morison and Commager have written: "Tecumseh's league would have been formed and Tippecanoe would have been fought if there had not been a single Englishman in Canada. Unfortunately, however, it is not the truth but what people believe, that makes history. The notion that every defensive move of the Indians was due to British machinations not only served to cover and excuse the frontiersmen's lust for Canada, but to convince thousands of people who desired no extension of territory that the only safety for the West lay in driving British power from North America."[8] On this pretext between 1795 and 1809 the Indians had been robbed of close on to fifty millions of acres. It was the easiest thing in the world to make the chiefs drunk and then get them to sign away their hunting grounds. That Tecumseh should attempt to interfere with that happy process was intolerable. He was therefore crushed.

In that crushing the Catholic settlers, who were mostly French, took little if any part. Rather they suffered from it themselves, because they had been on good terms with the Indians. In such circumstances it was impossible, at the moment, to evangelize even those tribes who were anxious to have

[7] See *op. cit.*, p. 161.
[8] *The Growth of the American Republic*, Vol. I, pp. 309–310.

Black Robes among them again. But once the Indians had been subdued, all the whites of the West found themselves in a common bond, and the new arrivals were too busy with other affairs to do other than accept with a reasonable amount of tolerance the fact that the French should have what they looked upon as the French religion. In the new life which was so closely occupied with the clearing of their settlements and the establishment of their families, Protestant Americans tended to forget their former bigotry. A kind of rough brotherhood was engendered once the westward trek had got under way. The French, being whites, were included in it.

Protestant ministers did not have much standing on the Frontier. Timothy Flint afterwards bitterly complained that he had been invited to the West for no other purpose than to "boost" a settlement. "A minister, a church, a school, are words to flourish in an advertisement to sell lots." Yet the very fact that this method of promotion was deemed advisable indicates that the West was already seeking to appear civilized and did not confine itself to the leatherstocking virtues. As few ministers could be persuaded to go, lay preachers, who were hunters or trappers or farmers during the week, made some attempt to perform sacred functions. The character of their ministrations may be imagined. Even the formally ordained ministers who made their way to the West were usually of the type that went in for orgiastic camp-meetings. These and "revivals" were social outlets for the people. Then group frenzy descended. Men and women got the "jerks"; they barked like dogs; and only too often these mystical manifestations ended in gross sexuality. In contrast to this, it was obvious that Catholicism was a severely intellectual religion. It was also obvious to everybody that the Catholic priest was a scholar and a gentleman. Where the itinerant lay exhorter or minister was addressed as "Preacher," the Catholic missionary was addressed as "Priest." The title of "Father" was not yet in common use; even in clerical correspondence the usual title is "Mister." But "Priest" represented a recognition among Protestants that the Catholic man of God was in some undefined but unmistakable way different from the Methodist and Baptist rabble-rouser.

Catholics accommodated themselves, to some extent, however, to the religious conditions prevalent on the Frontier. Because priests were few, and because they could visit the settlements only rarely for the saying of Mass and the hearing of confessions, laymen were often appointed to read prayers on Sundays, to administer baptism, and to register marriages. It was perhaps inevitable that some of the men who read the Mass prayers for these little groups, should take it upon themselves to expound the Gospel of the day or to offer their own homilies. We hear some strange things in Sister Gilbert Kelly's *Catholic Immigration Projects*—of one Stallo, for whom Stallostown was named, being threatened with an interdict for exceeding his functions; of Father Kundell's Slavonic colony where the services were made more interesting with brass bands and gunpowder. Not always were the laymen, even when they kept within due bounds as to the reading of prayers, very exemplary characters. Bishop Spalding records in his *Flaget*[9] how at the close of 1809 a priest who visited Vincennes (soon to be the seat of a bishop) was obliged to order Zepherin Chesnet, the officiating layman, to do nothing more of a sacred character. At the same time it must be acknowledged that at this stage of missionary activity laymen did good service—however imperfect may have been their qualifications—in keeping the Faith alive.

Long before the erection of a bishopric at Bardstown in 1808 a handful of French had been working in the backwoods of the West. It was because the Sulpician, Benedict Joseph Flaget, had been in the Indiana territory from 1792 to 1795 that he was now sent out as bishop. He knew the conditions there. It was in vain that he and his Sulpician colleagues protested to Carroll against the appointment, saying that they had prayed God to avert it: Carroll's answer was that undoubtedly the Holy Father had also prayed in making it. Nor was an appeal to Emery any more successful, though Flaget went to France to throw himself at his Superior's feet. Emery's first words were, "My Lord Bishop, you should be in your diocese!" The only comfort he got was the assurance that he would still be accounted a Sulpician and have three Masses said for the repose of his soul by every member of the Society when he died.[10]

Bardstown was the beginning of a new hierarchical organization that by 1840 was to stretch as far West as Dubuque and that ten years later had three bishoprics on the Pacific coast. So rapid were the strides that by then a loud outcry was made that Rome was carrying out a gigantic plot to capture the en-

9 P. 120.
10 Herbermann, *The Sulpicians in the United States*, p. 146.

tire Mississippi valley. It was to be the favorite theme of Lyman Beecher after he had gone to Cincinnati in the early thirties. Popery and despotism were allies: Catholicism in the West threatened the very existence of American republicanism.[11] If not the precipitant of the Nativist storm by then gathering—for that was caused by the influx of the Catholic Irish to the cities of the East—the Western "conspiracy" was useful to belabor the Church. It became such only because of what the Western bishops and their clergy achieved. It could be used as such because so many of the later immigrants were Catholics and were therefore imagined to be hand-in-glove with European autocracy.

Yet the poverty of the first missionaries was extreme. When Bishop DuBourg received a present of a bed from a friend who was shocked to find on what kind of a cot he slept, the letter of thanks read: "My palace is too small to admit so decorative a piece of furniture. You will therefore, my friend, allow me to exchange it for something more useful. Bread is what I need, I and my household. Everything here is unreasonably high and I dare not treat myself to the smallest piece of furniture. Would you believe that we have but a single writing desk, which passes from one member of the household to the other!"[12] Flaget after his consecration had to confess to Carroll that he did not have the money to carry him to Bardstown; it had to be scraped together from a few Baltimore friends. And though details of this sort come through only by accident—for bishops and priests were not much given to self-pity and, in any event, were too busy to leave a record of personal matters for posterity—their situation can be pieced together. When Flaget, accompanied by a couple of priests and three seminarians, arrived at Bardstown, having made their way on foot, except when they were in an Ohio flat-boat, nothing in the shape of a church awaited them. As O'Gorman puts it, "His installation in his cathedral was a fiction at law." He was less fortunate even than Portier, the first Bishop of Mobile, who twenty years later arrived in his episcopal city to find a wooden cathedral fifty feet by twenty. In Kentucky and Tennessee there were ten small log-cabin churches and six thousand Catholics, scattered here and there and attended by six priests who had to be continually moving in circuit. But

[11] See Billington, *Protestant Crusade*, p. 70 *et passim*.
[12] Herbermann, *op. cit.*, p. 176.

word also reached Flaget of a few churches at northern points —at Chicago and Prairie du Chien for example—and all that territory, though very far off, fell within the jurisdiction of Bardstown.

The Bishop's "palace" was a log-cabin, sixteen feet square. It contained nothing but a bed (the priest who shared the room with Flaget had a mattress on the floor), six chairs, a couple of tables, and some planks nailed to the wall as bookshelves. Nevertheless by 1811 we find the seminarians building a cathedral sixty-five feet long, and also the Nazareth convent. As everybody enjoyed the poverty and hard work there is no need for us to be sorry for them. But not once did Flaget ever have occasion to refer to the excellent French cookery book Emery had kindly given him when he left France under command to become a bishop! As for work, he took as his motto: *In coelo quies*; there would be time enough for rest when he got there. His salary was two hundred dollars a year. All this for the man whom Henry Clay called "the best representative of royalty off a throne"![13]

The life of the Bishop was largely a matter of going in search of Catholics, many of whom, for lack of a priest, had abandoned the practice of religion. This meant incessant horseback journeys. Badin, one of his priests, estimates that he must have ridden a hundred thousand miles while working in Kentucky, and Flaget did his share of this and more. Yet as bishop he contrived to get some help. Louis Philippe, whom he had met in exile in Cuba, remembered him when he became king and sent him some valuable paintings for the little cathedral in the backwoods. A religious order was founded of devout working men whose special vocation it was to erect churches as they were needed. And since 1806 the Dominican Fathers had been in Kentucky.

They had gone there under Edward Dominic Fenwick, the future Bishop of Cincinnati and the descendant of an old Maryland family. Soon they had a college and a novitiate in the wilderness. The Trappists, too, arrived about this time, but wandered about disconsolately without making as yet a permanent home. The fact that these orders penetrated to the Frontier was a signal proof that the Church had a vision of what was to happen. Nor were nuns lacking. The Sisters of Charity of Nazareth were founded by John Baptist David, who

[13] McGill, *The Sisters of Charity of Nazareth*, p. 357.

was auxiliary to Flaget. Already the West was stirring with Catholic activity.

DuBourg, after having been President of Georgetown and having begun St. Mary's College in Baltimore—assisting also in Mother Seton's projects—was nominated to the see of New Orleans in 1812, though the bulls were never issued. He was, however, appointed Administrator by Carroll and in 1815 became Bishop of Louisiana and the Floridas, soon transferring his see to St. Louis. To that city he brought the Vincentian Fathers, one of whom, Joseph Rosati, became his coadjutor and his successor, and the Religious of the Sacred Heart under that remarkable woman now beatified, Rose Philippine Duchesne. I say nothing about her at the moment, because we shall meet her in a later chapter, fulfilling in old age her dream of working among the Indians.

There was one rather unpleasant episode in the early Catholic history of the West. Nerinckx and Badin got at loggerheads with the Dominicans. In part the quarrel was theological: the foreign priests were tinged with the spirit if not the positive errors of Jansenism.[14] It was also, in part, traceable to Badin's

---

[14] For instance, the Dominicans had to complain that these missionaries demanded that under no circumstances should their penitents dance; otherwise they would not admit them to the sacraments. It may not have been the fault of Badin and Nerinckx, but of their narrow training, that they were imbued with this sort of false asceticism; it is enough to say that it was quite unCatholic.

However, we should remember that Badin had received part of his theological training at the seminary at Baltimore, where one might suppose he would have been in no danger of getting tinged with Jansenism. And, for what it is worth (since even the sourest Calvinist is sometimes by nature a very jolly fellow) Badin was relished in Kentucky because of his wit even if his strictness with his people was not at all popular. One of his jokes, which is recorded by Father Thébaud in *Forty Years in the United States of America*, is worth repeating. Badin one day lost his horse on the road and was chaffed about it when he reached the nearest inn on foot. A Presbyterian minister present said, "I hope that before your horse died, you had time to anoint him," but had to retire quickly in confusion when Badin instantly shot back, "Unfortunately I could not anoint him because the scoundrel turned Presbyterian." (P. 180.) He was also a gifted Latin poet. Nerinckx was less severe with his penitents, but was never known to jest and rarely smiled. But both were heroically devoted missionaries. It is interesting to recall that Badin later tried to join the Dominican order. The hostility of Nerinckx unfortunately never diminished.

sharp practice with regard to the Dominicans' property. It is a curious fact, often observable, that the "unco' guid" are not always to be trusted in business matters. Badin later tricked Flaget in much the same way as he had tricked the Dominicans—and then boasted of his cleverness! Mildly the Bishop said, "If I suffer any longer such conduct on the part of that man, I am afraid of failing in my duty; if I punish his delinquency, I feel that by his stubbornness and open rebellion he will stir up great scandal and perhaps break out into schism." He was therefore patiently suffered by his bishop on account of his admitted zeal. The correspondence between the two seculars and the Friars Preachers was, however, acrimonious. Father O'Daniel explains the matter thus: "Father Badin was a Frenchman; Father Nerinckx a Belgian. Three of the Dominicans were British. The other was an American; but he was of English origin, and had spent the greater part of his life abroad with Englishmen. Nearly all the people of Kentucky were Americans, but of English descent."[15] But this hardly explains Badin's trouble with Flaget, a Frenchman, like himself. We may at any rate be thankful that this is about the worst instance of serious internal dissension to be recorded. Compared with the turbulent East, the West was happy and at peace.

Cincinnati was erected into a diocese in 1822 on the advice of Flaget. He had visited it in 1814 and found there the nucleus of a Catholic congregation in what was then a settlement of log-cabins, and had said Mass in the house of a Mr. Scott who had come from Baltimore in 1805. But it was not until 1822 that what is now so great a city received its bishop or saw the building of its first Catholic church, which was also the cathedral. This was only a log-cabin outside the city limits and not for some time was permission given to set it on rollers and put it in a more central location. Even then Fenwick was without priests or schools. When he took charge there were about fifty Catholic families in his diocese; when he died ten years later the Catholic population was seven thousand. In the interval he had founded a theological seminary, first known as the Athenaeum, and a diocesan paper, the *Catholic Telegraph*. It was a magnificent missionary effort. Well might Fenwick dedicate his seminary to St. Francis Xavier.

15 "A Long Misunderstood Episode in American History," in the *Catholic Historical Review*, Vol. VI (1920), p. 22. Some of the letters of Badin and Nerinckx are in the same issue, pp. 66–88.

Only one more of these early Western bishops can be mentioned here, perhaps the most charming and saintly of them all—Simon Bruté de Remur. His career reads like a romance. Born at Rennes, he was a boy of fourteen during the Terror, but old enough to have been obliged to take part in the youthful firing-squads that executed priests and other suppositious enemies of the revolution. His mother quickly put him into her printing business so that he might have sufficient excuse for not absenting himself from work. Nevertheless he attended some trials, of which he has left us an account, as he has also done of the clerics who found hiding in his mother's house. Being only a boy, he was able to go with the disguised priests into the prisons without exciting suspicion; and it was he, not the priest, who carried the Blessed Sacrament concealed on his person.

When things had quieted down he studied medicine and became a doctor, though he never practiced. Instead he decided to become a priest and, after ordination, with difficulty refused Napoleon's offer to appoint him one of his chaplains. He was with the Sulpicians when Flaget fired his imagination with the idea of going to America. There he settled down to teach, and was hoping to end his days in studious retirement at Mount St. Mary's—where, because of his sanctity and sweetness of disposition, he was known as the "Angel of the Mount"—when in 1834, at the age of fifty-five, he was summoned, much against his will, to the new diocese of Vincennes.

His appointment was opposed by John England—not so much because Bruté was a Frenchman, for that did not matter in the West—as because he was too bookish. But there was another reason, expressed by Bishop Kenrick to the future Cardinal Cullen. It was that "an old man, with the most strange eccentricities of mind [should be] sent in the decline of a life spent in Collegiate exercises, to be the Apostle of a new diocese." And in truth he was and knew himself to be so eccentric that he called himself in one of his letters to William Gaston, "poor crazy Bruté."[16] Yet even England had such veneration for him that in a letter written long before

---

[16] The letter is one of a series of 140, all very long, half in French and half in English, written to Gaston and preserved in the archives of Notre Dame University. In one of these he at least half-seriously proposed to the widowed Judge that he take holy orders that he might become the Bishop of North Carolina!

Bruté's appointment was thought of, he inadvertently addressed him as though he were already a bishop.

An extraordinary thing happened now. The eccentricity which Bruté had felt free to indulge while he was merely a college professor, he laid aside the moment he was raised to the episcopate, realizing that it would now be out of place. But he retained his bookishness and amazed Vincennes with his library, though he had little time to read. At bottom he was an adventurous soul, one who had frequently dreamed of missionary work in China or India. Now late in life, and aged beyond his years, he unexpectedly fulfilled his earliest ambitions. His life has been written by Archbishop James Roosevelt Bayley, the nephew of his old friend Mother Seton, by a nephew of his own who bore his name, by Bishop Alerding, and more recently by Sister Mary Salesia Godecker.

Vincennes was, after Kaskaskia, the oldest settlement in the West. The Indians were still close at hand, and Alerding describes the white settlers as being almost as savage. Among these people descended the gentle Bruté with his emaciated face, his wide smile, his boxes of books, and nothing else except zeal. Fortunately he was often able to preach in French; his English was atrocious. Unlike Nerinckx, who is said to have mastered the language in four months, he never mastered it in thirty years. That he had lost most of his teeth did not improve matters. But this was of little consequence in Vincennes. What was lacking in enunciation was made up by his expressive and beaming countenance. One look at him was enough to make people recognize a saint.

What few worldly possessions he had were at anybody's disposal. The first poor man he met got the shirt off the Bishop's back. As for his priests, he was not only their father but their mother too. Never would he go to bed without seeing that they were snugly tucked up for the night. When, as frequently happened on his journeys, he had to sleep in the same bed with one of them, it was discovered that it was necessary to stay awake until the Bishop was asleep or else he would denude himself of all the blankets. On his visitations it was his custom to take his own dinner with him so as to put his host to no expense—and it was the plainest of food. The clerical destitution was so great that we sometimes hear of one knife and fork being shared between two or more men. All his riches were those of the mind. However absorbed he was in theology and the administrative details of his diocese, it was never difficult to get the old man to reciting La Fontaine—whom hc kncw from beginning to end by heart—or scenes from Racine or Corneille or passages from the Latin poets. His interests remained intellectual: both by correspondence and personal visits when in France he did his utmost to win back Félicité de Lamennais to the Church.

Bruté's services as bishop lasted only five years. Then he died of the consumption one suspects he had even before going to the West. In that short time and hampered by poor health, he founded St. Charles Seminary and St. Gabriel's College at Vincennes, personally conducting classes in both institutions. But he never forgot that he was a missionary and made constant journeys on horseback. On these he sometimes found that the fact of his being a doctor of medicine as well as a doctor of divinity came in very handy. I should like to linger longer upon him. But I must content myself with saying that his memory, with that of Cheverus, is like a strain of music, an odor of frankincense over the period. There were no doubt men of greater driving power than these two; there were none of greater charm, none in whom apostolic simplicity bloomed more exquisitely.

While the West was being organized by its bishops, and even before any bishop was seen there, interesting attempts were made to found Catholic settlements. The Irish did not as a rule migrate beyond the Appalachians; like most of those coming from abroad they were not woodsmen, and familiarity with the American axe was indispensable. Even the Irish colony at Benedicta, Maine, did not prosper, for few of the Irish immigrants were farm workers, as the peasant, however poor, tried to remain on his native soil. Those who did come were generally too indigent to get beyond the port of disembarkation or, if they did penetrate inland, soon found the loneliness of the American countryside intolerable after the sociability of the Irish village commune.

These colonization projects were the idea, not of the bishops—who had their hands full of other matters—but of some enterprising individual or speculative company. Often, in fact, they worked completely at variance with ecclesiastical authority, as when a scheme was concocted in 1789 on behalf of the Indians of upper New York State to have a Frenchman appointed as their bishop. In the same way a project was set on foot to have a Benedictine named Didier consecrated and sent out to the Gallipolis colony. It was part of the program of the Scioto Land Company for "boosting" its holdings and inducing French settlers to go to America. The Sulpicians were themselves so strongly attracted by the idea that at one time they thought of establishing themselves on the Ohio. Fortunately they changed their minds and offered themselves for Baltimore instead. But Propaganda, though it did not make Didier a bishop, appointed him Vicar-General for seven years, on condition that his jurisdiction did not conflict with Carroll's.

Didier was soon discouraged and retired to St. Louis, where he died in 1799. The Gallipolis colony dwindled in numbers. Concerning its Catholicism Carroll wrote to Propaganda to say, "Many of [its members] are refugees from Paris who have brought with them the vices of the large cities, and a hatred for religion." The energetic, if afterwards troublesome, Badin reported in 1796 that Gallipolis contained only eighty men, all without religion; and Dilhet, visiting them in 1805, found them in the same deplorable condition.[17]

A project that did succeed was that of Prince Demetrius Augustine Gallitzin at Loretto in western Pennsylvania, which was then part of the Frontier. This extraordinary and eccentric character was born at The Hague in 1770 where his father, who was a friend of Diderot, d'Alembert and Voltaire, was Russian ambassador. At seventeen Demetrius became a Catholic, to which religion his mother, a Prussian, belonged first in a nominal and eventually in a very fervent fashion. She even tried to convert Goethe, as he himself relates and, when he fled the house, she climbed into his carriage, going with him as far as the first posting-station, pleading with him all the way, much to his embarrassment. The son was destined for a military career and did serve for a short while as an officer in the Austrian army. With his family connections and his friendships—one was with the prince who became King William I of the Netherlands—a brilliant future was assured. But on a visit to the United States in 1792 he fell in with Bishop Carroll, entered the seminary at Baltimore, and was ordained priest in 1795, afterwards electing to be known as "Mr. Smith."[18]

His father philosophically accepted the situation. Long before this he had said of his son, "Mitri always wants to go

[17] Guilday, *Carroll*, Vol. I, p. 405.
[18] Though Badin was the first priest to be ordained in the United States, Gallitzin was the first to receive all the orders in this country.

against wind and tide." But he tried to get the young cleric to return to Europe where it would have been easy to pull wires for his ecclesiastical promotion. This was not Mr. Smith's idea at all: his true mission in life began when he crossed the Alleghenies in 1800 and settled at Loretto. There he sank his fortune—or rather his expectation of fortune—ultimately ruining himself by buying a large tract of land which he resold to Catholic colonists at a quarter its face value. He put up a tannery, a flour-mill and a saw-mill for them, going heavily into debt, but hoping to manage on the subsidies his mother sent him. Some of his creditors, however, were as generous as himself. Thus the Russian ambassador at Washington, Baron von Tuyl, to whom he owed $5,000, asked him to dinner when the note fell due—a dinner at which Henry Clay, Gallitzin's political hero, was also present. Afterwards as the men sat smoking, Tuyl took the Prince's note out of a drawer and put it in the candle-flame to light his cigar. And the King of Holland came to the rescue with $10,000. So despite everything, Gallitzin contrived to keep his enterprises afloat and died, as he had always prayed he might, free of debt.

He retained something of the cavalry officer. We hear of him in the war of 1812 teaching swordsmanship to his parishioners. He was also, to the end, the Russian aristocrat, even if he did call himself Mr. Smith. Among his people he was a martinet, but they willingly submitted to the domination of so benevolent a despot. He was in addition one of the most notable controversialists of his time, with an English style that was vigorous, graceful and witty, even though it betrayed at times the fact that it belonged to a foreigner. His polemical letters have recently been republished.

Towards the close of his life he was hurt from a fall and was paralyzed, but went his rounds still, dragged along on the rough roads in a sled. It was then that Peter Henry Lemcke, a convert who had in his youth served in the wars against Napoleon and who—oddly enough—received conviction of the truth of Catholicism by reading Luther's works, was sent to him as assistant. He wrote a racy account of the Prince, which Orestes Brownson's daughter draws upon freely in her biography.[19]

[19] Since this was written a translation of Lemcke's book has been made by Father Joseph C. Plumpe and published by Longmans. I could not use it, but find that Sarah Brownson has most of it in her book. Lemcke himself is worth a few words, and more. He founded

When Kenrick of Philadelphia sent him to Gallitzin he warned him: "He is a singular old saint; many others have tried to live with him, but it seems as if no one could get along with him." Lemcke nevertheless was willing to try and at once hit it off with the Prince. His first sight of the old man was in his sled, in a shabby overcoat and a peasant's hat which, he said, nobody would care to pick up in the street, and carrying a book in his hand. Lemcke rode up to him and asked, "Are you really the pastor of Loretto?" "Yes, I am he." "Prince Gallitzin?" At this the cripple laughed loudly but admitted, "Yes, I am that very exalted person."[20] As Lemcke had an admirable sense of humor he relished the exalted person's harmless foibles, and when, in 1836, he himself started an offshoot to the Loretto colony he wanted to name it Gallitzin. But here Mr. Smith put his foot down; so Lemcke had to be content to call his village Carrolltown.

We have in Lemcke not only a portrait of a character, but a vivid picture of Catholic life in country parts—the farmhouse, with its huge fireplace at which baking and cooking were going on at the same time, suddenly transformed into a church with the arrival of the priest. Then the people would gather on the porch, in the wood-shed, or under the trees, with their prayer-books in their hands, waiting for their turn to go to confession, and for the Mass in the large living-room that followed. It is a pity there were not more of such rural Catholic communities. Instead the immigration was dammed up in the cities, especially the Irish immigration. And cities, as the American Church has at last discovered, are anything but conducive to a healthy (or even normal) human life. But it would be unjust to blame mortals for being unable to foresee the future; the home was still taken for granted in urban centers, and it seemed unavoidable, because of the shortage of priests, that new arrivals should be encouraged to live in places where they could be easily reached. That was the declared policy of Archbishop Hughes, and it looked as though it were the only possible policy to adopt, especially as the Irish immigrants did not want to go to the country and did not have even the amount of money that was required for a small

---

several Benedictine abbeys, including the one at Atchison, Kansas. A bit of a character too!

[20] Sarah Brownson, *Gallitzin*, pp. 397, 398.

holding. Yet allowing for all this, what the Prince accomplished at Loretto might still be taken as a model before it is too late—though it is not necessary to imitate "Priest Gallitzin" in all his financial vagaries.

CHAPTER FIFTEEN

THE CATHOLIC INVASION

Immigration to the United States during the first years of the Republic was slow; then the war of 1812 and the last phase of the struggle with Napoleon made it almost impossible. Not until the "Jacksonian Revolution" of 1829, when America became more than ever the hope of the average man, did the immigrants really begin to pour in. At that time and for a long time afterwards the largest group among them were Irish and Catholic.

It has been estimated that the Catholic population of America in 1790 was 35,000. By 1820 natural increase should have raised that number to 84,000, and during the intervening thirty years probably another 80,000 came from abroad, while the new territories brought in 30,000 more, and there had been perhaps 5,000 converts. This would make 199,000; but as many of the Catholics were only nominal and many others lapsed, the true figure probably should be considerably lower,[1] though Bishop Canevin puts it at 243,000. After that it increased slowly but steadily until 1830, but during the next decade rose to about 650,000, while the dioceses increased from eleven to sixteen, and the number of priests from 232 to 482. From that point on the increase was by leaps and bounds.

[1] I am not qualified to make a close statistical analysis of these figures. This, however, has been done by Bishop Shaughnessy, whose conclusions have superseded the generalizations of John Gilmary Shea and others. The Bishop, who inclines to caution, puts the Catholic losses before 1820 at 225,000, but is not willing to admit that there were wholesale defections after that date, though this does not appear to be borne out by contemporary observers. However, merely because a man was a contemporary, he did not necessarily have the means of estimating the matter correctly. Thus John England put the losses up to 1836 at three and three-quarter millions. Even if a final nought were knocked off the figure would still be too high, in spite of which England's wild guess was used as a starting point for the rather disingenuous claims made by the Cahenslyites. England's statement is quoted in full in Shaughnessy's *Has the Immigrant Kept the Faith?* (pp. 234–236). The whole book should be carefully studied.

In 1850 there were a million and three-quarters of Catholics in the country, and by 1860 the figures had doubled. Meanwhile the dioceses, which were twenty-one in 1844, were forty-one ten years later, and the number of priests had mounted from about five hundred to over fifteen hundred. Though they were still few as compared with the army of Protestant ministers, it was the proportional increase which now alarmed so many Americans of the narrower sort. It is this alarm that explains what has to be related in this chapter.

America had not yet become the melting-pot; there was no problem of assimilating hordes who did not speak English. The Germans and Italians did not come *en masse* until later. But when America saw 600,000 immigrants pour in during the decade beginning 1830, and 1,700,000 in the decade beginning 1840, and the numbers as high as 2,600,000 in the next decade, it was but natural that they should fear being swamped.[2] Yet there was no thought of restricting immigration. America needed settlers for the western lands and laborers for the canals and railroads that were being built, as also hands for its industrial development. At the same time many Americans began, somewhat illogically, to resent the presence of those who came.

That resentment was mainly turned against the Catholic Irish. The Germans, whether Catholics or Protestants, for the most part went off quietly to the West where, as they kept largely to themselves and retained their own language, they could be regarded as foreign colonies. The ordinary citizen rarely came in touch with them. But the Irish looked upon themselves as Americans from the moment they landed—a claim which seemed impudent to the older inhabitants.

The trouble was that most of the Irish newcomers were papists; the Protestants among them were accepted readily enough. When the Nativist cry of "America for Americans!" went up, what was really meant was "America for Protestants!" For though there was also a vague nationalist apprehension on the part of Americans of the original stock, and an opposition on the part of the working classes to an influx of cheap labor, Nativism was fundamentally a religious prejudice, stemming

2 The figures for 1850 given by Thompson and Whelpton (*Population Trends in the United States*, pp. 94, 99) show that the Irish were 42.8% of the foreign-born, the Germans 26%, and England and Scotland and Wales a bad third with 16.9%. The Irish figures do not distinguish between Catholics and Protestants.

directly from the prejudices that had been so rampant in the Colonies up to the time of the Revolution. The fanatical bigotry of the Orange lodges, now being imported, inflamed that bigotry further, but did not light the fire.

In spite of what Catholic Irishmen might say, it was affirmed that no Catholic could possibly be a good American, for he had a divided allegiance, owing obedience to an Italian Pope and to his local bishop who, as often as not, was a foreigner. All this was of course a sad degeneration from the spirit of those who had founded the Republic, but by this time America, in several respects, had grown less liberal and urbane. Much was made of the fact that large contributions for missionary work were being sent by societies in Europe, and as one of these—the Leopoldinen-Stiftung[3]—had its center in Vienna, it was supposed to be an instrument of the Holy Alliance for the subjugation of the young Republic. As for the Catholic immigrants, they were looked upon—quite literally—as constituting an army of invasion. America was in deadly peril.

This frame of mind was, naturally enough, most often encountered in New England. The descendants of the Puritans had indeed permitted themselves to be charmed by Cheverus, but he had left Boston for a French see in 1823, and in his time Catholics were an insignificant handful. Now Boston and all New England were being overrun by Irish Catholics and it frightened everybody out of their wits. However much the Catholic Irish might be despised, they were also hated and feared.

During the years that had followed the Revolution and the

---

[3] With regret I relegate these societies to a footnote. The Leopoldine Association of Vienna was, at any rate in certain parts of America, outdone by the Society of the Propagation of the Faith of Lyons. This society contributed, for example, close on to a million francs to the dioceses of St. Paul and Dubuque between 1839 and 1864. (See Hoffman, *The Church Founders of the North West*, pp. 370–374.) Loras, the Bishop of Dubuque, as a native of Lyons, was of course in a favored position. The Vienna Society mainly helped German parts of the country, but was by no means confined to narrow nationalistic concepts. The third society was the Ludwig-Missionsverein of Munich. If smaller than the other two, it was, considering the resources of Bavaria, the most generous of all. But the patronage of King Ludwig was not quite disinterested. He could be appealed to on the ground of his anti-French sentiments. The history of the *Verein* has been written by Father Theodore Roemer.

establishment of religious liberty the various denominations had lived at peace with one another. It was immigration that roused the Protestant imagination to a roaring blaze. Though Governor Morris had only made himself ridiculous when he wrote to Governor Dinwiddie of Virginia in August, 1755, "The French might march in and be strengthened by the German and the Irish Catholics who are numerous here"—there were, at most, 1,300 of them—this new thing was no laughing matter. George Washington could visit Georgetown University and cause no adverse comment; but when General Harrison visited Mount St. Mary's in 1835 a petition against his harmless action was presented to Congress: so much had times changed. The intolerance that had been sleeping so long woke in a rage.[4]

There were, however, a number of factors that brought this about besides the Irish influx. A number of events all falling together precipitated the issue. Catholic emancipation occurred in England, to be followed by the restoration of the hierarchy. Little as this immediately concerned America, it was the occasion of much inflammatory Protestant writing which found its way to our shores and was applied to American conditions. Coincidentally there was the First Provincial Council of Baltimore. It should have allayed American fears, as the prime mover in the matter was John England, whose diocesan constitution proved his "democracy." Instead the Council seemed an instance of Catholic aggression, as did the establishment, about the same time, of the *United States Catholic Miscellany* and of other Popish periodicals. The one at Boston, unluckily named the *Jesuit*, was taken to be a flaunting of Catholic arrogance. And one of the facts upon which bigots could seize, and even well-intentioned persons misunderstand, was the Hogan and other schisms. Those who knew nothing of canon law concluded that the rebellious congregations were being defrauded of their rights by tyrannical prelates. The stage was therefore all set for an anti-Catholic uprising.

[4] This provoked Charles Constantine Pise, a professor at Mount St. Mary's, and afterwards the only Catholic who was ever chaplain to the United States Senate (he was appointed in 1832, while a pastor in Washington), to an outburst beginning:
"They say I do not love thee,
Flag of my native land!"

I think it must be granted as at least arguable that the American of this period was not a particularly attractive person, or at any rate that America contained a large number of persons who were all too willing to make themselves objectionable under the least pretext. They had, no doubt, their rough virtues, but they were, after their frontier experiences and the war of 1812, not much given to the cultivation of suavity or even decorum. They were suspicious, quick to take offence, and had an extravagantly high opinion of themselves. The line of the great Virginian gentlemen and of the Adamses had yielded to the blunt, though able, Jackson.

It is true that when Harriet Martineau wrote her book about her American visit she recorded the "sweet temper . . . diffused like sunshine over the land," and set it down to "the practice of forebearance requisite in a republic." And we may be sure that her American hosts were hospitable, as they were also among the most cultivated of the nation. But Anthony Trollope's mother, writing in 1832, only five years before Miss Martineau, after an unsuccessful attempt to run an emporium in Cincinnati, gave in her *Domestic Manners of the Americans* a highly unflattering account of them. And a keener observer than either, Charles Dickens, who came here in 1841, said some sharp things in his *American Notes* and was savagely satirical in *Martin Chuzzlewit*.

Even the note he appended to each book after his second visit, following the Civil War, merely emphasized his former criticism. He acknowledged that he had noticed a vast improvement; he did not retract a single word. However much the America of the forties and fifties may be admired for its crude vigor, it cannot be admired for its refinement. The cuspidor and the cuss were very much in evidence, as were the "quick feeders" the appalling boarding-houses, the "Rowdy Journals," the "Cities of Eden," decaying by their swamps, the Mrs. Hominys, the General Chokes, and the Jefferson Bricks. The American historian, John B. McMaster, has said, "The decade covered by the 'thirties is unique in our history. Fifty years of life at high pressure had brought the people to a state of excitement, of lawlessness, of mob-rule, such as had never before existed. Intolerance, turbulence, riot became the order of the day. Differences of opinion ceased to be respected. Appeals were made not to reason but to force; reforms, ideals, institutions that were not liked were attacked and put down by violence; and one of the least liked and first to be assaulted was the Church of Rome."[5]

More nauseous than the violence was the extraordinary complacency. Those who objected to the idea of using force against Catholics devised the ingenious argument that the influx of papist immigration must be due to the mysterious designs of Providence, to which they fancied they had glimpsed a clue. The crafty plot of the "Jesuits" would recoil on their own heads. The very people whom they had sent over to conquer the citadel of liberty would be converted by it—whereas at home there would be no way to penetrate their spiritual darkness. Then the last vestiges of Catholicism would be stamped out the world over. Thus America would destroy those who had intended its destruction. This was what might be called the highbrow thesis; the mob had cruder and more direct methods.

But I want to be fair to the Nativist movements. Even when they are considered strictly as a manifestation of intolerance, they cannot be blamed without qualification. The adherents of Nativism honestly believed[6] that the Catholic Church was by its very nature a persecuting and bloody affair, and that it was already planning to introduce the Inquisition into America. Everything they saw seemed to confirm their dread.

To this must be added the economic argument. The flood of cheap labor was lowering the American standard of living. And it was notorious that some European countries were using the United States as a convenient dumping ground for their own paupers. Certain German states openly offered pardon to petty criminals on condition that they leave the country; and where could they go but to America? As for England, it provided small bounties for paupers who would be so obliging as to emigrate. It is true that the British object was to people its own colonies, especially Canada. But many of those who went to Canada—in particular the Irish—used it merely as a

---

[5] "The Riotous Career of the Know-Nothings," *Forum*, Vol. XVII (1894), pp. 526–528.

[6] We must except, however, the many adventurers who joined these movements for their own profit: the hosts of ex-nuns who soon appeared in print and on lecture-platforms, and such apostates as Hogan who deliberately exploited religious prejudice by way of settling personal scores with Catholic authorities. At least Hogan knew that the charges he brought against the Church were utterly false.

stepping-stone to the United States. There was reason to believe that far more immigrants entered than those whose names appeared on the shipping-lists, as it is incontestable that thousands arrived only to become public charges. One cannot blame Americans for not relishing this state of affairs.

Even the Irish who did useful work with spade and pickaxe were not looked upon as very desirable members of society. Their shanties on the outskirts of the cities were slatternly, and those crowded into them were often drunken and disorderly. The workmen on the Erie Canal and similar projects were constantly getting into fights. Gangs recruited from different sections of the "old sod" pitted themselves against one another. They rarely lacked the grievance that this or that foreman would only hire men from his own county. Then there would be battles with fists and shovels, the men of Cork against those of Connaught, the "Far-ups" against the "Far-downs."[7] The same fights between various county groups of the Irish occurred sometimes even in the cities—apparently merely for the pleasure of the fight.

This was what the sober citizen noticed. He failed to notice that the majority of the Irish lived peaceably and respectably, even if they were poor. Nor did he guess that it might have been America that made the Irish more turbulent than they had ever been at home. To many newcomers American liberty meant a right to do what they pleased. They could not help being affected by their environment, and in this environment violence, even before their coming, was common, however much their presence may have increased it. The judgment of Marcus Lee Hansen must be accepted: "If the Irishman was often shiftless, untidy, improvident, so also was the American backwoodsman of the same period, and the latter's log cabin was hardly more habitable than the former's mud hut."[8] It was not that the Irishman preferred his shanty to anything else; it was that he too was a pioneer—doing his pioneering in the East instead of the West. If the Irish lived as they did, it was in many instances out of self-sacrifice: they were saving all they could to send to their relatives at home; only in this way could an old father or mother be saved from starvation, or wives and sisters and children have their fares paid to the land of promise. Had Americans but realized it, a compliment

---

[7] See Godecker, *Bruté*, pp. 361, 362.
[8] *Atlantic Migration*, p. 209.

was being offered to America. All the more, therefore, did the Irish resent the discrimination they believed practiced against themselves. Why, they wanted to know, should a drunken Yankee be left unmolested by the police when a far less tipsy Gael was sure to be haled before a magistrate! Everything was an injustice to the Irish. They supplied the country with the labor it needed. And if some of the old stock did leave the East because of them, this served to send up land values in the West. The Irish knew their worth, if nobody else did.

When everything else failed, ingenious appeals were made to the Irish hatred of England. For instance, a newspaper in 1852 placed the following case before them: "We wish the Irishmen in this country could see how England still contrives to make them pay taxes. Indeed the London Times says they will never begin to be profitable to England until they reach this country. By coming here and voting the Democratic ticket they assist that policy which supports English manufactures and sends back all the spare money in the country to pay for English goods. . . . Are Irishmen ready to do this? Do they wish to encourage English manufacturers? We think not."[9] The appeal was in vain: American money continued to be sent to help relatives in Ireland. If this money was, in part, used to pay British taxes and to support British trade, well, that was an incidental result that could not be avoided. On the other hand, the Nativists could hardly be expected to view the situation without anger.

There was another aspect of the situation that must be allowed for: it was the problem of Americanization. How could so vast a horde of newcomers be indoctrinated in the principles of true democracy? Again the Irish resented the implication. They felt themselves to be as good Americans as any; and it must be confessed that Americanism, as understood by the Nativists, was a somewhat spurious article. To have directed against the Irish—nakedly against them—naturalization laws that required an inordinate period of residence before citizenship could be conferred was monstrously unfair. It was, however, urged that, unless this were done, all the Irish would go to the polls in a body, led by their priests. The only thing that saved them from such laws was that local politicians perceived the advantage of cultivating the Irish vote. But as for their Americanism, it was to become apparent in the course

[9] Quoted in Noonan's *Nativism in Connecticut*, pp. 158–159.

of time that the Irish, with their natural aptitude for politics, were the most useful of all possible instruments for the Americanization of other foreigners, especially of Catholic foreigners. In this process the Irish clergy, who were rapidly becoming dominant in ecclesiastical circles, played a notable part. And although Irish-Americanism was perhaps rather generally of the narrow sort that laid undue emphasis on the importance of twisting the Lion's tail, it accorded pretty well with the type of Americanism common at the time.

A certain sneaking sympathy for Nativism, stated as a general philosophy, was not lacking among some of the American Catholics of the old stock.[10] They did not like the Irish, whom they blamed for the disturbances in the Church. A few, ashamed of the Irish poverty and disorderliness, even abandoned a communion now being overrun by such people. Others, for whom Orestes Brownson was a spokesman, made allowances for Nativism—also because of dislike of the Irish. This was to cost him dear when in 1854 John Henry Newman was appointed Rector of the new Catholic University in Dublin. He at once wrote to Brownson offering him a chair—any chair he chose. Then Brownson's Irish enemies in America brought pressure to bear, so that Newman had to drop the project.

After a stormy career this tall, gaunt, fierce Vermonter, who had been a minister in half-a-dozen denominations and had even tried to found the "Church of the Future," was received into the Catholic Church by Fitzpatrick, the coadjutor Bishop of Boston. "Do not hide your light under a bushel," the Bishop advised, somewhat superfluously. Upon which Van Wyck Brooks comments, "As well urge a bull not to pretend to be a lamb." He had dabbled in Transcendentalism, with a vehemence to which Transcendental circles were quite unaccustomed, and much to the distress of the gentle Emerson. Before long this bull was trying to drag Thoreau with him into the Church, to which he was plowing his way by sheer force of ratiocination. He made a set also at George Ripley, and nearly

10 Nor was it lacking in some Catholics who, being foreigners, could regard the American scene with detachment. Thus Father Augustus Thébaud, in his *Forty Years in America* (1839–1885), makes it clear that in his estimation Know Nothingism had a social rather than a religious origin. The good-humored French Jesuit does not pretend to be a historian, but his picture of the America of his time is of considerable value to historians. (See especially pp. 238–241.)

succeeded in his case, as he did completely in the case of Ripley's wife.[11] But Brownson was always constitutionally inclined to overdo things. Having taught himself Latin, he paraded his knowledge at Brook Farm, horrifying the exquisite Latinist Bradford with his false quantities. One night Bradford had a dream: he had entered the Church and was making his confession to Brownson. Then the confessor said to his penitent, "Now repeat this Latin psalm after me"—and Bradford awoke in a cold sweat groaning "O Lord, my punishment is more than I can bear!" Mr. Schlesinger, Brownson's latest biographer, writes, " 'The unpolished, vehement and positive man,' as young Georgiana Bruce called him, was not altogether popular on the Farm. The starry optimism of the dwellers frequently stirred him to debate where, argument failing, he sought to overawe by sheer physical massiveness, raising his voice, pounding on the table, and giving way to anger when his opponents failed to grasp his point.'

Nor did the Irish grasp his point much better, or have any more liking for him than he had for them. It is true that in 1854, at the height of the Know Nothing movement, he declared in his *Quarterly Review*, "Know Nothingism is no Yankee invention, no American production, but an imported combination of Irish Orangism, German radicalism, French socialism, and Italian astuteness and hate." Yet even in that year, while vigorously condemning what Nativism had developed into, he continued to believe that it had at bottom certain true and good ideas. I think we may perhaps still concede that much. Nobody will concede more.

With that formidable logic of his, Brownson had argued that there was no need to defend Catholics on the liberal Protestant ground that they might conceivably become good citizens "in spite of their religion." The truth, he asserted, was rather that no Protestant could really be a good American.[12] Certainly the sense in which many Protestant crusaders

[11] Ripley kept up a friendship with another ex-Transcendentalist, Father Hecker, and had a kind of understanding that Hecker was to receive him into the Church on his death-bed. When dying, he did actually send for him, but the message was not delivered, so that Hecker got the news only later from another source. Hastening to Ripley, he found him unconscious.

[12] On the other hand too many Catholics were assuming, like their opponents (into whose hands they played), that "Irish" and "Catholic" were synonymous terms, and were behaving as though

tried to propagate their religion was at variance with the religious liberty won by the Revolution. The best that we can say of the Americanism of Nativism is that it represented a throwback to the persecuting spirit of colonial times.

Though it had social and political as well as religious manifestations, it came to a head in the 'thirties as a violent attack on the Catholic Church. Lyman Beecher was almost beside himself with terror when he thought of the Pope's designs upon the Mississippi valley. Meanwhile Samuel F. B. Morse, the artist turned inventor, took a more general line of attack. In his case it would seem that his hitherto controlled prejudice was turned into frenzy when, on a visit to Rome, his hat was knocked off because he had failed to remove it at a procession of the Blessed Sacrament. That hat, as Professor Billington remarks, "became something of a symbol to American nativists."[13] His bigotry made him their leader. But their political history at this time was brief. In 1836 Morse ran for the mayoralty of New York on their ticket. In 1841 the Nativists formed themselves into the American Republican Party. By 1847 they were in total eclipse.

Yet not before doing a vast amount of harm. For they have to be considered, not so much as a definite organization as a movement that attracted to itself disparate elements, most of which had little in common except a determination to effect the destruction of the Catholic Church and the repression of the detested Irish.

There are two sides to the movement: that of controversy and that of action. The controversy was of two kinds. One, represented by Lyman Beecher and Morse and Brownlee and Breckenridge, was, despite its acrimony, dealing with matters open to debate: the supposititious errors of Catholicism and the supposititious designs of the Catholic Church on the United States. The effect of their unbridled speech, however, was to spur the unthinking into violent action. The other form of controversy (which had an even more deplorable effect on the mob) was about the basest that can be imagined—the production of a series of revelations on the part of ex-nuns

the Church in America was an Irish institution. Brownson saw clearly that the Church would never reach its full growth until it had become acclimatized to America, and that it would not become American so long as it remained Irish. (See Schlesinger, *Orestes Brownson*, p. 213.)

[13] *The Protestant Crusade*, p. 137.

(most of whom had never been nuns at all) who told of the immoralities that went on in convents. Such works as were written by ex-priests exposing Romanism, though usually equally salacious, lacked the delicious filthiness of the feminine confessions. They were therefore not nearly so popular as the tales told by ladies who had escaped from convents after discovering them to be brothels in which nuns bore to priests children who were strangled at birth and sent blissfully winging to paradise.

The most notorious of these ladies was Maria Monk. She gave out in her *Awful Disclosures* that she had been educated at the Hôtel Dieu at Montreal, and had become a Catholic while there, with the intention of becoming a nun. She had, however, wavered and had married, but had afterwards gone back to the convent to be duly professed and to drink the cup of horror and unspeakable iniquity before escaping. Eventually it transpired that the book which had appeared under her name was really the work of a clergyman, that Maria Monk had never been in the Hôtel Dieu in her life, and that (according to her own mother) she had been confined because of delinquency in a Catholic reformatory for girls. It was from this institution that she had escaped, and the child she said was fathered by a priest was really by a lover. As for the Hôtel Dieu, two Protestant ministers, and afterwards the Nativist editor, Colonel Stone, were allowed to go over the whole convent from attic to cellar. When the ministers confessed that the Hôtel Dieu they had inspected did not in the least resemble the building described in the book, Maria Monk's backers maintained that structural alterations had been made to deceive them. And poor Colonel Stone was dismissed as either in the pay of the Jesuits or else "Stone-blind."[14]

In the end Maria Monk was dropped even by her friends, though her book continued to sell and is still issued by the

[14] See Billington, *op. cit.*, p. 101 *et passim*. His *Protestant Crusade* is the most complete account of the anti-Catholic movements of 1800–1860, fully documented and devastatingly impartial. Its weight is increased by his Protestantism. There are many Catholic monographs of Nativism and kindred subjects, among which these by Fathers Riley and Noonan should be mentioned. But the most satisfactory Catholic study is that of earlier American anti-Catholicism, without which Nativism cannot be understood, Sister Mary Augustina Ray's *American Opinion of Catholicism in the Eighteenth Century*.

purveyors of pornography. In 1838 she produced a second illegitimate child, and when that mishap was accounted for as having been "arranged" by the Jesuits to discredit her, the explanation was considered insufficient to exculpate her for her arrest and conviction for having picked the pockets of a man in a New York bawdy-house. When another of the ex-nuns of the time, Sister St. Frances Patrick, also bore an illegitimate child in 1838, people began to wonder whether the charges of immorality brought against convents by such witnesses were to be relied on.

If anything further was needed it was supplied by the antics of the nunnery inspection committee appointed by the Commonwealth of Massachusetts. In 1855 it went over an academy at Roxbury, trying to nose out conventual enormities, twenty men tramping all over the house, though officially there were only seven on the committee. Afterwards they regaled themselves with a champagne dinner and passed on to Lowell. They thought it no more than just to charge their expenses to the state, but as these included the services of a Mrs. Patterson, whose profession was only too well known, there was some unkind comment. The Boston *Pilot* was cruel enough to record that at least one member of the committee had visited "nuns of the type who got him intoxicated and stole $71 from him."[15]

But although in the controversy Catholics scored all along the line—for the questions at issue here were not of opinion but of facts—this did not mean that the Nativists changed their views. Even the lucubrations of ex-nuns continued to be read and believed by the gullible. The Massachusetts Committee for the Inspection of Convents was set up long after the frauds of Maria Monk had been exposed.

There was in truth almost no limit to the credulity of the bigoted. As an amusing instance of this, take the hoax perpetrated by John Hughes, the future Archbishop of New York. As a young priest in Philadelphia he sent in 1830 a contribution to the *Protestant* under the pseudonym of "Cranmer." In it he attacked the Catholic Church, though being careful to impart to his remarks a tinge of absurdity. The article was printed and with it an editorial eulogy of the anonymous

15 Billington, *op. cit.*, pp. 414–415, 431. Shea puts the matter rather more euphemistically and merely remarks that one member of the committee was accompanied by "a lady who was not his wife." (*Op. cit.*, Vol. IV, p. 510.)

Cranmer which asked for more of the same true-blue stuff. Upon this Cranmer went a little further along the path of the ridiculous: not too far, just enough, for he did not know how much the editors and the readers of the *Protestant* would swallow. Seeing that they gulped it down greedily, he went on writing articles, pitching the strain a little higher with each. Perhaps he had overdone it this time; surely they would know that he was making game of them! No need to worry; the more absurd, the better they liked it. Only when he had wearied of writing nonsense did he print a letter in the *Catholic Truth Teller* telling how he had befooled the other magazine. The answer of the editors of the *Protestant* was, in the first place, that they did not believe him: there *was* a genuine Cranmer; but in the second place, they charged him with "deception and all the other abominations which it is essential to the craft and character of a Jesuit to perpetrate." Well, he had unquestionably been guilty of deception, even if he was not a Jesuit. But after Hughes' hoax Nativist papers were more careful about the credentials of their contributors.

This, however, was only a pyrrhic victory. Catholics might win their verbal battles, but the Nativists grew so much in strength during the 'forties and 'fifties that (in their later development) they fully expected to achieve their ambition of putting a President in the White House. And apart from political action, they inflicted on the Church, at Charlestown and Philadelphia, disastrous wounds, however much these atrocities may have alienated the sympathy of fair-minded Protestants.

The Ursuline Convent of Charlestown was considered one of the best schools of Boston and was attended by the daughters of many prominent non-Catholic families, especially those of the Unitarian persuasion. All was going well until a postulant, named Read, who had left the Sisters wrote a dull book entitled *Six Months in a Convent*. Miss Read hinted at awful doings, but had nothing of consequence to relate, being without sufficient imagination to be a convincing liar. What she said, nevertheless, was enough to set rumors in circulation, so that, when shortly afterwards Elizabeth Harrison, one of the nuns, became slightly deranged from overwork and fled, all Boston was in a turmoil. It did no good to say, what was the truth, that Bishop Fenwick had had a talk with her the next day, as a result of which she had asked him to be allowed to return: it was given out that she had been carried back by force and was now incarceratcd in a dungeon. Just then Lyman Beecher returned from the West, full of his theme of the Pope's plot to seize the Mississippi valley, and preached a sermon on the subject on the Sunday of August 10, 1834, to a large congregation.

The very next night the convent was burned to the ground. The Reverend Mother tried to appeal to the mob and—that failing—rather tactlessly warned them that "the Bishop has twenty thousand Irishmen at his command in Boston." Unfortunately they were not at Charlestown; had twenty of them been present, the vandals would not have dared to approach. While fire companies looked on without doing anything to help, the convent was set on fire. The nuns and their pupils had to escape the flames in the middle of the night.

Indignation meetings were held and the mob was denounced. Yet of the few men eventually arrested only one was brought to trial, and he was acquitted to wild cheers in court. He was even showered with so many presents for his godly deed that he was obliged to acknowledge them generally in a newspaper. As Dr. Billington remarks, the majority of people "probably were more pleased than horrified at the destruction of the Ursuline school."

At intervals during the next day similar instances of vandalism occurred, though none of quite the dastardly character of the one just mentioned. Catholic churches in other places were also fired; so too were a few Protestant churches in retaliation. It is not, after all, a particularly safe proceeding to step on the tails of an Irishman's coat. The embattled Gaels of Boston were by now spoiling for a fight and were with difficulty held off by Bishop Fenwick. Elsewhere there were stories of Irishmen, flushed with fervor and whiskey, marching in bands and demanding of all they encountered, "Catholic or Protestant?"—and dealing with the answer in what they considered the appropriate fashion.

Thcse incidents nevertheless pale into insignificance when set beside what happened in Philadelphia ten years later. The issue there was precipitated by the question of Bible-reading in the public schools. Bishop Kenrick had pleaded that it was unjust to make Catholic children listen to the Protestant version of the Scriptures and had asked that they be permitted the use of the Douay translation. This was not only refused but the request was twisted into an attack on the Bible itself, however often Kenrick patiently explained that he was making no objection to the Authorized Version for non-Catholics. The Nativists were looking for a pretext and had found one. They roared that this was the beginning of the Inquisition, the tocsin for a St. Bartholomew's Day massacre, and all the rest of it. In defence of their religious freedom they rose to wreak their wrath on the Irish.

To some extent perhaps Bishop Kenrick was to blame—at least John Hughes, now Bishop of New York, thought so. His temperament was too peaceable. He did nothing except issue reasonable explanations and stick up placards. What was wanted was what Hughes supplied in his own diocese—strong measures, the positive threat that the Catholics would defend their churches. His decision prevented the destruction of Catholic property in New York; Kenrick's ineffectual mildness resulted in continued attacks on convents and churches in Philadelphia and a riot in which thirteen lives were lost and fifty men wounded.

It was really much more than a riot. It was a battle that lasted three days. Not only two churches and the seminary but whole rows of Irish houses were burned, with the police and the firemen looking on, either because they feared the mob or sympathized with anti-Popery. Boys were employed—greatly to their satisfaction—to fire off pistols with blank cartridges during the night and so keep up the martial spirit. St. Michael's Church went up in flames. The Mayor tried to save St. Augustine's by standing on the steps and telling the crowd that their suspicions were unfounded; there *were* no arms inside. That was just what they wanted to know; they could destroy it in perfect safety. The rioters even got hold of a couple of cannon and fired them point-blank at the door of St. Philip Neri's Church. In the end a company of militia had to be called out, and then reinforcements, before the artillery was captured. Yet there is reason to believe that the same people among the official and more substantial classes who voiced their disapproval in public, in private whispered very different sentiments.[16] The grand jury ascribed the riots to "the efforts of a portion of the community to exclude the

[16] See Billington, *op. cit.*, pp. 230, 236, and Kirlin's *Catholicity in Philadelphia*, pp. 320 *et seq.* But we should also remember that Bishop Kenrick was sheltered by a Dr. Tyng, a minister, and that a Protestant layman did the same for the priests, who took with them the Blessed Sacrament. (Kirlin, p. 324.)

Bible from the public schools," and indicted for murder several Irishmen who had tried to protect their homes.

The fact is that even those who deplored the violence of the mob were in many instances perfectly convinced that the Catholics—and especially the Irish Catholics—were a menace. The country was swept by a hysteria that discovered Popish plots everywhere. When the news of what had happened at Philadelphia reached St. Louis there were riots in that city, so infectious is example. The medical school conducted by the Jesuits was barely saved from attack.[17] The cadavers used in the anatomical classes were supposed to be bodies of the Protestant martyrs put to death in exquisite tortures by the local Inquisition![18] The West had long been known to be a part of the country on which the Pope had fastened his baleful eye. Though the term, fifth columnist, had not then been thought of, fifth columnists were imagined to be everywhere. The Jesuits were on the prowl in the Mississippi valley "under the names of puppet show men, dancing masters, music teachers, peddlers of images and ornaments, barrel organ players and similar practitioners."[19] When the Irish could not be accused, Italian hurdy-gurdy men served. Nor did women escape the finger of suspicion: of course there were female as well as male Jesuits (and both were accustomed to employ disguise); this was testified to by some of the lady lecturers who avowed that, before seeing the light of the Gospel, they too had been Jesuits.

The age was one in which any activity by a Catholic was sure to be grotesquely misrepresented. The temperance crusade of Father Mathew in the 'forties was thought to be a means of enrolling regiments for attack on the Republic under the cloak of getting them to take the pledge. It mattered little that the priest was welcomed by many ministers and that he, for the reason that he was attempting a moral reform rather than dogmatic instruction, willingly worked with them. That itself caused trouble. For some of the Catholic clergy looked askance at the reformer, sorry that he associated with men

[17] Ten years later in this city, during the 1854 election, there was an anti-Catholic riot in which nearly a dozen men were killed, and the following year Louisville, Kentucky, had riots in which twenty men perished.

[18] See Billington, *op. cit.*, p. 237.

[19] The issue for Christmas Day, 1834, of the *American Protestant Vindicator*, quoted by Billington, p. 120.

whom they knew to be bigots and fearing that his line of argument implied that drink, as such, was an evil, a proposition to which they could not assent. Therefore the very ministers who used Father Mathew considered him an exception and continued to denounce what they called the iniquitous Catholic connection with the drink traffic.[20] Papists were damned whatever they did.

Not even in the South did the Church wholly escape, despite its having too few adherents, outside of New Orleans, to be regarded as a serious threat. Moreover, most of the Southern Catholics were of old families about whose Americanism there could be no question. Not many, it is true, were rich, but an aristocratic tradition leavened the whole body and gained a respect for Catholics in the general community that was lacking elsewhere in the United States. Few Irish immigrants had come among them, and those who had done so had been absorbed by the mass of quiet, inoffensive people. Though the Charleston and Norfolk schisms had been caused by groups largely Irish, these same men felt themselves to be old settlers and therefore superior to the newcomers.

These circumstances, however, did not altogether save the Catholics in the South. Even if there was little actual violence (except in speech) in that region, the Southerners had their own reasons for disapproving of the Irish influx into the North. They did not recognize, or would not admit, that the Irish declined to go to the South because they would have to compete there on unfair terms with negro labor; therefore they resented the immigration that was giving the North a preponderance which every year increased. Since the thirties, with the nullification issue and the bad feeling that was being engendered by abolitionist propaganda, the anger of the Southern states was mounting against the populous industrialist North. That the Irish were not abolitionists, that they were even—despite the pleading of Daniel O'Connell—strongly anti-negro somehow failed to register below the Mason-Dixon Line. They were accordingly lumped with the German immigrants, whose opposition to slavery was an actual fact. Indeed, the Irish were sometimes suspected—in their rôle "agin the government"—of fomenting slave insurrections.

[20] These ministers conveniently ignored the fact that the Fourth Provincial Council of Baltimore of 1840 ordered that priests were to debar from the sacraments saloon-keepers who sold liquor on Sundays or permitted drunkenness on their premises.

But all this was of course rather vague. The only real appeal of Nativism to the South was the fear that the vast tide of foreign immigration was likely to engulf American institutions. That and the obsessing question of slavery. For this reason some Catholics in Louisiana sought and received admission into the Know Nothing party when it was founded, though they withdrew before long in protest against the proclaimed anti-Catholicism of the Know Nothings of the North. So far as the South was concerned, the general attitude towards the Irish was a mere grudge—a confused resentment that they refused to come South, and a satisfaction that they stayed away. To the Catholics already there there was accorded an admission that, however bad the principles of Popery might be, they themselves were not such bad fellows.

In the North the Catholics found a redoubtable leader in John Hughes. He had been sent to New York in 1837 as coadjutor to Dubois, and at once made himself felt. Poor Dubois was hardly the man to cope with his internal difficulties, let alone the external threat. Yet he made a gallant fight against the trustees of his cathedral when they refused him his salary. "Well, gentlemen," he told them, "I am an old man and need very little. I can live in a cellar or a garret. But whether I come up from the cellar or down from the garret I shall still be your bishop." Hughes, however—who was a fighter—carried the war against the trustees and won. But this was only because the aged Dubois' failing health made it necessary to give all authority to the young coadjutor. The old man tried at first to resist but had to yield at last. His form of protest was to keep as far away as possible from his supplanter—his former student at Mount St. Mary's—whom he persisted in referring to as "Mr. Hughes."

Mr. Hughes—or "Cross John" or "Dagger John," as the Nativists styled him—had bigger game to go after than a former senile professor. He routed the trustees. He threatened the newly elected Nativist mayor, James Harper, at the time of the Philadelphia riots that, if the city administration would not protect his churches, he would do so himself. "So you are afraid for your churches!" His Honor sneered, to get the reply, "No, but I am afraid for yours." The Bishop amplified this: "If any Catholic church is burned here," he vowed, "New York will be a Moscow." And "Dagger John" was known to be a man of his word.

He was never what can be called discreet. Did the Nativists

assert that there was a Catholic plot to capture the West? He would admit it. In 1850, preaching in his cathedral, he boomed: "Protestantism pretends to have discovered a great secret. Protestantism startles our eastern borders occasionally on the intention of the Pope with regard to the Valley of the Mississippi, and dreams that it has made a wonderful discovery. Not at all. Everybody should know it. Everybody should know that we have for our mission to convert the world —including the inhabitants of the United States—the people of the cities, and the people of the country, the officers of the navy and the marines, commanders of the army, the Legislatures, the Senate, the Cabinet, the President, and all." Many Catholics were appalled by such words, which were instantly circulated as proof positive of the Popish plot that had hitherto been denied. And perhaps Hughes might have made his effective point a little more graciously. But he was born with a chip on his shoulder, and he recognized that the time had come to hit back. There can be no argument as to his success.

He failed, however, in what was his greatest fight, that on the school question. His contention was that, because of the fewness of parochial schools and the reading of the Protestant Bible in those conducted by the city, many Catholic children were able to attend no school at all. In this he was supported by Governor Seward on the ground that, unless the children of immigrants were educated, they would not become good citizens. Nevertheless the Common Council of New York declined to allocate any share of the public funds for the support of papistical institutions. Hughes addressed the Council for three hours, presenting his case; then the Protestant partisans orated two whole days in reply, avoiding the issue but denouncing the enormities of Rome, and won. "If the fearful dilemma were forced upon me," declared one of the speakers, a minister, "of becoming an infidel or a Roman Catholic, according to the entire system of popery, with all its idolatry, superstition, and violent opposition to the Bible, I would rather be an infidel than a papist."[21] The reverend gentleman has had his ideal carried out—in the complete secularization of the public schools with the resultant emptying of almost all vitality from American Protestantism. If the Catholic Church has suffered too—as it has not even yet been able to

21 Quoted by Billington, *op. cit.*, p. 147.

establish enough parochial schools, or to prevent a large number of Catholic children from attending those run by the state —it has at all events suffered less than Protestantism. As Dr. George Shuster, the President of Hunter College, has written, "The Protestant churches ought to have discovered long ago that only schools frankly denominational in character and supported as such from the public treasury can, in the long run, serve the interests of religion."[22] But on this issue the Catholic Church, which had seemingly come near to obtaining the only reasonable solution of the educational problem—the support of Catholic schools from the taxes paid by Catholics —was defeated. It might have succeeded in a more propitious time; during the period dominated by the Nativist fury, it was doomed to fail. Catholics were therefore forced to pay for their own parochial schools and also for the endowment of a system of education which has shown itself increasingly irreligious or, at best, unreligious.[23]

The Nativist fury manifested itself most dramatically in the Bedini episode. Perhaps in this case it may be argued, as Dr. Billington argues, that Rome "blundered," and no doubt there were Catholics who could have been more tactful than they were, though why they should be expected to be so very polite in the face of extreme provocation is not quite clear. On the face of it, Bedini's visit was perfectly harmless. He bore an autographed letter from the Pope to President Pierce, and though he may have had the intention of examining the advisability of setting up an Apostolic Delegation in the United States (which in any case was nobody's business except that of Catholics), his immediate and more important function was to inquire into the trustee troubles[24] so as to be able to report to the Holy See. It is worth noting, in this connection, that he strongly advised against the appointment of bishops

---

22 *The Catholic Spirit in America*, p. 5.

23 The distinction I make has no real value and is offered merely as a concession to those who wish to maintain it. An unreligious education, even when given by people who happen to belong to some religious body (including the Catholic Church) inevitably instills the idea that religion is something of no consequence.

24 That these troubles were still in need of settlement is shown by the fact that Bishop Timon, who was appointed to the see of Buffalo in 1847, was actually shut out from his own pro-cathedral by rebellious trustees.

on the basis of racial proportions—or, in other words, in favor of the policy of Americanizing the immigrant.

Bedini had the misfortune to arrive at the wrong moment. The Know Nothing movement was rising to its height. And he reached American shores just when the ex-priest, Alessandro Gavazzi, also arrived with the double object of denouncing Bedini and exposing the tyranny of Rome. It was all strong meat and drink to Nativists.

Gavazzi was a tall handsome man, black-haired, burning-eyed, and a powerful orator. What he had to say sent thrills of horror down American spines. He accused Bedini of having been directly responsible for the execution in northern Italy of Ugo Bassi, a Barnabite friar who had led a rebellion against the Austrian government. It was even given out that Bassi, before execution, had been flayed alive and, as some papers said, scalped.

The facts are these. Bedini, so far from having anything to do with Bassi's execution, was carefully kept in ignorance of it by Gorgkowski, the Austrian governor of Bologna, precisely out of fear that he might attempt to get the Holy See to use its influence with Austria to save the condemned priest. As for the flaying alive and the scalping, this was a fantastic reference to the ceremony of clerical degradation, which in part consists of a ritual scratching of the surface of the palms with a pin. In any event, Bassi had not been degraded, his offence having been purely political. But it was useless to point this out to a public in no mood to listen. Already Nativist animosity had been whipped to frenzy the previous year when Louis Kossuth, the Hungarian revolutionist, had visited the United States. As a victim of the Austrian monarchy he had paved the way for Gavazzi. The only conceivable reason why this should have been considered the concern of the Nativists—who so loudly proclaimed their "isolationism" and indifference to all Europe's concerns—was that Kossuth was a convenient stick with which to beat the Pope. He was therefore accepted as a symbol of the struggle against Catholic autocracy, and on his arrival in New York a minister preached a sermon entitled, "The Coming of Kossuth Illustrative of the Second Coming of Christ."[25]

[25] See Billington, *op. cit.*, p. 331. In spite of this, the American public soon lost interest in the man. A crowd of two hundred thousand had welcomed him in New York; not a soul went to see him off when he sailed for Europe.

Bedini was personally very charming, able and courageous, and he treated the demonstrations against him with dignified silence.[26] He was followed from city to city by Nativist agitators who stirred up the people so much that in Cincinnati he barely escaped being lynched. (The church in which he had preached was destroyed.) But as these doings were mainly the work of Italian *Carbonari* and German radicals—the function of the American Nativists being that of egging their foreign brethren on—it was made clear that the motive was not one of protecting America but merely of damaging Catholicism.

Catholics were naturally very indignant at this treatment of the Pope's representative. They were still more disgusted at the hypocrisy that underlay it. At a reception for Bedini at Georgetown College on January 17, 1854, the then fifteen-year-old James Ryder Randall, the future author of "Maryland, My Maryland," declaimed a poem of which these lines formed part:

> The rabblecrew who thus have stained our sod
> Are stranger-born, are recreant to God,
> A plague-spot of this land they'll ever be
> Who 'neath a mask pretend to liberty.

Not very good verse; but the strict truth.[27]

I have told the story of the Nativist movement as though it constituted a continuous whole, and therefore have felt free to go backwards and forwards through the 'thirties to the 'fifties. And it *was* a continuous whole, since it all sprang from the same cause—a hatred of the Church and a dislike of the Irish. At the same time it might be remarked that there were two chronological phases, or rather three. At first the movement remained unorganized. Then there came the attempt to enter politics under the name of the American Republican party. This collapsed in 1847 because the war with Mexico, which the Nativists had expected to aid their cause, deflected attention from it. Finally there was the culminating phase of the Know Nothings.

When Nativism emerged as Know Nothingism, after having lived underground with its bigotry undiminished, it had

[26] See Guilday, *John Gilmary Shea*, p. 44.
[27] The best account of the Bedini affair is that by Dr. Guilday in *Records and Studies*, Vol. XXIV (1933), pp. 87–131. The weakest chapter in Dr. Billington's book is the one dealing with it.

learned a lesson from the past. It had, in fact, learned several lessons. One of these was the advantage that might be derived from taking a leaf out of the Masonic book and cultivating a secret ritual. This is all the more remarkable in view of the anti-Masonic furore of 1826–1832 which, though in no way connected with Nativism as such, inflamed much the same type of minds as gave Protestant bigotry its driving force. The Masons suffered because a certain William Morgan, who had once belonged to the order, had threatened to expose it. When a body, which was assumed to be but was never proved to be his, was found afterwards under Niagara Falls, the inference was drawn that he was murdered to prevent his giving away the masonic secrets, whatever they were. Therefore, as Dr. Billington puts it, "Masonry and Catholicism, dread oaths and the Inquisition became linked in the minds of the people."[28]

In spite of this—or perhaps because of this—Masonry had a dark fascination for the moronic mob. Why not fight the Church, with its abominable mysteries celebrated in the darkest recesses of convents, by using its own weapons? In 1849 Charles Allen of New York founded a society to which he gave the name of the Order of the Star-Spangled Banner. It was merely one of many such societies—nearly all of which had a Nativist tinge (and a convivial character) to their professed patriotism—until James W. Barker, a well-known dry-goods merchant, saw its possibilities and bought Allen out. It was an anticipation of the history of the Ku Klux Klan of our own time, though in this case there does not seem to have been any prominent mercenary motive. Barker gave his followers a ritual and an esoteric grip and passwords and a code of signals, including one to be used when danger loomed. Being an excellent psychologist, he warned that it must be used only in extreme emergency. With these allurements he drew in those whose dull lives found in secrecy itself the delicious shiver of excitement. The society was now known as the Order of United Americans.

Its success was phenomenal. In Massachusetts, as the American Party (only unofficially did its members call themselves the Know Nothings), it elected the Governor in 1854 as well as all the State's officers and the entire Senate. Only one of the 378 representatives of the legislature was not a Know Nothing. And though that was its most complete triumph, the

[28] *Op. cit.*, p. 41.

party carried Delaware and in the following year added Rhode Island, Connecticut, Maryland and Kentucky, and was in virtual control in New York, California, Pennsylvania, Virginia, Georgia, Mississippi and Alabama, while holding the balance of power in many other states. To overawe the electors, the Maryland Nativists assembled at the polling booths armed with shoemakers' awls for the persuasion of those who needed it. These bands proudly entitled themselves the "Plug-uglies." Another of the many groups of the same type, all of which had horrific names, was the "Blood-tubs"—who wore little models of these as their distinguishing emblem. It was by such means of intimidation that they ensured the election of their candidates. By 1856 they expected to put their nominee in the White House; all except 9 of the 149 electoral votes were regarded as being already "in the bag."

How then did it happen that the American Party accomplished nothing, after all? The explanation usually given is that the slavery question, which it had been hoped had been permanently settled by the Missouri Compromise, cropped up again at this time to cause dissension in the party and to make Nativism appear a matter of small consequence compared with the black shadow gathering overhead. That this was the immediate cause of the Know Nothing ineffectiveness is true. But the deeper reason is that the American Party was thoroughly un-American. Even had it succeeded in electing Millard Fillmore,[29] even had it gained a majority in Congress, the most it could have done would have been to pass discriminatory naturalization laws. Against it stood the constitutional guarantees of religious freedom. Congress was explicitly deprived of the power of making any law on the subject of religion. Had some other Chief Justice than the Catholic Roger B. Taney then presided over the Supreme Court, that court would still have been obliged to uphold the Constitution.[30] There and not in the shibboleths of Know Nothing

[29] Fillmore was not a strong candidate for the reason that he did not really share the Know Nothing views, and had accepted their nomination only as a matter of political expediency. The news that he had been nominated by the American Party reached him at Rome —just after he had had an audience with the Pope!

[30] I anticipate my story here to point out that it was the Supreme Court that ruled against the Oregon School law of our own time, thus preserving the right to existence of the parochial school. It can never be anything else but the Palladium of religious liberty.

lodges lived true Americanism. Theoretically of course it would have been possible to have changed the Constitution. But this would have involved bringing under debate all the principles upon which the Republic reposed. In such a debate the mass of moderate American opinion would have prevailed, for however much the country was against Catholicism, it still retained a hearty predilection in favor of the Constitution as it stood.

I do not want to close this chapter, with its record of violence and ill-will, on a political note, and therefore turn in conclusion to that very city where in 1844 the fiercest explosion had occurred. For there, during the very height of the fury, Catholic scholarship had flowered in Francis Patrick Kenrick and Catholic sanctity in John Neumann. They were even better representatives of the Church than the belligerent John Hughes of New York.

The mild, the too mild,[31] Kenrick had been appointed in 1851 Archbishop of Baltimore where he was admirably qualified, because of his learning and gentleness, to serve as Metropolitan and to preside as Apostolic Delegate over the First Plenary Council of Baltimore in 1852. Its legislation was directed towards regularizing Catholic discipline, but the specific details need not be discussed here. It is sufficient to say that its work was, in the eyes of Propaganda, almost too thorough. For a letter was sent from Rome on September 26, 1852, which, while approving what had been done, warned that a too rigid uniformity might give the semblance of a *national* Church.[32] They were to be Americans—true; but they must never forget that they were also Catholics. Under the impact of Nativism, there was a danger of Catholicism itself becoming too nationalistic. It was part of the Universal Church and not the Church of the United States.

Kenrick was succeeded in Philadelphia by John Neumann, a Bohemian and the Provincial of the Redemptorists. He tried his utmost to escape the episcopate, until one evening, going up to his room, he found a ring and pectoral cross lying on his desk. Then he knew that Archbishop Kenrick must have been there in his absence, and that his pleadings had failed. There is no space to tell here the story of his life. But the im-

[31] It was a pacifist principle that led him to say to his friend, Dr. William Keating, "Rather let every church burn than shed one drop of blood or imperil one precious soul." (Kirlin, *op. cit.*, p. 324.)

[32] Guilday, *A History of the Councils of Baltimore*, p. 181.

pression it left is seen in his being the only American bishop whose Process towards Beatification was begun at Rome. Not without significance is the fact that it was his see that had been the center both of the worst trustee schisms and the worst manifestations of Nativism.

CHAPTER SIXTEEN

IMPERIAL EXPANSION

The Mexican war was but a new instance of the aggressive nationalism that had come to look on America's expansion at the expense of her neighbors as what was described as manifest destiny. The euphemism was magnificent, though from hardly any angle can this phase of history be regarded as redounding to the national honor. To make matters worse, it was hardly illustrative of any clean-cut policy. The grand phrases employed could at most mean that it was somehow noble of Americans to yield to the desire to grab. The best one is able to say is that they were caught in a vortex of confused sectional issues and did not always know that they were allowing themselves to be swept along by party or merely predatory passions. The true destiny of the United States as the guardian of justice and liberty was lost sight of. If in the end good did result, and the American ideal reasserted itself, there is no need, on that account, to praise either the politicians or the populace who mistook resounding speeches for sound thought, however much we may now admit that in the cross-currents of the time some of the currents were directed to better objects than immediately appear.

New England was opposed to the Mexican war, for the reason that it was opposed to the extension of slavery involved in any acquisition of new territory by the South. This had its genuine humanitarian aspect, and was expressed with homely raciness by Lowell's *Biglow Papers*. Texas might well be called another pen in which to cram more slaves. Other aspects of the matter were less admirable. One was the Northern determination to maintain ascendency. But another again was that New England was the center of the Nativist movement, and for this reason looked upon the war as a heaven-sent opportunity for humbling a Catholic power and so proving the predominance of Protestantism. Yet even here there was confusion: for there were apprehensions about obtaining new territories where so many of the inhabitants were Catholics. The Nativists therefore wanted war and at the same time did not want it. Only the South was perfectly clear in its mind.

From Texas it hoped to carve several slave states that would balance the growing free West. If it was not always candid in saying so openly, at least it knew what it wanted. Solidity of sentiment there, combined with the appeal to the Middle-West of the idea of expansion, gave Polk the support he needed to force the issue.

There is no need—or any space—to record here the political history of the annexation. But certain factors must, in fairness to those who were least scrupulous, be pointed out. Mexico was anything but an orderly nation. In 1824 Iturbide, after the casting off of the Spanish yoke, had himself crowned Emperor, only to be soon deposed and banished and, when he ventured to return, executed. After that things remained in a state of confusion, with one adventurer after another seizing momentary power, and each in turn being overthrown. Only Santa Anna contrived to keep hold of the reins, though even he had his vicissitudes. Americans therefore had some reason to feel uneasy about Mexico.

Mexico would have been none of their business except for the fact that numbers of Americans had been settling in Texas. Under the grant made to Moses Austin by the Mexican government in 1821 only those were to be admitted who were Catholic in religion and who were prepared to take an oath of allegiance to Mexico. Both the loyalty and the religion of most of these settlers was extremely dubious, yet as they were prepared—tongue in cheek—to fulfill the technical requirements, they could not be kept out. They were even powerful enough to obtain a special exemption from the Mexican laws prohibiting slavery. And they bided their time.

Their opportunity soon came. On the pretext of objectionable taxes the Americans in Texas rose, ejected the customs officers, and drove the Mexican garrisons across the border. They had never had any intention of living except as they chose. Early in 1836 Texas proclaimed its independence.

To restore order, as he described it, Santa Anna marched north, was resisted in the famous siege of the Alamo in San Antonio in early March, 1836, and then butchered all the surviving defenders, to be himself routed the following month by Sam Houston and an American force at San Jacinto. The road was now clear, the Texans hoped, for their annexation by the United States.

For that, however, they had to wait until Polk became President. Van Buren was opposed to the annexation, knowing that it would mean war with Mexico. And when, during Tyler's administration, an offer came from England of a loan to Texas, on condition that it renounce slavery, the South took alarm: Texas had to remain a slave state until it could be annexed. Some men of both political parties feared this would mean the revival of the old sectional strife. But the South was willing to run that risk and the West, in its zest for expansion, was blind to it. Meanwhile a group of Machiavellian Whigs hoped that the Democrats, by taking Texas, would overreach themselves. Which was precisely what happened, so far as the South and its interests were concerned. As Morison and Commager point out: "The real trouble was that Polk wanted much more than the Rio Grande boundary. His eyes were fixed on the Pacific."[1] The farsighted Calhoun was opposed to seizing too much, well understanding that it would bring about internal strife over the question of slavery. But other Southerners were not so wise, and the Mississippi valley was all for America's manifest destiny. Texas was therefore duly annexed, and when a Mexican force invaded its soil the President perceived that he had a splendid chance for declaring war, so issued a proclamation that "by the act of the Republic of Mexico, a state of war exists between that government and the United States." This very conveniently removed his obligation of consulting Congress. But however technically correct Polk was, it was the United States after all that had committed the act of aggression.

With the war a new age opened. When Jefferson had made the Louisiana Purchase its constitutionality had been questioned. But Jefferson had been dead for twenty years, he and John Adams dying on the same day, July 4, 1826—"a damned Yankee trick" on Adams' part, as one of Jefferson's friends called it. Now a new generation was in the saddle. The caution of the Founding Fathers was definitely outmoded. The period of American imperialism had begun.

Nor, it must be confessed, is there any conclusive sign that it has ended. Trotsky prophesied shortly before his death that the United States would develop into the most gigantic imperial organization ever known. Although strong forces are at work against it—for American idealism deplores such adventures—it is difficult to set bounds to a process once it has be-

[1] *The Growth of the American Republic*, Vol. I, p. 487.

gun. At least with one side of its mind America approves an almost unlimited expansion. In the case of Texas what occurred could be explained as America's inheritance of the ancient English suspicion of Spain, so that according to this point of view the war of 1846 may be regarded as the first phase of the struggle of which the war of 1898 was the second. It was so uplifting to believe that America had a positive duty to eject the corrupt and disorderly Latin, and so grand an excuse for expanding its territory. Sooner or later, it was argued, those loosely held provinces of Mexico were bound to drop into the American lap. All that needed to be done in 1846 was to shake the tree. Had there been no other reason, the protection of the value of the Texan bonds that were held in such quantities in the United States would have been reason enough.

A fuller discussion of the political issues involved would be outside the scope of this book. I have brought them up at all because they are illustrative of the American temper of the time. Similarly I need not give any account of the war itself, except to say that it was popular, except in the North Atlantic states, and even there some satisfaction existed over the chastisement of the Catholic Mexicans. What I must limit myself to is such aspects of the matter as bear directly upon the story of the Church.

The more bigoted Protestant partisans lost no time in circulating rumors about the defection of American Catholic soldiers to the enemy and of Catholic plots to poison Protestant soldiers. That there were some desertions is true, though they were insignificant and rarely occurred among Catholics.[2] The shoe was rather on the other foot. Many Protestant soldiers went off to the war licking their pious chaps over the loot of Catholic churches they expected. And though in this they were usually disappointed, papists with the American forces were as a rule obliged to attend Protestant services, where they had to listen to sermons that tried to whip up patriotic fervor by denunciations of Catholicism. It was for this reason that Polk—acting out of a plain sense of justice—appointed two Jesuits as chaplains to the army, so bringing upon himself

[2] The charges are discussed in Thomas F. Meehan's "Catholics in the War with Mexico" in *Records and Studies*, Vol. XII (1918), pp. 39–66.

the Nativist charge that he was violating the Constitution.[3] The Presidential sense of fairness (though this was conveniently linked with astute policy) was also manifested in his proposal to employ Bishop Hughes of New York to "disabuse the minds of the Catholic priests and people of Mexico in regard to what they erroneously supposed to be the hostile design of the government and people of the United States upon the religion and church property of Mexico."[4] Hughes prudently refused because of the storm that was at once raised at the bare suggestion of employing a Catholic bishop in such a mission. His biographer, Hassard, remarks: "The Bishop often alluded darkly to this affair but he would not tell the whole story, because he thought it would not be proper for him to repeat anything of what transpired in a confidential interview with the chief officer of the government. Even with his most intimate friends he used to make a little mystery of it." There really was not much mystery: it was natural that a Catholic prelate should be thought useful to bring about peace.

He would never have entertained the Presidential proposal had he not known that annexation would be of service to the Church in Texas. Ecclesiastical conditions there were anything but satisfactory. While it had been a republic there were only two clerics in the whole vast territory, and neither of them was in good standing. Though they said Mass now and then they gave no instructions and heard no confessions.[5] Matters were indeed improved somewhat in 1841 by the appointment of a Vicar-Apostolic, John Odin, who afterwards became Bishop of Galveston. But at the moment he could do little except survey the field, when he discovered that there were thousands of Texans who had never seen a priest since they had left Europe.[6] Having founded a convent at Galveston he left for Europe to see whether he could gather recruits for the mission. By the time he returned war had broken out. It was its cessation that made possible his appointment as Bishop and more extensive building upon the foundations he had already laid down.

[3] One of these chaplains, Father Rey, was killed—so much to the grief of General Scott that he wept at the news. The other was the celebrated Father McElroy.

[4] Polk's *Diary*, Vol. I, p. 408.

[5] See Sister M. Salesia Godeker's *Bruté*, pp. 372–373.

[6] Shea, *op. cit.*, Vol. IV, p. 288.

Texas proper was not the only part of the territories acquired by the United States that benefited by passing under a new ecclesiastical jurisdiction. There was, for instance, the work done by John Baptist Lamy in New Mexico and Arizona. His story has been told in Willa Cather's novel, *Death Comes for the Archbishop*—an example of how the non-Catholic artist can find thrilling literary material in what those of the household of faith are inclined to take too much for granted. He was an Auvergnat, a Frenchman of Frenchmen, but had worked in the dioceses of Louisville and Cincinnati before being made Vicar-Apostolic of New Mexico in 1850. It was his special mission to bring about friendly relations with those Spanish Catholics who would probably have resented the intrusion of any other American. The fact that he was a Latin helped; the fact that he was a man of much tact and charm helped even more. For he had somehow to bring under better discipline a lax and lazy clergy long accustomed to being a law unto themselves. With great courage and humor he set about his task, aided almost equally by his *bon sens français*. His was a life in the saddle and often his bed was the bare ground under brilliant stars. Nor did it change in any essential when he became Archbishop of Santa Fé in 1875, though by then he was over sixty. He remained the missionary whose function it was to build up a neglected diocese. We can estimate the progress of his achievement when we know that by 1865 there were a hundred thousand Catholics in New Mexico alone, with eight thousand more in Arizona and Colorado. In that year he was able to announce to Propaganda that he had built forty-five churches and had repaired eighteen more. Not until 1885 did he at last hand over the reins of government to John Baptist Salpointe, who had worked as one of his missionaries until 1868 and since then had been Vicar-Apostolic of Arizona. Now the old man could retire from his labors. But his heart being in the West, he remained in Santa Fé in retirement, and there in 1888 death came for the Archbishop.

Almost simultaneously with Texas and New Mexico, California—the real objective of Polk's policy—fell into American hands. Indeed, had it not been for California there would probably have been no war with Mexico. For that country, while it never officially recognized the independence of Texas, had come tacitly to accept it as an accomplished fact. Minor boundary questions could easily have been settled by negotiation. But though Mexico's hold on California was weak, it did not wish to relinquish so rich a province. Equally the soil and climate of California—its deposits of gold were not as yet known—were a good reason for the United States wishing to obtain such a prize.

In the whole region there were at the time only about 6,000 whites, American traders who had no legal right to be there at all and Mexicans of Spanish descent who lived a large luxurious life on their ranches. When trouble with Mexico was obviously brewing, Commodore Sloat was sent secret orders to seize San Francisco as soon as he heard that war had been declared. Meanwhile the American consul at Monterey had been instructed that though "the President will make no effort and use no influence to induce California to become one of the free and independent States of the Union," it would be welcomed if it chose to become such of its own accord. The hint was sufficiently broad, and was all the more pointed by the strange coincidence that Frémont happened to be in California on an exploring expedition.

Concerning this Paxson blandly writes: "He does not appear to have been ordered [there] as part of the impending war."[7] But there is no need for us to show such beautiful simplicity. The Hitlerian technique—however much it may be regarded as the last refinement of its special method—is not particularly new. The Führer did not invent the Trojan Horse. All that need be noted is that Frémont was at hand when news came of the outbreak of hostilities between Mexico and the United States—when at once he, assisted by other Americans, raised the Bear Flag and proclaimed California an independent republic. They could count on the annexation that soon followed.

But again the Catholic Church was to profit. California had had a glorious missionary history, but the secularization effected in 1835 had undone the work of Serra. The Indian converts drifted away; the churches were falling into ruins; few priests were left; and the property, which under the Franciscan regime had been considered as belonging to the Indians, was now plundered by avaricious officials. With the entry of the United States the work had largely to be begun all over again, but it was put upon a much better basis.

Because the story of the Church in California is in itself so noble, it would be advisable to interrupt the progress of events

[7] *Op. cit.*, p. 353.

to go back to the work accomplished in the eighteenth century —which in turn largely rested upon those explorations of the great Eusebius Kino in Lower California that have recently been related with such a wealth of detail in Professor Bolton's *Rim of Christendom*.

The Jesuits were unable to continue their activities because in 1767 Charles III issued his edict banishing them from Spain and the Spanish possessions. It was for this reason that the Franciscans entered upon the scene. In 1769 Junipero Serra went north with Governor Portolá and began that chain of missions which extended from San Diego to Sonoma, a length of about six hundred miles. Making his headquarters at Monterey, the presidio, he built at nearby Carmel the church dedicated to San Carlos Borromeo in which he is now buried.[8] Up and down the *camino real*, a mere footpath then, hobbled Serra on his half-crippled legs, baptizing thousands, confirming thousands more (for which he had special faculties) and founding the missions whose names sound like poems: San Luis Rey, Santa Clara, San Juan Capistrano, San Antonio de Padua, San Luis Obispo, San Gabriel, San Fernando, San Buenaventura. I have not given a complete list, and many of the missions were founded after Serra's death in 1784.[9] These I have not mentioned at all. The work is all the more astonishing when we remember that the Californian Indians were of a stupid and degraded sort, often showing such stubbornness that Serra and his fellow-friars had to labor for years before they could make a single convert. The eventual system established shows on what firm foundations they had built.

This system was everywhere the same. At each mission a guard of half a dozen soldiers was maintained, but these were subject to the padres and had as their main function the administration of temporalities. The missionaries had nothing to do with such matters, being paid a fixed salary by the government. The lands and the buildings of the station belonged to the converts themselves.

A strict discipline was of necessity maintained. The Indians

[8] I had the honor to be present at the translation of his remains and wrote an article about this for the first issue of the *Commonweal*.

[9] When Serra died his work was taken over and extended by Fermin Lasuen, whom Bancroft ranks even higher than the pioneer as the builder of the missions. Perhaps the best account of him is in the article by Dr. Charles E. Chapman of the University of California in the *Catholic Historical Review*, Vol. V (1919), pp. 131–155.

had to be induced to work at various trades, which of course they had to be taught. Those who did not live in the village attached to the mission were provided with quarters in the mission quadrangle, one side of which contained a dormitory for the girls, another a dormitory for the young men, and the other the workshops. There the young people remained as a rule until they married, after which they joined the village. Everybody was under the authority of the missionaries, for without such authority nothing could have been accomplished for these wretched savages. Correction, however, was mild and administered by the Indian chiefs. By such means the people were made Christians and lifted from their debased condition. One of the features of the missions was that the Fathers saw to it that the people were provided with plenty of harmless amusement. They were taught the Spanish dances, and not a station but had its orchestra. The priest was in a very special sense the Father of his people, all of whom had to be regarded as children if anything were to be done with them at all. But the paternalism was intended to be only a stage towards the development of independence.

The prosperity of the missions was to a great extent the cause of their downfall. A vast amount of grain of different kinds was raised on the farms, and on the ranches there were at one period nearly a quarter of a million head of cattle, and even more sheep, as well as thousands of horses, mules, hogs and goats. This wealth—communally held, with the friars acting merely as administrators—was coveted when, upon the shaking off of Spanish rule, Mexican politicians cast their greedy eyes in the direction of California. Salaried commissioners were appointed by the government, and the lands which the Franciscans had always maintained belonged to the Indians themselves were under one subterfuge or another confiscated. The friars were ejected and secular priests, who were given no opportunity to do anything for the development of the Indians (and who generally had very slight interest in it) were put in their place. What had been built up in sixty years was destroyed almost at a blow. Yet while they were in charge the Franciscans had baptized a hundred thousand souls, of whom all except a small percentage belonged to the most degraded and hopeless savages in the world. The one good quality they possessed was amiability. It proved enough to permit the missionaries to make a silk purse out of a sow's ear. One of the tragedies of history is that the friars were not allowed to bring their neophytes to the high degree of civilization at which they were aiming. This experiment with what seemed the poorest of human material produced in a short space of time results so striking that one can only speculate sadly on what might have been achieved if Christians had not wrecked the work of Christianity.

If the Indians were destined to pass as completely as the padres, so also was Latin civilization destined to pass from California. The Spanish power had been held there, almost against its own will, by the enthusiasm of the missionaries. And though these had only a spiritual motive, their presence —by keeping Spain to its task—had kept out the Russians who, early in the nineteenth century, under Rezanov,[10] had schemes for annexing the whole Pacific coast. Had the Muscovite once found lodgment there he would have been difficult to get rid of. For its Pacific states America can thank Serra, and Serra's successors. Of Spain nothing now remains except a few ruined or restored churches as memorials to the past. Of these Californians are legitimately proud, as giving additional glamor to a land of entrancing loveliness.

The Mexican bishop of the Two Californias, Francisco Garciadiego, died at Santa Barbara in the spring of 1846. The new ecclesiastical organization, under the Spaniard, Joseph Alemany, who had been Provincial of the American Dominicans, was virtually a rebuilding from the ground up. He did, however, manage to save from the debacle part of the interest on the forced sale of the lands of the missions.[11] But by then

[10] He fell in love with the daughter of the Governor of San Francisco. After his death she became a Dominican nun. Their romance has been told in one of Gertrude Atherton's novels.

[11] Engelhardt tells in his *Missions and Missionaries of California* (Vol. IV, p. 745) how after a long suit before the United States Land Commission the Church was awarded tracts of land formerly belonging to the missions as Church property. The question of the money of the Pious Fund was finally settled only in 1902 before the Hague Tribunal, when an award of $1,420,682 in unpaid annuities was demanded of Mexico for the United States in the name of the California hierarchy. By the same decision Mexico was obliged to pay annually $43,050 *in perpetuum* to the United States for the same purpose. This sum was one half of the interest at 6% of the confiscated fund. (See Engelhardt, Vol. I, pp. 676, 677.) Had it not been for the American possession of California, in other words, the Church there would have been robbed without any hope of redress.

California had been ceded to the United States and two years later it was admitted to full statehood.

The completion of the westward advance of the United States was achieved—except for the pan-handle of the Gadsden Purchase of 1853—with the acquisition of Oregon. This territory (which included the present Washington and Idaho as well as Oregon, just as "California" included what were to become several other states) had remained under joint American and British occupation until 1846, when the expansionist urge that had seized America demanded its formal surrender to the United States. In his inaugural address of 1845 Polk rather truculently asserted the claims of his country and explained to a Congressman, who thought he had taken too strong a line, that "the only way to treat John Bull was to look him in the eye." The American slogan was now "Fifty-four-forty or fight!" And no doubt there would have been a war before Great Britain consented to so unjustifiable a demand had not the outbreak of hostilities with Mexico made even the most bellicose American expansionist wonder if it was altogether advisable to fight on two fronts. As events turned out, Great Britain consented to withdraw—at the advice of Dr. John McLoughlin, the agent of the Hudson Bay Company—despite the fact the region north of the Columbia River contained at that time only a dozen Americans as against over seven hundred British subjects. What McLoughlin saw was that England could not permanently hope to retain so deep a southward dip from Canada, although if actual occupation be any argument it was clearly entitled to the country. On the other hand, the United States withdrew its claim to the 54° 40′ bulge into Canada, and the matter was sensibly compromised on the basis of a straight line drawn from the Lake of the Woods to Puget Sound.

The legend is that it was the Presbyterian minister, Dr. Marcus Whitman, who saved Oregon for the United States in the face of the wicked machinations of the Catholic missionaries who were supposed to be hand in glove with Dr. McLoughlin, now and since 1843 a Catholic. The fact is, however, that Dr. McLoughlin always aided the American Protestant missionaries and protected them when the only law then prevailing in the territory was that of his administration—and this even against the wishes of the Hudson Bay Company.[12]

[12] O'Hara, *Pioneer Catholic History of Oregon*, p. 55.

Nor did the French Canadian missionaries make any attempt to influence the course of politics. As for the greatest of the missionaries to the Indians, De Smet—of whom we shall hear more later—he was definitely pro-American.

It is necessary to say something at this point about the charges brought against the Catholic Church in connection with the tragedy of Marcus Whitman. If I pass over the discussion of the matter in Bishop O'Hara's book and Father Peter J. Paul's article,[13] it is because they are Catholics, and so may be thought to be prejudiced. No such suspicion can be entertained of William I. Marshall's careful studies or of what Professor E. G. Bourne has written on the subject. They utterly demolish every point in the myth.

The facts are these. Whitman, a medical missionary, first went to the Oregon country in 1835, going out again the following year, this time with a wife and a Dr. and Mrs. Spalding. They were consistently befriended by McLoughlin as well as by the Catholic priests. Indeed, without McLoughlin they could hardly have maintained themselves.

In 1843 Whitman made his famous ride to the East which —so his legend had it—was made for the patriotic motive of saving Oregon for the Union. Actually he went to the East because word had arrived that the Protestant missions were in danger of being withdrawn by the missionary society which had commissioned them. Further, he wished to gather recruits to stem the tide of "Romanism." It is true that in one of his letters he wrote (without warrant) that "The Papal effort is designed to convey over the country to the English"; but in another letter he says, "We very much need good men to locate themselves, two, three, or four in a place and secure a good influence for the Indians and form a nucleus of religious institutions and keep back Romanism. This country must be occupied by Americans or foreigners; if it is the latter, they will be mostly papists." In other words, he was mainly interested (as was quite proper) in the propagation of his faith; only *per accidens* was he working in the American interest. But equally the Catholic missionaries were not working for the political advantage of Great Britain; they were concerned solely with converting the Indians.

It was the terrible murder of Whitman and his wife and others in 1847 that induced Dr. Spalding—twenty years after

13 In *Records*, Vol. XL, 1929.

the event, be it noted—to concoct the myth of the patriotic ride and, worse, to suggest that the Whitman massacre had been instigated by the priests. Actually it was Father Brouillet who saved Spalding's life by warning him, as soon as he had heard of what had happened, of his danger. As for the murderous Indians, they were not Catholics but those among whom the Protestant missionaries were laboring. But Spalding was never perfectly sane on the subject of Catholicism and after the massacre what remnants of sanity he had were shattered. Even so, only after a long period of morbid brooding did he produce his fantastic story.

If some exculpation can be offered for him, none whatever can be offered for William Barrows, who published his *Oregon* in 1893 and amplified the lies and legends. Yet as Marshall pointed out in the *Annual Report of the American Historical Review* for 1910, Barrows had at his command in the office of the Massachusetts Home Missionary Society about four thousand pages of letters from Dr. Whitman and his associates and these "utterly annihilate every proposition that Barrows advances as to the origin and the purpose of the Whitman ride." On the dastardly mendacity concerning the Whitman murder, Shea's caustic comment is enough: "It is scarcely credible, and is a reproach to human nature, that Rev. Mr. Spalding, who owed his life to Vicar-General Brouillet, and so acknowledged at the time, in later years interpolated his early accounts so as to charge that the Indians were instigated by the Catholic missionaries."[14]

Until the settlement of the Oregon claims the Catholic ecclesiastical organization in Oregon was under the direction of Francis Norbert Blanchet, a French Canadian and the Vicar-Apostolic. After the settlement he was appointed Bishop of Oregon, and the same day (July 24, 1846) was named Archbishop, his brother Augustine being elected to the see of Walla Walla four days later. He had so strongly urged upon the Holy See that the vast territory under his jurisdiction be divided that a number of other bishoprics were constituted under his metropolitanate, but as several of these remained on paper, he himself acted as administrator for the dioceses

[14] *Op. cit.*, Vol. IV, p. 327. Yet it was in the year following Shea's fourth volume that Barrows wrote, and the complete demolition of the Whitman legend had to wait for Marshall and Bourne. Even so, it still has a certain currency, so hard is it to refute a lie once set in circulation.

of Princess Charlotte's Island and New Caledonia, while his brother acted for Fort Hall and Colville. Eventually Walla Walla was itself suppressed and Augustine Blanchet translated to Nesqually, which has also disappeared under that name. It covered the present state of Washington.

The work of the two brothers continued until 1880, both resigning within a couple of months of one another. It was they who established the Catholic Church north of California, and again the work was that of Frenchmen, though in this case French Canadians. But they had been obliged to seek their earliest recruits in France, the first action of the Archbishop being to sail in search of them. America owes much to them as it does to the noble open-hearted, open-handed giant, Dr. McLoughlin, the true Father of Oregon. After the settlement of the boundary question, he became an American citizen and lived in retirement in the country over which his rule had once been absolute. All these men achieved what they did because they put the claims of God and humanity over political interests. They were able to be so loyal to their new allegiance because they sought above all else the good of the Church. They recognized that this could be effectuated only by their complete identification with the United States.

They were sadly to witness, however, the pushing back by the incoming white men of the Indians, whom they knew from the beginning to be doomed. Nor did the finding of gold in California at all aid anything like a steady, settled Catholic development. For the inhabitants in their parts migrated almost *en masse* when the news arrived of the precious bane. This, fortunately, was before long offset by the railways that linked the East and West and by the mining opportunities that the north Pacific states discovered within their own borders. And with these there opened up other possibilities of wealth in live-stock, agriculture and lumber. By being on hand before the boom which they foresaw, the priests were ready for the arrival of a new huge wave of settlers. The Church was here in advance of the Frontier as it had been in the Ohio and Mississippi valleys.

So much for the Catholic connection with the expansion of America towards the West and the South-west. A few concluding words might be said about the general temper of the country during those driving years. Looked at from one angle, the energy of America at that time seems to be hardly more than a crude greed, to be pardoned merely because it was naïve. The judgment would be distorted that pronounced so definitely. A deeper insight might perceive, even in the most corrupt of politicians and the narrowest of the new million-aires that were beginning to arise, a secret streak of altruism. Or, if that is too much to say, at least these men, hurried on by something which they did not fully comprehend, may be said to have served a cause not altogether ignoble. I am no imperialist and dread the birth of a society whose chief vigor is devoted to acquisition. But over-simplifications must be avoided: the acquisition, though sufficiently ugly, was not alto-gether undecked in a few seemly gauds and feathers. Nor was the imperialism, in the event, other than a blessing for those whom it rescued from a worse despotism and a cynical ineffi-ciency. But, allowing such considerations to remain on one side, it must be pointed out that then, as always, in America there was a genuine idealism which manifested itself in a hundred sometimes very different ways. The period was, for example, the hey-day of Fourierism and the Owenites (with their New Harmony colony), of the "perfectionism" with which the Oneida community attempted to meet the de-mands of sex and of the universal celibacy with which the Shakers avoided it. It was the age of Brook Farm and Fruit-lands and the *Dial* and the Transcendentalists and Alcott's quaint educational experiments and the feminism of Marga-ret Fuller and Frances Wright. And although it would be un-fair to lump all these movements and people together, we might roughly say that America at this time was, in many ways, the kingdom of the crank. However absurd the American of that kingdom might be, he balanced with his starry opti-mism the coarser optimism of the Frontier.

In religious opinions the same apparent divergences may be seen. Brigham Young, the masterful organizer, led his follow-ers to Deseret—being directed thereto, it is somewhat amusing to note, by Father de Smet.[15] It was there that he established

---

[15] As a rule the Catholic missionaries got on rather well with the Mormons. Joseph Smith, for example, always sent a barge, manned by strong rowers, whenever the German Dominican, John George Allemann, had to cross the Mississippi. When Father Allemann thanked him, the Prophet explained, "Never mind, Father. Next to the Church of the Latter Day Saints that of the Catholics is the best." The real explanation is that Smith had observed that the Catholic clergy minded their own business and confined themselves to work-ing among their flocks, whereas the Protestant ministers who had

a theocracy reposing upon a theology which for sheer illogicality has never been surpassed—polygamy imposed upon a Christian framework. But this rough, rowdy, jovial, humorous Puritanism must be admitted to have populated Utah; and the hard-headed practicality and business sense of Brigham Young made Deseret blossom like the rose—or at any rate flourish on sugar-beets.

That was one side of the American religious originality, and I confess preferring it to the other—the spirituality of Mrs. Eddy that was soon to make such an appeal to a very different group. She dissolved all flesh to spirit where Brigham Young, taking over Joseph Smith's theology, had to solidify his pantheon into flesh. Both succeeded as they did because they were the twin lobes of the American mind of the time.

But of course these two movements represented that mind as cut off from the past and making a completely new start in a new world. They had slight intellectual foundation—Mrs. Eddy's perhaps even less than Joseph Smith's. They were thoroughly American in the sense that only America could have produced them. It is true that Mormonism was obliged to renounce its central tenet—or the practice it implied—in order to exist unmolested in a country that recognized normal Christian morals. Christian Science was more fortunate: having little to offer that conforms to human experience, it continued to expand, vague, pervasive.

What Christian Science did was to loosen the dogmatic concepts of traditional Protestantism. Rather than have that befall, it would have been better for America to have retained the fierce bigotry of Nativism. But even that wish is futile: Protestantism as a coherent system had already begun to fall apart. Mormonism tried to hold it together with a new revelation; Christian Science escaped into the intangible.

What might be remembered, however, is that the eccentricity which was the first sign of the break-up in America of dogmatic Protestantism was kept somewhat in check by cool Catholic common sense. It was greatly to America's advantage that during these years it had so many satirical Irishmen, so many classically rational Frenchmen within its borders. Most

been sent to the West from denominations in the East "did little else than meddle in politics and write home misrepresentations, especially against his own people, the Mormons." (Hoffmann, *The Church Founders of the Northwest*, pp. 176–177.)

fortunate of all, there was present the Catholic Church with its keen consciousness of historical continuity. It alone knew that Americanism derived from a body of doctrine of which most other Americans were quite unaware. Therefore it was able to adapt itself to new conditions, never losing its identity or its special character when it appeared as American. It could be that as well as anything else for the simple reason that it was universal. The imperialism of the 'forties, the westward drive of American aggression were political affairs with which Catholicism, as such, had no concern. But the Church was always there, at once American and Catholic. So that when the fifth decade of the century closed, the Church was ready for all that even "manifest destiny" had in store.

CHAPTER SEVENTEEN

THE GRAVE OF CALHOUN

From the beginning the fact of slavery had been regarded as an anomaly in the Constitution. The very machinery of American government functioned around the Declaration of Independence that all men were created equal. Yet it immediately proceeded to except a large class of human beings who, so far from being equal to the rest, were as much the property of other men as were their horses and dogs. There was no need of a very keen sense of logic to be affronted by the fact or a very keen conscience to be wounded by it. Yet America had perforce to accept the anomaly and allow it to eat like a cancer in the soul.

One anomaly of course immediately led to another. The Southern states, to which, at the time of the Revolution, slavery was already virtually limited, demanded that slaves be counted as though they were citizens when it came to apportioning the number of representatives sent to Congress. As it was only on that basis that they would accept the Constitution the North reluctantly compromised to the extent of agreeing that slaves should be so counted, but only three-fifths of them—a compromise as illogical as the extreme demand. Therefore, as the wealth of the industrial North grew, the question was asked with increasing insistence: if slaves, as property, were to give South Carolina a representation far in excess of its citizenship, why should not Massachusetts have a proportionate representation for its ships and mills? If that question was not very logical either, it was at least as reasonable as the false principle written into the nation's fundamental law.

The North was—at all events in the beginning—not at all idealistic in its objection to slavery. Its objection was simply to human chattels being counted when other forms of property were not. Further to confuse the issue that subsequently arose, it was precisely the State that became the center of abolitionism—Massachusetts—that had first thought of secession from the Union long years before South Carolina formally declared its secession and so precipitated the Civil War. Everything became more and more confused as new factors entered into the situation. Neither party—or none of the extremists in either party, those who brought on the clash—retained much hold on principle. Each was largely actuated by self-interest and altogether inflamed by passion. The rhetoric of their respective orators tended to obscure the whole question under discussion. When Calhoun asserted that the "peculiar institution" of the South was a positive good, he was talking nonsense, however dazzlingly. When Garrison said that slavery was under all circumstances an absolute evil, he too was talking nonsense, in admirably lucid and forceful English. There was, in truth, a certain amount of idealism on both sides. But the determining fact—practically never admitted—was that anti-slavery was coming more and more to accord with the economic interests of the North and Middle West. That was why the idealism of Garrison found political support. It also happened that slavery accorded with the economic interests of the South. And that was why the idealism of Calhoun seemed so beautiful to Southern politicians and property-owners.

What we have to consider is a gradually changing temper on both sides of the Mason-Dixon line. As early as 1696 the Quakers went on record with the opinion that slavery was opposed to the principles of the New Testament—yet some of them continued to hold slaves. Delaware had prohibited the slave-trade in 1776, and Rhode Island two years before had declared that all slaves brought there were to be free. As for Vermont, her constitution forbade slavery (1791), and when Quock Walker sued his master in 1781 in the Massachusetts courts, pointing to the declaration that all men were free and equal, his argument was upheld. But all this was mainly because slave labor was not profitable in the North.

Nevertheless in the South itself voices had been raised against slavery. "I tremble for my country," said the slave-owning Jefferson, "when I reflect that God is just, that His justice cannot sleep forever." It was his influence that led Virginia to prohibit the slave trade in 1778, though slavery itself was retained. Nor did Jefferson's views change. Rather he saw with increasing clarity the eventual strife that it would cause. When Alabama was admitted in 1819 as the eleventh slave state to balance the eleven that were free, he described it as "a fire-bell ringing in the night." So, too, Patrick Henry held slavery in abhorrence, but accepted it. And the will of Charles

Carroll of Carrollton is typical of the nobler minds of this period. It read in part, "I have always regarded slavery as a great evil, producing injury and loss to the whites principally, an evil for which we are not responsible." He therefore provided that his slaves should descend to his children, with the injunction that, if they were sold, it should be within the family, and with the wish "that my children will not transmit them to my grandchildren." Men's minds were then far from easy on this matter.

With the passage of time, however, they became more easy. Ingenious arguments were found to justify what had formerly been merely tolerated. The real argument, which was rarely mentioned, was that Whitney's cotton-gin had made slaves more profitable than before. Now that the price of field-hands had so greatly risen, owners went to history and the Bible to prove that slavery, instead of being an unavoidable evil, was eminently good in itself and of benefit to the slaves. To listen to some people talk you would think that the planters kept human beings in bondage solely out of pure kindheartedness!

It is usual to say that this argument was advanced mainly because some means had to be devised of meeting the challenge of the Abolitionists. Such is not the case: the argument antedated the challenge. It was advanced because the tender consciences of the Founding Fathers were somewhat calloused in their children. As Cecil Chesterton points out with plain good sense, the "Progressive" thesis that evils tend by the process of evolution to disappear, is not borne out by the facts. Quite the contrary. "Time," he remarks, "so far from being a remedy—as the 'progressives' do vainly talk—is always, when no remedy is attempted, a factor in favour of the disease."[1] Had the thing not been violently uprooted it might have endured to this day. Which is not to affirm that the right remedy was used. But certainly those who, after the event, proclaimed their belief that slavery would have gently disap-

---

[1] *A Short History of the United States*, p. 130. The book is well worth reading, though it is not always accurate. Chesterton wrote it while in camp in England in 1917—not, as his brother says in his *Autobiography*, while he was in the trenches. A prodigious textual memory was relied on, but even the best memory needs to consult books of reference. The result, however, was what is by far the most readable short history of America, one that has recently been republished in the Everyman Series.

peared of its own accord are out of touch with human psychology.

It is difficult in all this controversy to come across anything that makes much sense. Even the bootleg trade in "black ivory" found defenders: the negroes, it seems, were being captured in Africa and brought to America for their own good! The fact was conveniently passed over that slaves were getting too high-priced and so a new cheap supply was needed. In the same way we may scornfully dismiss the canting attempt to defend slavery from the pages of the Bible—for in pre-Christian times the institution was universal and unquestioned, and the Church itself arose in a civilization that took the thing for granted. The nauseous insincerity of much of the "idealism" that prevailed is proved by the motives of the American Colonization Society. It wanted to reship free negroes back to Africa out of a fear that they might prove a focus of disaffection for the enslaved. Many people who joined the Society did so for humanitarian reasons, but the organizers, so far from wishing to free the blacks, affirmed roundly, "You cannot abolish slavery, for God is pledged to sustain it." Even with God on their side, they were apprehensive lest the peculiar institution be undermined.

The practical argument that could have been used was that the slave suffered less than his master, and much less than the "poor white trash"—a class that did not originate after the Civil War but that was already sinking in the social and economic scale by having to compete with bondmen. The peculiar institution was so very peculiar that no group of people was more fierce in resistance to abolition than that of these poor wretches, whose one paltry consolation was that their freedom at least separated them from the slaves. They were too ignorant and stupid to see how slavery was already dragging them down tobacco road.

Then there was the horrifying, but absurd, argument that emancipation would end in miscegenation. As Professor Hart puts it, "Southerners sincerely believed that the object of the abolitionists was the amalgamation of the two races."[2] Actually racial amalgamation came nearer to being a consequence of slavery. The negro women, being the property of their masters, could be used sexually without restraint. Many a small planter had his own children working in his tobacco or cotton

[2] *Slavery and Abolition*, p. 216.

fields. Nor do we need to stop even there: many living negroes are descended from very illustrious forebears. Morality was hardly possible to the slave; immorality was all too easy to the slave-owner. Had slavery been given sufficient time the South would have absorbed all black blood.[3]

But there was another argument, equally horrifying, that had more substance. It was that of the danger of slave insurrections. Few such outbreaks occurred, and they never have in the history of slavery anywhere. But when they *have* occurred, they have had a ferocity all their own. People in the South vividly remembered the Nat Turner rebellion of 1831. This was connected in their minds with Abolitionist agitation, though the correct explanation is that Turner was a religious fanatic, probably insane. He raised a band of sixty men—all of them inflamed with brandy, except for the pious abstainer, Turner—and proceeded to massacre men, women and children, sixty-one in all, before being rounded up. By Turner's own confession they drank the blood of at least one victim to make them "brave and encouraged." Over the whole affair hangs the murky light of voodoo. Of the fifty-three arrested—several were killed in fight—seventeen, including a woman, were hanged; twelve were transported out of Virginia; three, being freedmen, were condemned by the State Circuit Court; the others were released. But the South was now convinced that nobody could be safe unless the blacks were kept in subjection. For that nothing except slavery sufficed. The rising therefore put back the process of gradual emancipation that had been gaining ground; there was no other slave rising until the one under John Brown at Harper's Ferry.[4]

[3] I do not want to press this too far. No doubt the majority of slave-owners were moral men. When Abolitionists talked of the whole South as being "one vast brothel" they were using the same language that the same type of person (who was often the same person) had used regarding convents. There is nothing quite so dirty as the puritanic and pharisaic imagination. But making all due allowances for exaggeration, human nature being what it is, irresponsible sexual immorality was one of the fruits of slavery.

[4] Garrison denied any connection between his propaganda and Nat Turner's rebellion, and this was supported by the confession Turner made in prison. The leaflets distributed in the South were aimed at the whites; as a rule the blacks would not have been able to read them had they ever fallen into their hands. But the whites naturally took the abolitionist leaflets as incitations to rebellion, and some of the slaves may have been affected, as by things "in the air." Turner

The danger of such risings was not of course a valid argument in favor of slavery, if the matter be philosophically considered. It was none the less powerful. For even if slavery had in the abstract to be considered an evil, one might not unreasonably take the position that it had to be continued—and even made more stringent—in order to avoid worse evils. True, that the negroes were in America by compulsion; true, that the problem raised by their presence was the creation of those who had brought them here. All the same, what troubled the whites in the South was the fact that negroes were among them in large numbers; therefore, whoever was originally to blame, they had to meet a threatening situation as best they could. If they had stuck to this line of reasoning, they would have had a case. Instead they disingenuously argued that slavery was a positive good because they were at once desperately afraid of the slaves and desperately keen on their own profits.

We must nevertheless sympathize with the Southerners when we remember the more objectionable variety of Abolitionist. Though the masters were mistaken in believing that their negroes were being incited to rebellion, that was their strong belief, and it must be allowed for. And there is no doubt at all that the negroes were being incited to run away and were being helped to escape by the vast conspiracy of the "underground railway." This was simply organized theft of private property. Moreover, many took part in it, not out of humanitarian conviction, but for mere sport. Worst of all was the general feeling throughout the South that its whole culture was in danger of being destroyed by the North—the same North that was sucking the planters economically and overwhelming them politically. No wonder that Southern tempers, never of the most equable, flared into rage, and that political philosophers like Calhoun glorified the institution the Abolitionists were attacking.

---

said he had been ordered to do what he did by a heavenly voice. We must bear in mind, too, the psychological effect upon both whites and blacks of the massacre at Santo Domingo and the risings in the South in 1800, 1822 and 1829. Before these there had been a slave riot in New York in 1741. It was suppressed with the execution of eighteen men and the transportation of eighty others. The fear of the masters made them take such frightful reprisals that risings rarely occurred. But even after the reprisals the fear remained, and must be allowed for. It was something that always weighed down and darkened the minds of Southerners.

There was a great deal to the contention that what was really at issue was the struggle between the industrialist North and the agricultural South. Thus Reuben Davis of Mississippi orated, "There is not a pursuit in which man is engaged (agriculture excepted), which is not demanding legislative aid to enable it to enlarge its profits, and all at the expense of the primary pursuit of man—agriculture. . . . Those interests, having a common purpose of plunder, have united and combined to use the government as the instrument of their operation and have virtually converted it into a consolidated empire." What made anti-slavery seem like cant was that honest idealists were being used by cynical realists, again for the swelling of dividends. The South did not forget that the slave trade had been mainly in the hands of New Englanders, that it was men from the North who conducted the infamous "breeding farms" of Maryland, and that "hard-boiled" Northern overseers were required if slaves were to be driven in an increasingly competitive market.

It was because of the Southern mood of exasperation that Senator Hammond bluntly referred to the "nowhere accredited dogma of Mr. Jefferson that 'all men are born equal.'" With equal plainness he asked, "Supposing that we were all convinced and thought of slavery as you do, at what era of 'moral suasion' do you imagine that you could prevail upon us to give up a thousand millions of dollars in the value of our slaves, and a thousand millions of dollars more in the depreciation of our lands?" One wishes that all Southerners had been as forthright, for precisely there was the real difficulty: the South could not—or believed it could not—abandon slavery without being ruined. It certainly had no intention of abandoning it at the behest of Northern manufacturers working in concert with Northern fanatics.

Nobody will now deny that slavery was an enormous evil. On the other hand few will deny that the slaves were not as a rule treated with undue harshness.[5] Even Harriet Beecher Stowe represented most of her Southerners as kindly gentlemen; her Simon Legree was from the North. Yet to argue that

[5] We need not on this account attempt to make a pretty picture of slavery. Even recent scholarly defenders of the South like Lloyd and Flanders on occasion try to prove too much. We can believe that most masters were sufficiently and sometimes very kind. But the suggestion that the negro women of Charleston often appeared in the height of Parisian fashion is laying it on a bit thick!

it was not to the interest of the slave-owners to ill-treat their slaves is a shallow sophistry—Dickens in his *American Notes* cut through it in a single stroke. "Is it to the interest of any man to steal, to game, to waste his health and mental faculties by drunkenness, to lie, forswear himself, indulge hatred, seek desperate revenge, or do murder? No. All these are roads to ruin. And why, then, do men tread them? Because such inclinations are among the vicious qualities of mankind. Blot out, ye friends of slavery, from the catalogue of human passions, brutal lust, cruelty, and the abuse of irresponsible power (of all earthly temptations the most difficult to be resisted), and when ye have done so, and not before, we will enquire whether it be to the interest of a master to lash and maim the slaves over whose lives and limbs he has an absolute control!" A lady told Calhoun that his plantation was a more eloquent argument for slavery than all his orations. But there were others of a very different kind. Nothing, after all, can gild the ugliness of slavery. All that we can sadly say is that Calhoun's warnings were justified: merely the form of slavery was changed; the negro race remained, and still largely remains, in virtual servitude—as, for that matter, does a large proportion of white men in many lands.

The other side of the picture is the harm slavery did to white men. The large, dignified, kindly plantations of the South where life was lived graciously did exist. But because of the over-blown romanticism of the South every owner of a few slaves, however ignorant and degraded he might be, regarded himself as a "cavalier"—on the ground that he did no manual work. Professor Hart tells us that of twelve and a half millions of persons in the slave-owning communities, only about 384,000, or one in thirty-three, was a slave-holder. "About 77,000 owners had only one slave apiece, and 200,000 more owned less than ten slaves each; while only 2,300 families owned as many as a hundred slaves."[6] On the other hand, blacks who were freedmen and had the necessary property qualifications could and did vote in all the states except South Carolina and Georgia until 1835 when—thanks to the Abolitionist propaganda—the situation of all negroes became worse. Freedmen were themselves in some instances slave-owners, and Hart gives an amusing instance of a negro minister being

6 *Op. cit.,* pp. 67–68.

bought by his congregation.[7] One wonders if they whipped him when his sermon failed to give satisfaction!

The times were indeed preposterous in many ways. For example, according to the plan of the "Ostend Manifesto" signed by the American ambassadors to France, Spain and England on October 18, 1854, Spain had to be forced to sell Cuba to the United States, and the quaint argument was advanced that she could use the money to develop her country to attract the tourist trade and "her vineyards would bring forth a vastly increased quantity of choice wines." If Spain was unable to appreciate this piece of beautiful American altruism, then Cuba should be seized. Among those who signed was Buchanan. Apparently even Texas was not a big enough pen to cram slaves in. If such projects were mooted, it was because the South was desperate with its grievances. There can be no denying that there was a steady and remorseless tipping of the balance against the Southern states, and though this was not by any means solely due to slavery, slavery was entwined with every aspect of the Southern question. It had become the obsession of men already exasperated beyond all bearing.

Although the South must bear the blame for finally precipitating the Civil War, and chose its moment badly, the North cannot be absolved from the blame of persecuting the South, or at least of irritating it beyond endurance, which amounted to much the same thing. The Abolitionists did not free the slaves, nor did they intend to bring on the war. On the contrary they would have been glad to have allowed the South to secede. But as the Abolitionist propaganda was the chief irritant, some attention must be given to it here, for the Catholic Church was involved in the matter, if only as a counter-weight to the fanaticism of the extremists on both sides.

First, however, it might be pointed out that the earliest of all Abolitionists were not Protestants but Catholics. It was Las Casas who led the fight in the sixteenth century, and it was the Spanish Crown that passed humane laws trying to curb what it could not altogether abolish. Nearly all the slave-traders from Sir John Hawkins down were Protestants, even if their religion consisted chiefly of a pious itch to plunder papists and cut their throats. This is worth mentioning be-

[7] *Ibid.*, p. 127.

cause Abolitionism came to be entangled with Know Nothingism and anti-Catholicism in the North. That there is no necessary relationship between a radical Protestantism and anti-slavery was shown clearly enough in the South. Nevertheless the Abolitionists completely misunderstood the Catholic position in this matter, which was almost the only sane factor in a world deranged.

But before coming to the part the Church played in the controversy, it would be as well first to take a glance at the Abolitionists themselves.

They were broadly of two classes. The one that was most distinguished—and least effectual—consisted of idealistic intellectuals and writers, and of highly cultivated Unitarian clergymen. They were mild, benevolent and not unreasonable; therefore they did not accomplish much. When Channing complained that Garrison had aroused "bitter passions and a fanaticism which shut every ear and every heart against argument," the rejoinder was, "We are not to blame that wiser and better men did not espouse . . . the cause of our oppressed, coloured countrymen. . . . We Abolitionists are what we are—babes, sucklings, obscure men, silly women, publicans, sinners, and we shall manage this matter just as might be expected from such persons as we."

That is precisely what they did. Even their ostentatious humility was immensely arrogant—and immensely effective. I find it hard to muster much admiration for the character of the more typical—that is, the more violent—Abolitionists: men like Garrison and John Brown. Their courage and sincerity are, of course, incontestable, and any man who possesses these qualities is entitled to respect. But when Garrison and Brown—and even Theodore Parker—said openly that anyone attempting to capture a runaway slave should be killed, it is evident that in them fanaticism had destroyed reason. In Garrison's case, however, it had not destroyed, but rather heightened, a command over words. Not because I subscribe to the sentiment but for the mere pleasure of copying out an unsurpassed piece of powerful English, I quote from the famous article he contributed to the first number of the *Liberator*, issued on New Year's Day, 1831: "I shall strenuously contend for the immediate emancipation of our slave population. . . . On this subject I do not wish to think, or speak, or write, with moderation. . . . I am in earnest—I will not equivocate—I will not excuse—I will not retreat a single inch—AND I WILL BE HEARD."

As for John Brown, if his action had been confined to his seizure of the arsenal at Harper's Ferry, I could think of him simply as a good, brave but misguided man. But I cannot blot from my mind the cold-blooded murders and mutilations he had previously perpetrated in Kansas. The only possible extenuation for these is that he was insane, as would seem to be borne out by his confession that he had, in disguise, questioned those whom he had marked down as his victims and had made the remarkable discovery that, without exception, every one of them had "committed murder in his heart." The proper place for him was not a gallows but a padded cell. It is a disheartening commentary on war hysteria that the North, when it marched to battle, chanted the song in which a sadistic lunatic was made a hero.

How wrong-headed the whole Abolitionist agitation was is shown by the fact that the British Parliament by its Emancipation Act of 1833 had pointed the way to a just and peaceable solution of the question of slavery—and that this was ignored. Under the British law the owners of slaves were to be compensated and slavery abolished by degrees, with 1840 as a terminal point. Its only effect on Abolitionists was to give a new impetus to the American movement—without imparting any wisdom or moderation.

In general therefore I can view the Abolitionist propaganda only with disgust. It was bigoted and deliberately mendacious, and therefore almost wholly mischievous. Though I cannot accept Dr. Arthur Young Lloyd's suggestion that the Abolitionists were out for no other purpose than to further the economic interests of the North—for that was merely an accidental consequence—it can hardly be questioned that the Abolitionists were unconsciously used by people who cared for nothing except their own dividends. But let us hear what Dr. Lloyd has to say: "In viewing the radical abolitionist attack upon the South after approximately a hundred years, it seems that the violence of the propaganda appealed only to the sectional interests of the North and merely served to antagonize and alienate the South. If the abolitionists were genuinely interested in ameliorating the condition of the slaves, why did they fail to make use of the anti-slavery sentiment among the Southern people? Instead of using Southern opinion, which might have aided the cause of emancipation, the radicals soon smothered it under an avalanche of vituperation. If the abolitionists really hoped to benefit the Negroes, their attack was a failure because of their incendiary propaganda which necessitated greater coercion and stringent discipline from the slaveholders and left the blacks totally unprepared for freedom when the day of emancipation came. On the other hand, if it was the intention of the abolitionists to discredit the Southern agricultural states, to create new sectional and political alignments, to encourage the development of sectional bitterness and hatred, and either to dissolve the government or allow its domination by Eastern industrialism, their tactics were highly successful."[8]

We may turn with relief from the fanatics to Abraham Lincoln's pronouncements. On March 3, 1837, when he was a member of the Illinois legislature, he signed with another member a statement that "They believe that the institution of slavery is founded on both injustice and bad policy, but that the promulgation of abolition doctrines tends rather to increase than abate its evils." In 1854 he wrote again, with that admirable logic of his which was perhaps founded upon his fondness for the study of mathematics, "If A can prove, however conclusively, that he may of right enslave B, why may not B snatch the same argument and prove equally that he may enslave A? You say A is white and B is black. It is color then; the lighter having the right to enslave the darker? Take care. By this rule you are the slave of the first man you meet with a fairer skin than your own. You do not mean that exactly? You mean the whites are intellectually the superiors of the blacks, and therefore have the right to enslave them? Take care again. By this rule you are to be the slave of the first man you meet with an intelligence superior to your own. But, you say, it is a question of interest, and if you make it your interest you have the right to enslave another? Very well. And if he can make it his interest he has the right to enslave you." After which one can only write *Q.E.D.* If the South had but had sufficient sense to entrust the solution of the problem to Lincoln, an equitable adjustment would have been possible without the need of a long bloody war. Unluckily for everybody concerned, the South was not guided by reason but by passion, and as it had been exasperated by the fanaticism of the Abolitionists it answered with a fanaticism of its own.

[8] *The Slavery Controversy, 1831–1860*, pp. 100–101.

Through all this period the Catholic Church kept its head. By which I do not mean to affirm that all Catholics, as individuals, were sensible people. They were not; some of them talked as much nonsense as anybody else. But though among them strong partisans were to be found for each of the extreme positions, as a body they took up a middle ground, and those in authority in the Church were among the few Americans who acted and spoke with moderation. Bishops and priests, like the laity, had their personal views, but they agreed to allow them to remain personal. There was no attempt made to commit the Church either to slavery or anti-slavery. Instead Catholics as a group tried to apply principles and to distinguish—with the result that they were often accused of straddling the question and (by the more reckless of the Abolitionists) of even being in favor of slavery.

Let us see what their position really was. In 1839 Gregory XVI issued his Apostolic Letter, *In Supremo Apostolatus*, on the slave trade. In this he followed previous papal pronouncements on the subject and wrote of course with the Catholic sense of history. He could not but remember that the Church arose in a servile society and had gradually—not by positive legislation but by moral suasion—mitigated the lot of the slaves until, after they had passed through the intermediate status of serfdom, they gained the freedom the Church considers natural to man. The Church also knew by experience that the lot of the slave, however hard, was not incompatible with the slave's eternal salvation; and the salvation of the souls of men is the Church's sole business. If the rich can reach heaven only by squeezing through the needle's eye, still harder must be the salvation of those whose wealth consists in the ownership of their fellows. From this point of view the Church was more concerned about the master than the man. In any event it did not wish to make matters worse by being in too much of a hurry. Gregory therefore took the line that, while slavery was a social evil, it was not a *malum per se*—that is, not necessarily an evil for the slave under a kind master, and not a positive detriment to his hope of heaven. At the same time the Pope, like previous Catholic authorities, condemned the slave trade. Slavery, as such, was neither condemned nor condoned. And this, after all, though embittered minds failed to see it, was the very distinction which had been enshrined in the American Constitution. The only difference was that the Church based its solution upon the ground of reason, while in the Constitution it was based upon nothing better than a political compromise. The Church and the Constitution were at one, however, in believing the solution neither perfect nor permanent, but a way of meeting a difficulty which was not, for the moment, to be met on any other ground.

The Papal Letter was, as might be expected, misunderstood and criticized by the extremists of the opposing factions. Bishop England therefore wrote in 1840 his *Letters to Forsyth* —this was John Forsyth, Secretary of State under Van Buren— in which he argued that Gregory had not made an absolute condemnation of slavery. Yet his own views of the matter were emphatic. In 1833 he had written to Propaganda saying that he was working "under a system which perhaps is the *greatest moral evil that can desolate any part of the civilized world*"[9] (the italics are his own), and in a letter in the *United States Catholic Miscellany* for February 25, 1841, he said, "I have been asked by many, a question which I may as well answer at once, viz: Whether I am friendly to the existence or continuation of slavery? I am not—but I also see the impossibility of abolishing it here. When it can or ought to be abolished, is a question for the legislature and not for me." The consequence was that he was accused of being an Abolitionist. At the same time he was accused of being proslavery, because he had advised Daniel O'Connell not to interfere in the matter, as it was a purely American concern.

England's position may be taken as typical. As a bishop in the South he would no doubt have espoused the cause of the Confederacy had he been alive at the time of the Civil War. His protégé and successor, Patrick Lynch—who was born like him in Ireland—did just that. Yet neither man approved of slavery. They hoped it would pass; they also hoped that, so long as it continued, the Church could effect amelioration by preaching mercy to the master and obedience to the slave. But Southern Catholics recognized that American slavery was not quite the same thing as that of classical antiquity. Then the slave, as a captive of war, might be the equal or even the superior in blood, culture and former social standing of his owner, whereas the American negro belonged to a race which needed to be educated before it was fitted for equality with the whites. The Church did not say that the negroes were

[9] Guilday, *England*, Vol. I, p. 531.

forever doomed to a subordinate position—still less that they ought to be doomed to it. But it looked facts in the face and thought of a gradual process of emancipation instead of that sweeping stroke which—by freeing the slaves in a single body —created a new negro problem. Again it was a matter of common sense.

England, though a bishop, wrote as an individual. Perhaps we should go to Francis Kenrick, who became Archbishop of Baltimore in 1851. In his *Theologia Moralis*, a text-book for seminaries, he argued that slavery was not demonstrably contrary to the natural law, without asserting its conformity or denying its being a social evil. In the Ninth Provincial Council, which sat under his presidency, the question was treated as a strictly political one, beyond the jurisdiction of the episcopate. "Our clergy," said the Pastoral Letter issued in May, 1858, "have wisely abstained from all interference with the judgment of the faithful, which should be free on all questions of polity and social order, within the limits of the doctrine and law of Christ." Slavery, it tacitly affirmed, did not fall within those limits. More specifically the Pastoral Letter said, "The peaceful and conservative character of our principles . . . has been tested and made manifest in the great political struggles that have agitated the country on the subject of domestic slavery. . . . Among us there has been no agitation on the subject."

This does not mean, however, that many Catholics had not vigorously expressed their personal views. As early as 1832 Judge Gaston, greatly daring, had addressed the students of the state University of North Carolina and had called upon them to help extirpate slavery, giving as his reasons that it worked against industry and enterprise and poisoned morals. As against this we have the letter, quoted by Hassard, written by Hughes of New York on May 7, 1861, to a Southern bishop. He claims that the Catholics of the North have, upon the whole, behaved themselves with great prudence and moderation, and then adds: "I regret I cannot say as much for the Catholics, and for some of their clergy, in the South."[10] But we must remember that this was nearly a month after the confederate guns had opened fire on Fort Sumter. Up to the time of the actual clash the Southern Catholics had been a restraining influence.

[10] *John Hughes*, p. 439.

Another factor should be borne in mind: the overwhelming majority of Catholics belonged to the Democratic Party, constituting its backbone in the North. Of these Catholics the majority were Irishmen who had scant sympathy with the negro, despite the fact that Know Nothingism had become more or less allied with Abolitionism. In vain were sixty thousand signatures obtained in Ireland in support of the anti-slavery cause; in vain the great O'Connell appealed to Irishmen in the United States. On this subject they turned him a deaf ear. They believed—or at any rate believed up to 1854— that they suffered from unfair competition with negro labor. They failed to perceive that their real enemy was slavery itself and that white men could never be really free so long as black men were held in bondage. Into their minds had entered something of that hatred William Cobbett had entertained for the emancipator Wilberforce. They knew that they themselves were far from being free and attributed it to the economic effect of slave labor. It needed the indiscreet scorn of Southern politicians for all who earned their living by manual work to open their eyes. At last it began to dawn upon them that they could never expect to receive the wages to which they were entitled so long as they were pitted against a slave who cost his master ten cents a day to keep. Even so, there were already too many free negroes in the North for their comfort; with these they could not escape a more direct competition on unfavorable terms. They therefore did not ever develop much enthusiasm for their colored brethren, though they took a notable share in the war.

As for the celebrated Catholic publicist, Orestes Brownson, his opinions, as was frequently the case with him, varied at different periods. He had opposed the anti-slavery of the New England intellectuals as a muddled matter (which it was), and pointed out that these gentle souls had got themselves into association with disreputable bigots. When war grew imminent, however, he changed his position that slavery was not contrary to the natural law and began to argue that natural law favored freedom—propositions not so contradictory as they might at first glance appear to be. Yet he agreed with Taney's decision in the Dred Scott case, while viewing it with misgivings that were justified by the event. During the war itself he urged emancipation as a war measure.

Perhaps the best statement of Brownson's views was that given in the commencement address he made in 1853 at

Mount St. Mary's College:[11] "You of the South consist of freemen and slaves . . . and so do we of the North. . . . While you have the manliness to avow it, we have the art to disguise it from the careless observer, under the drapery of fine names." As Mr. Schlesinger puts it: "In Brownson's eyes, the injustice of capitalism now exceeded those of slavery. If there had to be a laboring population distinct from proprietors and employers, he would prefer the slave system. 'As to our actual freedom one has just about as much as the other'; and the slave never tastes the terrible want and uncertainty which forever torments the free laborer."[12] Without subscribing to all the implications of that doctrine—which can be twisted to the support of the Bellocian "servile state"—it is perfectly true that the slavery issue was involved with many others: with that of industrialism versus agrarianism, with that of the danger to the gracious civilization of the South, and most of all—which is perhaps why nearly everybody had carefully excluded it from the discussion—with the fact that no true political democracy can permanently exist unless it find a basis in economic democracy. The capitalism detested by the South was quite as much the foe as the slavery detested by the North. And the end of that battle has not yet been decided. Writing in his *Quarterly Review* for April, 1862, in the midst of war, Brownson said, "It was not liberty for the black race so much as for the white race that we wished to secure." He was one of the rare minds who clearly recognized that one could not be demanded without the other—and that the slavery of industrialism must follow chattel slavery into the discard. It was this that the Irish Catholics—with their tradition of democracy and their aptitude for it—dimly perceived. Without understanding their situation we are likely to think of them as merely reactionary in regard to negro slavery.

Catholic thought about these questions—even that expressed by Orestes Brownson with such candor and force and

[11] The young man who was to be Lord Acton followed Brownson to Emmitsburg, hearing that he had gone there, but was delayed, as he relates, by the astounding cocktails provided at a hotel in Gettysburg, ten miles to the north of the college. Brownson's own character comes out in a letter he wrote to the President of Mount St. Mary's in 1848: "I found all our clergy from Boston to Emmitsburg wrong in their politics except Father McElroy (S.J.). He was wrong four years ago, but *I'm never wrong.*" (*The Mountain*, Vol. I, p. 462.)

[12] *Brownson*, p. 90.

pungency, and also with a strain of piquant inconsistency—
was moderate, and kept always in mind the fact that deeply
embedded evils have to be cautiously uprooted, gradually and
without a sudden jerk, unless worse ills are to follow. The
Church—or rather the Catholics who make up the Church—
may be criticized for moving too slowly. I am inclined to think
that they do so in the analogous case of capitalism. But at all
events the most extreme caution is to be preferred to violence
and revolution. It was these that the Abolitionists considered
the only possible weapons. Therefore they hurled the country
into a war that a compromising spirit could have easily
avoided.

The Abolitionists' antagonism to the Catholic Church did
not, however, originate in the Catholic habit of appealing to
principles and the lessons of history. They hated the Church
without that; the Church's attitude to slavery merely served
to increase their hate. But they were almost equally intolerant
towards Protestants who ventured, on whatever grounds, to
dissent from them. There was, for instance, the case of Mr.
Andrews of Georgia, who was elected a Methodist bishop.
Twelve years later he married a woman who owned slaves, and
at the next general conference of his denomination a resolution was passed that he should "desist from the exercise of his
office so long as the impediment remains." That he had acquired his slaves only through marriage was regarded as beside
the point. The upshot was a split among the Methodists, the
first of similar splits in most of the other Protestant bodies.
Contrasting with these dissensions was the Catholic unity
which no disagreement, however strong on a political and
social issue, had any power to affect. But of course this—like
everything else connected with Catholicism—merely infuriated
the amalgamation of the Abolitionists and Nativists, who
looked upon it as only another manifestation of Catholic indifference to what they considered "righteousness."

Nor did it help the Church very much that the Dred Scott
decision was handed down by a Catholic, Chief Justice Taney.
Here was further proof of the natural fondness of the Catholic
mind for oppression! Now Taney may have been right or
wrong, but he was doing no more than interpret the Constitution as a lawyer, and about his competence in that capacity
there can be no debate. What he was accused of having said
was that "a negro had no rights which a white man was bound
to respect." What he did say was something rather different.

Taking into consideration historical facts and the law as he found it, he delivered the judgment: "They had for more than a century before been regarded as beings of an inferior order, and altogether unfit to associate with the white race either in social or political relations; and so far inferior that they had no rights which the white man was bound to respect; and that the negro might justly and lawfully be reduced to slavery for his benefit. He was bought and sold, and treated as an ordinary article of merchandise and traffic whenever a profit could be made by it. This opinion was at that time fixed and universal in the civilized portion of the white race."

The decisive point is in the last sentence and makes no pronouncement as to the abstract right or wrong of slavery. As Chief Justice, Taney had to admit the force of the Constitution. In his private capacity he did not believe in slavery and had not only manumitted those slaves whom he had inherited at the death of his father but had pensioned his freedmen when they grew too old to earn a living. Years before, from the bench of the state Court he had said, "A hard necessity indeed compels us to endure the evil of slavery for a time. It was imposed upon us by another nation while we were yet in a state of colonial vassalage. It cannot be easily or suddenly removed, yet while it continues it is a blot on our national character; and every lover of real freedom confidently hopes that it will be effectually, though it must be gradually, wiped away, and earnestly looks for the means by which this necessary object may be best attained."[13] His pastor, the same Father McElroy of Frederick, Maryland, who served as a chaplain in the Mexican war, noted the great jurist's humility in insisting on taking his turn in the line of those waiting to enter the confessional, though most of those ahead of him were negro slaves. But as Chief Justice he believed that he could interpret the Constitution in no other way than he did in the Dred Scott case.[14]

What may be fully admitted is the unfortunate effects that flowed from this decision—or rather from the law as upheld by Taney. The South was naturally jubilant over what it considered a resounding victory. But the Republican Party, in order

---

[13] *Catholic Builders of the Nation*, Vol. III, pp. 49, 50, 51.

[14] Thaddeus Stevens, on the other hand, after Taney's death, denounced "the infamous sentiment that damned the late Chief Justice to everlasting fame and I fear everlasting fire." Well, it was something, after all, to be damned by that tough old cynic!

to get even, emphasized more firmly than ever its doctrine of high tariff. As the Supreme Court had upheld the rights of the slave states, and had taken from Congress the power to legislate against slavery, discriminatory taxation was the answer of the North. A new burden, grievous to be borne, was now by legitimate (though unjust) congressional action fastened upon the already breaking back of the South.

An impasse had been reached. Garrison fiercely described the Constitution with his gift for memorable and nonsensical rhetoric, as "a covenant with death and an agreement with hell." And Henry Ward Beecher when told that the Southern states were seceding, burst out "I don't care if they do!" Even Horace Greeley was willing to "let our erring sisters go." It was men of this stamp that had brought the nation into danger because of their intolerance. Men of more generous mind and larger vision and truer Americanism had to be summoned to save the Union, about which the Abolitionists confessedly cared nothing.

Nevertheless, Southern extremists have to share their guilt. In their truculent and arrogant way they had demanded their "rights," which included not only hunting wretched runaway slaves through the towns and countryside of the North but were in practice stretched to include, in some instances, the seizure of freed negroes. Calhoun might perhaps have averted the disaster had he lived, though it was he who had been the principal exponent of the new doctrine that slavery was a positive good. However, ten years before the outbreak of the war he died, seeing only too distinctly what was destined to happen. He protested with his last breath against the Missouri Compromise—a treaty rather than a law—knowing perfectly well that it would prove ineffective. He would have done his best to check the Southern mania for trying to force the "peculiar institution" upon the territories that did not want to accept it. His last speech had to be read for him in Congress, while he sat listening, in the last stages of consumption, hollow-eyed, gallant and magnificent to the end. On March 31, 1850, his great spirit passed away. Over his tomb at Charleston they carved a single sufficient word: CALHOUN. Walt Whitman later heard a soldier say that the whole ruined South was his grave. It would be truer to say that his grave was slavery.

END OF VOLUME ONE